TULA HATTI
The Last Great Elephant

TULA HATTI

The Last Great Elephant

PETER BYRNE, F.R.G.S.

ff

Faber and Faber

BOSTON AND LONDON

This book is for

Rara

STHOREEN   VEG   ORE

―――――――――

All royalties from the sale of this book are being donated to the International Wildlife Conservation Society, Inc.

Library of Congress Cataloging-in-Publication Data

Byrne, Peter, 1925–
    Tula Hatti : the last great elephant / by Peter Byrne.
        p.   cm.
    ISBN 0-571-12942-0 : $19.95
    1. Tula Hatti (Elephant)   2. Wildlife conservation—Nepal.
    I. Title.
    QL73 P98B97   1991
    333.95'9—dc20   90-36753
                                                                        CIP

Interior photographs from the collection of Peter Byrne
Jacket photographs by Celia (Dede) Killeen

PRINTED IN THE UNITED STATES OF AMERICA

CONTENTS

FOREWORD

My wife Gloria and I first met Peter Byrne in Calcutta, India in 1958. At that time he was running the American Yeti Expedition in the northeastern Himalaya of Nepal. Gloria and I were friends with the sponsors of that expedition, so when Peter found some bones in a cave in the mountains and wanted to get them to England for scientific examination—and as we were passing through India at the time—we offered to help. We were able to get the specimens to England, to the Regents Park Zoo in London.

After meeting us in Calcutta, Peter had to find his way back to the Himalaya (a nine day journey by rail and on foot), so we were with him for only a couple of days before he returned to the mountains. During that short time, however, we were able to learn something of his dedication to saving endangered wildlife and his concern for the environment.

Now, many years later, Peter has written a book which, in addition to being an expression of that dedication, is also an appreciation of the beauty of the wilderness—in this case the area known as the White Grass Plains, a hundred thousand acres of forest and grassland in the southwest Terai of Nepal that is the home of Tula Hatti, a great elephant, and his companion herd. This book and its messages are Peter's way of telling all of us about the importance of protecting our wildlife and, through that, the fragile and much abused environment on which depend our future and the future of our children.

Jimmy Stewart

Acknowledgments

I am grateful to many people for help and encouragement in the writing of this book and the making of the film, *Tula Hatti: The Last Great Elephant*. If in the following listings I have neglected anyone who has been associated with the work, I am sure they will understand that the omission is not intentional and forgive me accordingly.

Here, in the order that they come to mind and with a brief note on their participation in or association with the dual projects, they are: Erick and Eleanore Karlsson of White Salmon, Washington, for assistance that bought me precious time; Paul and Joella Dethman of Pine Grove, Oregon, for helping me to meet a deadline; Claire Haser of Mount Hood, Oregon (who now knows what a Hollywood python really does to its Hollywood victims), for executive secretarial services and kind personal attention to the twin projects; Ellen Pitcher and Ken Wright of Mount Hood, for keeping the inner man more than happy on more than one occasion and thus enabling me to return to the typewriter; Nick and Pam Bielemeier, portrait photographers at the top of their class, for dealing patiently with a difficult subject; Susan Garrett of Portland, Oregon, for allowing me, while "on the trail" to share her house with robins; unsung geniuses of the internal combustion engine, Lynn Winans and Larry Hoffman (The Grease Pit) of Parkdale, Oregon, for expert "underhand" work on our Suzuki camera car that allowed it to defy the threat of termite mounds, high road centers, stumps, and other nasties on location in Nepal; Bob and Dolly Fleming of Paulsbo, Washington, who, at Oriole Camp in the White Grass Plains, raised a glass with us to celebrate surviving a thousand miles of Indian highways, Paradeep to Palia; Jack and Kate Mills of Mount Hood, whose own feelings about the planetary ecoweb, expressed by positive action, are very much in line with those of the book; Monte Bricker of Portland, Oregon, who, deep in the forests of Bardia, had a close encounter of the tigerish kind, and his son David, for helping me to get my files in order; Mary Kay Bielemeier of Hood River, Oregon, for being a willing slave of the dreaded fax machine, and her husband John; Jim Janney, M.D., and his delightful wife Cindy of White Salmon, for medical counsel that kept all of us — especially Rara — in good health while on safari; Clyde Raven of Eugene, Oregon, for instruction in the delicacies of true sound recording; Basanta Karki of Portland, Oregon, for unswerving devotion to the cause in the smoke of a hundred Terai campfires; Bud and Mary Schlick of Mount Hood, for literary consultation and enthusiasm for the work; John Lindsay and David Richards of Oregon Public Broadcasting, Portland, for movie-making advice and consultation; Robert Pyle, author of the award-winning book *Wintergreen*, of Grays River, Washington (The Monarch Project), for lepidopteric identification and literary direction; Susan Petersen of Phoenix, Arizona, who, through many an hour on the back of a riding *hatti* in the White Grass Plains, saw "the vision splendid"; Karen Eberly of Yakima, Washington, who was at my side during the very first encounter with the last great elephant; Steve Matthes of Carlotta, California, who knows the forests as do only a few, and his wife Vera, for sharing with me their book, *Brave*, their own courageous venture into the world of writing; Tony and Joyce Weseman of Parkdale, Oregon, who have the capacity to see the humorous side of things, for ongoing assistance and interest; the undauntable Bob Pierce of Portland, Oregon, fearless veteran of a hundred high Himalayan treks and indefatigable courier, Portland to Kathmandu; George and Margo Earley of Mount Hood, for allowing us to see the pleasure of friends taking delight in the success of others; Academy Award nominee producer Bob Nixon and producer Gerome Gary of Santa Monica, California, for hospitality and sound professional movie-making advice; script writer Arnold Schulman (*A Chorus Line, Tucker*) for keeping me out of trouble in the swamps and depths of movieland; professional outfitter (Malla Treks, Kath-

mandu) Stan Armington, old *pundit* of Kathmandu, for looking after
my Sherpas; Dick Fisher and Teresa Powlovsky of New York,
New York, for dedicated professionalism through many a long
Terai jungle day; John Cordell, of Vancouver, Washington, who
breathed the air of the mountain rivers with us, and Jeanne Moreno,
who will see that he does it again; Dipenda Bista, of the Nepal Mis-
sion to the U.S. in New York, for keeping us in touch with the
changing Nepalese scene; Jerry Tinling of San Francisco, California, for cartographic assistance, and his wife Sassy; Loren Coleman
of Portland, Maine, for literary advice and publishing introduc-
tions; C. W. (Chuck) Ennis of San Antonio, Texas, for lessons in
humanity on a last safari down the Terai's great jungle river, the
Sapt Gandaki; Cynthia Fagen of New York, New York, for helping
us to shoo rhinos out of camp in the dark of the jungle night; Russ
Kinne of New Canaan, Connecticut, ace professional pho-
tographer, airman, and intrepid adventurer in his own right, for instructions on how to keep the lens cap off; Bill McKinney of Hood
River, Oregon, photographic doyen of the world of the magazine
cover, for reminding us to keep the eye to the viewfinder but also
to bear in mind, when the photo subject is a large wild animal, that
it is important to look up occasionally; Ron Rosner of New York,
New York, who, in the very beginning, shared the hyena laughter
of many a *phanta* night with me, and Jacqueline Martell, his lovely
wife, who guards him against people like Peter Byrne and the
dangers their wild and wooly adventures represent; Gerry and Kate
McCarthy of Mount Hood, for support for the White Grass Plains
Reserve and for donations of equipment; John and Claire Lyddon
of Hood River, for direction in the world of film distribution; Jack
Lemmon of Beverly Hills, California, for letters of introduction and
for trying to help; Bill Hartigan, of Schenectady, New York, news
cameraman without equal, who knew that we would never give up,
and John Stebila of San Francisco, California, who shared that belief; Academy Award-winners Sue Marx and Pamela Cohn of
Detroit, Michigan, for sharing their precious time with us; the in-
domitable Eleanor Sabin of Middleburg, Virginia, who was behind
us from the very beginning; Lucy Mack of Los Angeles, California,
who saw what could be done while the whole idea was still but a

seedling not yet grown; Bill and Beryl Green (my sister) of Touchen End, Berkshire, England, for encouragement, warm hospitality for jetlagged itinerants, and for helping to keep the wolf from the door when he was at times quite ferocious; dauntless shipping agent Vispy Patel of Colaba, Bombay, veteran of the Indian bureaucratic war, who helped to preserve my sanity in the heat and dust of the Bombay docks; ex-tea planter Jack Boyland of Willersley, Worcestershire, England, whose story (in the book) about the clash between the tiger and the leopard contributed much to a student of jungle lore, his wife Pamela and their children; ex-tea planter Bill Hudson of Chippenham, Wiltshire, England, whose sage words of long ago directed my footsteps on the original path; Cynthia Turner of Axminister, Devon, England, whose courage in the face of adversity continues to inspire; Phillip and Gael Cohen of Careel Bay, New South Wales, Australia, whose joy of life and love of adventure—especially on Himalayan trails and Terai jungle rivers—has my unending admiration; John Bonney of Glenorie, New South Wales, Australia, who walked the green halls of the Terai forests with me when Tula Hatti was but a growing teenager and about whom the Tarus of Kalkutta and Pachuie still ask twenty-five years later; film producer Belinda Wright of Calcutta, India, and Baraboo, Wisconsin, for personal interest in the works and much appreciated professional advice that has its roots in a career of high quality wildlife films (was the source of this the gift of a lion cub to a little girl in Ballygunj, Calcutta, many years ago?) and her husband Stanley Breeden of Palm Beach, Queensland, Australia, with whom she recently made the movie classic *Tiger!*, a National Geographic special presentation; Peter and Beryl Saunders, of Sutton In The Isle, Cambridgeshire, England, for youthful enthusiasm for the dual projects; Utpal Sengupta, hotelier par excellence and master puppeteer of the Shangri La Hotel, Kathmandu, for nourishing jetlagged or road-weary minds and bodies in Kathmandu's finest watering hole, and his ever effervescent wife, Caroline, and the heir to the fortune, Kanu; Guy Mountfort of Blackboys, Sussex, England, for contributing, a year or two ago, to the defeat of the myth that tigers will not walk through a campsite at night; Saeed Jaffery of Greenford, Middlesex, England, and Bombay, India, star of the original *Gunga Din* and intrepid Gurkha of Kipling's *The Man Who Would Be King*, for lifting our spirits with many an hour of jollity at the Shangri La, and his wife Jennifer; Captain Emil Wick of Cointrin, Switzerland, undaunted birdman of the airy heights of the Himalayas, for a hundred plus hours of airborne companionship and for practical (if somewhat hair-raising) demonstrations of the theory that *Mugger* crocodiles fiercely resent being buzzed by low-flying aircraft; and my dear friend Nancy de Herrera of Beverly Hills, for unending and gracious hospitality both during the work and during the long search for book publishers and film sponsors, and for many years of warm friendship.

I would also like to thank Jimmy Stewart of Beverly Hills, California, actor without equal, for his most generous contributions to both the book and the film, and his wife Gloria, in admiration of their enduring devotion to the cause of wildlife conservation and in particular to the greatest of beasts, the elephant.

A number of companies contributed to the making of the film and through it to the writing of this book. Locally, they include: MEG Telecommunications of Mount Hood, with David Cunningham; Mount Hood Executive Services, with Claire Haser; Columbia Photo of Hood River, with Thad Perry; the new and delightfully restored Hood River Hotel, with hosts Pasquale Barone and Jacqueline Brown; the book lovers' haven, Waucoma Bookstore of Hood River, with Sally La Venture and Peggy Dills Kelter; Radio Shack of Hood River, with Paul Henne; Parkdale Chevron of Parkdale, with Lynn Winans and Larry Hoffman; and Columbia Travel of Hood River. On the national scale about twenty companies contributed equipment or services and, while all are credited in the film, four, because of the excellence of their service or their equipment, are deserving of special mention. They are: the Coleman Company of Wichita, Kansas, for camping equipment that is obviously the finest on the market today; American President Lines, for superb cargo services carried out under the often near-impossible conditions of Indian ports of call; Johnson and Johnson (Eureka Tents), for first-class tentage which has proved itself under rugged conditions for many years. And Silent Safaris (P.O. Box 4631, Kathmandu; phone Nepal) for field services.

In the U.S. two institutions gave their support and allowed their names to be used with the field work. I am grateful for this to the International Wildlife Conservation Society, Inc., Washington, D.C., and its directors, Karl Jonas, Scott Whitney, and Leonard A. Fink, especially the latter for his special interest in the work. I am equally indebted to the Academy of Applied Science, Concord, New Hampshire, its president, Mr. Robert H. Rines, and the members of its board who generously allowed us the use of their facilities and gave the project their special interest and attention.

In Nepal a number of people personally helped us, as well as several government departments and one institution: the King Mahendra Trust for Nature Conservation. The King Mahendra Trust, co-producers of our movie, under the leadership of its august Chairman H. R. H. Prince Gyanendra Bir Bikram Shah, was the ship that carried us safely through the reefs and shoals of bureaucratic and other difficulties. Dr. Hemanta Mishra, Secretary to the Trust, was the helmsman who steered us on our way. And, most worthy of mention among his hard-working crew of young and enthusiastic people, Arup Rajouria, Conservation Education Officer, R. K. Shrestha, Administrative Officer, and Madhab Bhattarai, Chief Officer who, while on location with us, was our Government Liaison Officer.

The Department of National Parks and Wildlife, Kathmandu, willingly gave us the permits necessary to camp and to work in the White Grass Plains and I am indebted to its director, Mr. B. N. Upreti, for his personal interest and also, within the D.N.P.W. structure, Mr. Krishna Man Shrestha, Wildlife Warden of the Bardia Reserve.

Among those who helped on a private or individual basis in Nepal were the Bisht family of Mahendranagar, to whom all of us involved in the project are more than grateful for hospitality, assistance, and patience and acceptance of our inscrutable western idiosyncrasies. And their paterfamilias, Hikmat, old *shikari sahib*, who knows the jungles of the southwest Terai as few do; our Sherpa team: Pasang, Jangbu, Phurua, Jangbu "Two," and Lakpha, without whose loyalty, integrity, and devotion to the work on location things could have been a lot more difficult; Mr. Pant, steely-eyed guide during our location work and with him the headmen of Radhapur, Kalkutta, and Singpur.

A number of persons sponsored the project, either on a private basis or through foundations and I am indebted to them for their kindness and interest. Frank Pachmyr of Los Angeles, California, whose concern for wildlife goes back many years; Mrs. M. Machris of Bel Air, California, who took a keen personal interest in the projects and followed them through to their conclusion; Ms. Sandra Payson of Delaplane, Virginia, who believed in the importance of what we were doing; Mrs. J. C. Herbert Bryant of Middleburg, Virginia, whose concern for wildlife is legendary and whose special interest in elephants prompted her to most generously support our field project; and Mr. and Mrs. R. R. Ohrstrom of Middleburg, Virginia, whose original interest, sparked at a luncheon with me in Sun Valley, Idaho, was the prime mover of the twin projects. All of this latter group, in addition to sponsorship, gave generously of their time and attention to the work, asking in return only that they be allowed to visit the work on location and view the results of their sponsorship firsthand. Because of their belief in what they sponsored and their kindness, Tula Hatti is alive and well in the White Grass Plains. To all who were part of this special group, I am deeply grateful.

Toward the end of the list comes my wife, Dede, who for years will probably hear the endless tap tap tap of the typewriter from my early morning office intermingled with what I know she dreams about a great deal: the sounds, sights, and scents of the White Grass Plains — a place the real spiritual messages of which she understands as does no one else. To her I owe much.

And last but not least, my editor, Betsy Uhrig, to whom I owe more than thanks for patience and tolerance of one of the world's worst (albeit fastest two-fingered) typists this side of Suez, and for having the courage to take me on in the first place.

TULA HATTI
The Last Great Elephant

I

AN OLD FRIENDSHIP

t is night. From the cobalt pools of darkness outside the canvas
walls of our tent come the small sounds of the nocturnal hours.
The incessant drone of cicadas. The dry leaf rustle of hunting
lizards. The snuffling of a porcupine, rooting among the dead
branches for food. A crescent moon hangs in the west and a thin
yellow light etches on the roof of the tent the dark imprint of the
huge cotton tree that shades our campsite. Suddenly the air is rent
by the powerful scream of an elephant. It is awesome in its volume
and the sound echoes down through the corridors of the jungle. Instantly all the little sounds of the jungle night cease. The silence that
follows is one of creatures in awe, watching for the source of the
sound and waiting to see what is going to happen. Tula Hatti is
passing by and his presence is one that commands the instant respect
of the lesser folk of the jungle.

We sit up in bed and strain our ears. We listen for the snap of a
dead branch. The sound of dry leaves being crushed under the
weight of an immense foot. The swish of a tree limb whipping back
to its parent trunk after being bent by a powerful force. But we hear
nothing more. Nothing other than that single great scream. Tula
Hatti is passing our camp. He is moving down an Elephant Walk
no more than a hundred feet from our tent. But, like all of his kind
when they are in motion, he is as silent as a shadow. Soon the
renewal of the small jungle sounds tells us that he is gone. The moon
wanes and we sleep.

It is late in the winter of 1988–'89 and we are spending the last
few days of a series of safaris in a tented camp on the edge of the
White Grass Plains Reserve in southwest Nepal. The safaris, spread

3

across three winters, have centered around finding and filming the great elephant known to the indigenous people of the southern jungles as Tula Hatti. They have taken my wife and me from our home on the slopes of Mt. Hood, Oregon, three times to the jungles of the little kingdom of Nepal. They have involved more than 400 days of living in tented camps, more than 100,000 miles of travel, and a whole kaleidoscope of events ranging from the dramatic to the mundane, from the dangerous to the hilarious. Now the adventure — and in essence that is what it was for us more than anything — was coming to an end and what had begun as a simple interest in a single elephant was about to finish with international recognition of an extraordinary animal and a one hour television special planned for worldwide release. All of which would round off a saga that began back in the fifties when, one moonbeamed night, on the edge of the White Grass Plains, not far from where we were now camped, I first encountered Tula Hatti. Encountered him in a face to face meeting that revealed an animal not just of great size, but also of unique character and personality.

I was a hunter at that time, a P.W.H. or Professional White Hunter, and I was in my third year of running safaris in Nepal. I had been given a professional hunting license by the government in 1953 when I had gone there after a five year stint as a tea planter in north Bengal, east of Nepal, in India. My hunting concession included Bardia, Kailali, and Kanchanpur, the three most westerly districts of southern Nepal. My prime area and the one where most of my safaris were run was Sukila Phanta, the White Grass Plains, one hundred thousand acres of primeval forest in the center of which lay six thousand acres of golden grassland, the seasonally white-tipped grasses which gave the area its name. In those days, tigers were, as we used to say, thick on the ground. Leopards lived in the deep forest. The two little jungle rivers that flowed through the area, the Chaundhari and the Bauni, were the home of the big black and yellow crocodile, the silent saurian the indigenous Taru people called the *Mugger*. Wild boar ranged through the forest and the grassland. Herds of Axis Deer, the beautiful spotted deer known as the *Chital*, lived in the forest and along its edge in groups that

4

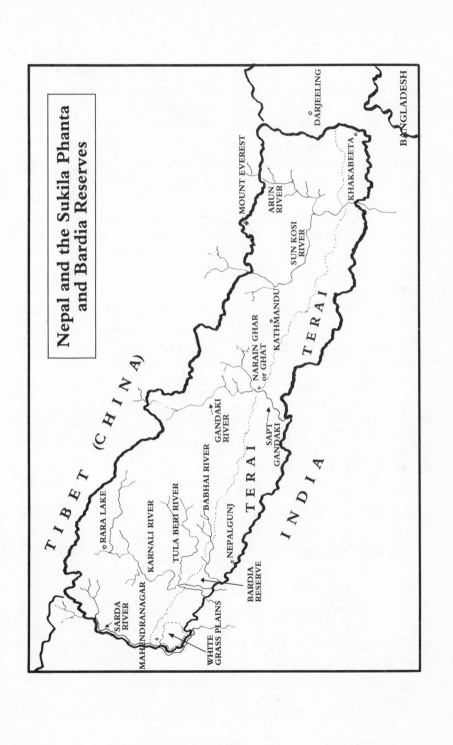

Nepal and the Sukila Phanta
and Bardia Reserves

TIBET (CHINA)

SARDA
RIVER

MAHENDRANAGAR

RARA LAKE

KARNALI RIVER

TULA BERI RIVER

BABHAI RIVER

GANDAKI
RIVER

NEPALGUNJ

WHITE
GRASS PLAINS

BARDIA
RESERVE

TERAI

SAPT
GANDAKI

NARAIN GHAR
or GHAT

KATHMANDU

SUN KOSI
RIVER

ARUN
RIVER

MOUNT EVEREST

TERAI

INDIA

KHAKABEETA

DARJEELING

BANGLADESH

numbered eighty to a hundred. Black Buck, the strikingly marked black and white antelope of the open *phantas*, were plentiful and their counterpart, the little bow-backed Hog Deer, found the thick cover along the edge of the Sukila Phanta swamp a perfect environment. In the mornings, with the first sun, one was often greeted by the sight of hundreds and hundreds of Swamp Deer emerging from the dense elephant grass of the swampland, a veritable sea of horns in the fall of the year. The red-coated *Sambhur*, largest of all of the deer of the Terai — the 500-mile-long strip of forest that lies in Nepal between the Indian border and the foothills — stirred the crystal clear air of daybreak with its bell-like calls, often answered by the strident, doglike alarm calls of the Barking Deer. The single herd of elephants that made the White Grass Plains their winter home numbered twelve animals at that time. Ten were wild and one was a domestic female that had broken away from bondage to join them. She still had, when I knew her, a small length of chain attached to her right front foot and sometimes in the night, when the elephants were ghost walking past one of my camps, as silent as the mooncast shadows that etched their jungle trails, the clanking of that little piece of chain would register itself in my slumbers. The twelfth animal was Tula Hatti, and while I knew that he did join the herd from time to time, probably when he came into *musth*, or rut, he mostly lived alone.

Safari hunting in those days was, simply, trophy hunting. Or, as P.W.H.s were inclined to call what their clients did, trophy collecting. My job as a P.W.H. was to organize and run safaris. Clients came alone or in couples and jungle safaris ran from a minimum of fifteen days to as long as three months, depending on what the clients wanted. Mountain hunts for wild sheep and wild goat, which I also took out, were usually longer than jungle safaris, added time being needed to walk in and out of the ten to fifteen thousand foot ranges of the Himalaya where the *Bharal*, the Blue Sheep, and the *Thar*, the Himalayan wild goat, made their habitat. Clients paid me a safari fee and paid the government of Nepal a license fee. They shot the game; we — I and my staff — jungle "dressed" it; they took it home, had it stuffed to suit their tastes, and hung it on a wall for their friends to admire. I hunted professionally in Nepal for sixteen years.

Then one day I folded my tents and walked away from it and, doing what many another white hunter has done, moved directly into the field of wildlife conservation. This was something that I had been thinking about for some years. But I had hesitated. What worried me and what prevented me from making a major decision — one that would mean a complete change of lifestyle — was the fear that life as a wildlife conservationist, lacking the dangers and excitement of big game hunting, would be boring. Danger in all shapes and sizes and the challenges that it generated was something on which I thrived in those days. To me, at that time, nothing equalled the cold, clean, spine-tingling exhilaration of stalking big game on foot in dense jungles, especially when the animal in question was in a state of provocation. If, as sometimes happened in the case of the big cats, the animal was a maneater, that was the ultimate.

Eventually, however, I found myself forced to come to a decision and when I finally did, several things caused me to make it an irrevocable one. One was the psychological impact of a series of bad safaris in the early part of the sixties. Another, changes in my attitude toward my profession. The third was a single incident that reinforced these changing attitudes, a brief moment in time during a safari, a period of less than a minute which created a turning point in my life and left an indelible impression on my mind.

One day in 1967, toward the end of an unpleasant safari with a particularly unpleasant client, sitting in my tent and nursing a bedtime scotch, I had something of a revelation about what I was doing. For the first time since I started hunting professionally in 1953, I found myself looking on my life as a P.W.H. in a different light.

I have always loved animals, especially the wild ones, since boyhood when I lived on a three hundred acre estate in Monagahan county, Ireland, and walked the woods with my father. Woods that in those years still had deer, badgers, foxes, hedgehogs, squirrels, hares, and rabbits. It was in those days that I first learned to hunt and fish. But while teaching me the basic techniques my father also taught me the basic rules, one of which was respect for whatever it was I hunted. Game that was brought home went into the cooking pot—or at least into someone else's pot—and if it was not suitable for eating, then it was not to be shot. In other words, if I was going to be allowed to take the life of an animal, then there had to be a very good reason. Those early lessons, many of them supported by actual experience, stayed with me all my life. Now, many years later, I found myself reflecting on them and their application to my profession.

In its heyday professional hunting was one of the most exciting and exhilarating occupations that any young man could enjoy. It was highly lucrative, adventurous, glamorous in the eyes of one's friends and associates, and in my case it allowed me, in line with the wet and dry seasons in Nepal, to spend five months on vacation after just seven months of safari work each year. It was also a profession that allowed me to enjoy the company of great sportsmen and women, to travel, to entertain and be entertained by them in their homes around the world, and to develop lifelong friendships. It was the kind of life that many a young person could only dream about. But professional hunting was a public business and more often than not the client, before he or she arrived, was a totally unknown entity. Once in camp, safari fee paid, the client was the responsibility of the P.W.H., who provided two to three weeks of hunting and everything that went with it, including whatever in-camp socializing was expected or requested, regardless of the personality or behavior of the client.

I have to admit that I have never had an unpleasant or disagreeable female client. On the whole, women handled themselves well on safari. But in the early part of the sixties I had a number of men as clients who were particularly unpleasant and unattractive. Quite simply, the safari brought out the worst in them, just as with a different kind of client it often brought out the best. This group of men, businessmen in their fifties for the most part, fat and unfit, included alcoholics who seemed to think that they could drink all day and hunt at the same time; incompetents who, because of their inability to hit the wall of a barn at ten feet, or cowardice, or both, expected their White Hunter to shoot their trophies for them, something no self-respecting professional would ever do; and out-

and-out killers, licensed or not, who wanted and expected to be allowed to shoot everything in sight, from porcupines to pythons, from monkeys to mongooses. I reached a point during these hunts, watching the game go down, where I secretly—and dangerously—began to wish for just one occasion where the position of collector and trophy could be reversed. The desire was particularly strong when, at the end of a shoot, some red-faced tub of blubber stood with his foot on the neck of his trophy, grinning into the camera for his "I did it" picture.

At the end of the 1967 season, I felt that I had had enough and I made the decision to fold tents on my safari business. In Kathmandu, up from the Terai to sign off for the season and close licenses, I took the time to talk with the government about my concession, the hunting area in southwest Nepal that I leased from the government. I told them that I was giving up hunting and I suggested to them that the prime part of my concession, Sukila Phanta, would make an excellent wildlife reserve. Describing it—and I was doing this for people who had never been there—I told them that I had travelled the length of the Terai from east to west and that nowhere had I found a place as pristine and beautiful as the White Grass Plains. They, the Department of Forests people who at that time also had wildlife under their wing, said that what I proposed was very interesting but that there was no money available.

We had a series of meetings at the end of which it was agreed that the heart of my concession, the White Grass Plains, could be made into a reserve if I could find the money to do it. I would also be required to do all of the work and in addition carry the responsibility for anything that went wrong. Political appointees all, in those days they lived in fear of losing the lucrative sinecures that they held at the whim of others higher up the ladder. Hence the delegation of responsibility, one that meant that if heads had to roll at least the first would be mine.

These talks took place in the spring of 1967 and I would have closed my operation there and then had I not had bookings—some of them made two years in advance—for the safari season of 1968. (Plus about $50,000 in fee advances which I had already spent!) Thus in the winter of 1967-'68 I ran my last season of hunting. I had five

9

safaris during that winter, two of which were with single woman clients and the remainder with five men, two pairs and a single. It was during the second to last of these that the incident took place which, added to the impact of the bad safaris of 1967 and the serious doubts I was beginning to have about big game hunting as a whole, made my decisions of 1967 irreversible.

I will not mention my client's name or even say if it was a man or a woman. Suffice it to say that toward the end of a twenty-day safari, one evening as the sun was going down, on the edge of a patch of golden elephant grass, a bad shot was fired. The client's target, a tiger, went off with a roar of rage and pain before I could get in a second and killing shot and I was left with the job of tracking it and putting it out of its misery. A nasty job at the best of times but on this occasion, with the short tropical twilight heralding the rapid approach of night, one a little nastier than usual. I sent the client back to camp in a Land Rover – standard procedure for wounded big game follow-up; clients were never allowed to participate – and with Pasang, my Sherpa gunbearer and my best man (of whom more later) tracked the big cat through the last of the light. There was high level, frothy blood spoor, indicating that the animal had been hit in the lungs, and following it was not difficult. But the night closed in on us and we lost the spoor so we walked back to camp and told the client that we would try again in the morning.

In the morning, before the dawn wind began to blow and with the client still sleeping, Pasang and I were back at the scene of the shot and taking up the trail. The follow-up took hours. The tiger, as many a wounded animal will do, had gone to water and to do this had traversed a mile of thick elephant grass. After drinking at a little stream the big cat had turned back into the grass to lie up and nurse its wound. As we could see from the spoor, blood clotting of the wound had reduced blood loss. It also reduced the amount of sign that we were using to track on. The sun was over the horizon and sending long bars of light into the jungle when we finally caught up with the animal.

We were walking a narrow game trail through the elephant grass when we found him. I was in front, with Pasang, carrying a shotgun, close behind. Ahead of us was a little clearing, well lit with the first rays of the morning sun and fringed with small bushes. The tiger was lying on the left side of the clearing, broadside to us, with just his head and neck showing. The instant I saw the animal I shot it and killed it. Then I reloaded and walked up to it, stopping about five or six feet away from it. It was then that I saw something that I shall never forget and that now, twenty years later, is as vivid in my mind as it was when it happened.

As an aside, I can say without bragging that during my hunting days I was a good shot. When I took aim at the cat and fired my single round, my confidence in my shooting and my ability to dispatch an animal like a tiger with one clean shot was such that I had no hesitation in walking right up to the big cat, something that is normally only done after death has been very definitely established. I knew that it would be dead.

It was; it lay supine, chin down on the ground and absolutely motionless. But its eyes were not. They were wide open and they stared right at me, full of fire and life. There is gold in a tiger's eyes and the glowing, golden light that I now saw, enhanced as it was by the morning sun—the very light of life itself—seemed to burn from great depths. I felt, looking into those eyes, that I was looking into another world, a world mysterious and unreachable, untouchable, a world which held the beginnings of life itself. I also felt an accusation in that steady stare and I felt it the more when, after a mere fifteen seconds, it slowly began to weaken. A gray cloud crept across the pupils and the light that blazed out of them began to darken. Then, quickly, almost as though I had been privy to some secret thing living in those extraordinary depths, the light faded and died. An opaque film clouded the irises and suddenly they were dead.

Pasang was not far behind me when all this took place and when I saw death sweep across those great pools of life I had to walk away and be alone for a while. I rejoined him a little later and we walked back to camp together. I did not tell the client what had happened, what I had seen and experienced. I just said that I had found the tiger and sent the men out with the Land Rover to pick it up and bring it back. I finished the safari, did one more, the last, and then folded my tents, sold or gave away all of my equipment, drove up to Kathmandu, sold my Land Rovers, paid off the men, and entered into a series of meetings with Department of Forest officials that led to an agreement about the establishment of the Sukila Phanta Reserve.

A professional hunting concession is, normally, a piece of land leased from the owners—in Nepal this was the government—by a professional hunter for a period of time. At this time, in Nepal, I was the only holder of a hunting concession. So when I closed down, big game hunting on the safari level virtually came to an end there. One other man, an American named Charles McDougal who subsequently became a well-known conservationist and wildlife author (his book, *The Face of the Tiger*, is well regarded in its field), tried professional hunting in Nepal for a while and then gave it up. Thus when the government agents started the bureaucratic procedure of converting a hunting concession into a reserve, they were encountering a first. Sensing that they would have problems, I left them to it and headed for Europe to look for money for the project.

For the building of two bridges on the Bauni River, for demarcation of the reserve, for drawing up of maps, doing a game count, training guards and providing them with equipment, we needed $75,000. I went first to Morges, in Switzerland, to the offices of the International Union for the Conservation of Nature. There I met with the Swiss officials and outlined my plan. I was given a reception that was quite cold and when the subject of money came up, it went from cold to freezing. The three bespectacled gentlemen who interviewed me, neat in pin-striped suits and dark ties, asked me only one question. Was I a scientist? When I replied in the negative, I heard them sigh with relief. If I was not a scientist—in other words if I had no credentials—they would not have to part with any of their precious funds and they could quickly get rid of me. Which is what they did, adding, as a parting shaft, that as the principal big game animal of the reserve appeared to be tiger, and as tigers were not endangered at this time nor likely to be endangered for a long time to come, my proposal was without merit or need.

From Morges I went to London to the World Wildlife Fund, deliberately emphasizing tigers in my proposal. Coming straight from the field, as it were, and with years of experience behind me,

I knew what the toll on tigers had been, not so much from licensed hunting as from poaching and the sale of skins, and I knew that they were endangered. My reception in London was a little warmer than in Morges. But I was told that there was no money available and that if the pundits of Morges and the I.U.C.N. said that the tiger was not endangered, then its status could not be anything but sound.

From London I flew to Rome, where an international conference on wildlife was taking place. I managed to get into the conference and to meet with some of the people attending. Again, the wise men of Morges predominated and my words and pleas fell on deaf ears. From Rome I flew to the U.S. I headed for Washington, D.C., and there directed my proposals to the World Wildlife Fund in the capitol. And once more I failed completely to convince anyone that in the far-flung country of Nepal there was an area of great beauty — pristine jungles, waving grassland, lakes and streams alive with life — that cried out to be protected.

Eventually, after months of fruitless talking I came to the conclusion that the only way I could make any impact on the seemingly closed ranks of conservationists was to move away from being an individual and turn myself into a corporate body of some kind, one with proper registration, sound credentials, and nonprofit status. Out of this thought came, with the help of two Washington surgeons, Lymon Sexton and Karl Jonas, and two Washington attorneys, Leonard A. Fink and Scott C. Whitney, the establishment of the International Wildlife Conservation Society, Inc. Jay Mellon, a former client and friend, agreed to lend his name as a Trustee and in time he was joined by three others: Lady Edith Bingham of London, the Maharaja of Baroda — an old friend of mine — and George Adamson of Meru, Kenya. Within a short space of time we found the funding needed for the new reserve and in late 1968 (at about the time the worthy gentlemen at Morges had awakened from their slumbers and were engaged in writing the tiger into the endangered species lists of the I.U.C.N.) I found myself back in the White Grass Plains. I was living once more in a safari tent, running my same Sherpa crew headed by my ex-gunbearer, Pasang, now camp manager, and spending my time trying to count tigers and elephants and

13

crocodiles, demarcating boundaries, laying out roads, building bridges, and trying to teach reserve guards not to be afraid of large animals and, for patrolling, to ride bicycles. I also found myself, to my delight, totally enjoying my new life as a wildlife conservationist (waking up in the mornings and saying, ah, no clients!). I found it completely fulfilling and, as time went by, much more meaningful than what I had been doing until then. I did not, however, forget my years as a hunter and what I learned during them. Nor did I forget the elephant I first encountered while on safari in 1955.

It was the latter part of December of 1955 when night temperatures in the open country of the Terai sparkle the grass with a sugar coating of frost and cold damp mists wreath the silent halls of the jungle. My safari client was a young woman from Washington state named Karen. A flight attendant with Continental Airlines, she was about twenty-six at this time, tall, lithe, and athletic. She loved the outdoors and was fascinated with the thought of encountering big game at close quarters. But she had absolutely no experience in hunting anything, let alone big game, and had probably fired a rifle twice in her life—at a beer can in her own backyard. However, she was eager to learn, a good sport, and unlike many a client, prepared to work hard for whatever she might get.

One evening, after a couple of hours spent scouting for tiger in the northern part of the White Grass Plains, we were driving back to camp in an open Land Rover with the canvas top off, the doors removed, and the hood folded down. The sun was an angry red eye as it lowered itself slowly into the line of *Simul* cotton trees that marked the course of the Sarda River, the western boundary of the reserve and the border with India. The temperature was dropping as the sun sank and long thin lines of gray mist were beginning to run between the little clumps of trees that dotted the *phantas*. Later, when the lines joined to form a solid gray carpet across the flat reaches, the picture one saw, stretching to the horizon, was of an open, desolate sea broken only by the dark silhouettes of tree clad islands.

We were within a couple of miles of camp and were closing on a giant *Peepul* tree, a lone monarch that signposts the north center of the grasslands, when I heard a Jungle Raven calling from a small patch of brush and elephant grass that lay behind the *Peepul*. Jungle Ravens and Jungle Crows are birds with a strong streak of curiosity. Add to this extremely sharp eyesight, a healthy appetite, and an ability to eat almost anything, and you have a bird that is not only nearly always the first to spot a potential meal but also invariably the first to the feast. The feast may be nothing more than a dead snake curled up in the grass, a desiccated fish at the side of a jungle pool, or the decaying carcass of a long dead deer. Or even, in some cases, something which is not yet dead but which, to the knowing eye of that indigo blue family of omnivores, is shortly to be so. They see, they hear, they noisily caw the news to one another and then, with infinite caution and a careful watch for those rivals of the feast who will soon be arriving—jackals, hyenas, and porcupines, who themselves home in on the calls of ravens and crows—they descend. At first, perches are selected both for safety—high above the scene of their interest—and for a view of the potential meal and the surrounding area. From these high perches, with much peering and head wagging and cawing, they begin a slow series of descents which will take them closer and closer to the waiting meal, until at last, satisfied that it is safe to land, they swoop down and start to eat.

Sometimes the food that attracts them may be the kill of a tiger or a leopard. The kill may be old, the big cat long gone and the bones picked almost clean by other scavengers, but it may also be new, with the possibility of the big cat lying up nearby to guard its food against Mr. Raven and his friends. And so when the calling of Jungle Ravens and Jungle Crows is heard in country where there are big carnivores, it is always worthwhile investigating the cause of their interest. Crows and ravens in flight are just birds passing over. But when these little grave robbers form a group in the trees and start putting their heads together and chattering, there is something afoot.

When I heard the ravens and crows calling, I stopped the Land Rover and switched off the engine. Telling Karen in a whisper what the calling might mean, I listened until I had the sounds pinpointed in the brush behind the big *Peepul*. Then I took a rifle and, asking my client to sit tight and telling her that I would be back in a few minutes, walked slowly and carefully into the brush. Within fifty yards of the Land Rover I came into a small clearing. The clearing may once have been a wallow because the floor consisted of bare patches of earth with small scattered clumps of coarse marsh grass. It was surrounded by elephant grass on three sides. Edging the fourth side, its eastern edge, was a patch of jungle, a dense stand of mixed growth entangled with a mass of trailing vine. Close to this edge lay the body of an Axis Deer. The animal was dead. The body was still warm and the big canine teeth holes in its throat told me it had been killed by a tiger. Blood oozing from the holes indicated that it had just died. Since it was unusual to find a tiger's prey lying unattended like this, I surmised that the tiger had been startled by the approach of the Land Rover and, wary of being seen by us, had dropped its kill and moved quickly into cover. There was no doubt in my mind that at this very moment the big cat was lying up close by, carefully monitoring my movements and waiting for me to leave. His body odor, acrid and pungent, hung heavily on the sun-down air.

I walked quickly back to the Land Rover and told Karen what I had found. I told her that a tiger had made the kill and that he was now very probably lying up close by. His making the kill meant that he was hungry, and as he had not had time to eat, he would al-most certainly be coming back very soon to claim his food. That if we moved quickly and got into a position where we could see him approach, she might be able to get a shot at him. I explained to her that as there was no time to build any kind of a *machan*, or blind, we would drive the Land Rover deep into the brush and sit in it, us-ing it as our hide. She agreed immediately and I started the Land Rover, jammed the gear stick into four-wheel-drive low ratio, and slowly forced the vehicle through the short, thick brush to the clearing where the kill was lying. At the western side of the clear-ing, where the sunlight had nourished it, the grass was thicker and taller and I backed the Land Rover into this, to a position that would allow for a clear field of fire between us and the deer carcass. Stop-ping the engine and telling Karen to get a jacket on, for the air was already turning cold, I took a short length of nylon rope out of the

Land Rover and walked over to the dead deer. There was a little tree stump close by and I dragged the animal over, lashing one of its hind legs to it. This was to prevent the tiger from coming in quickly, picking up the kill, and charging off with it before Karen could get her shot.

Back at the Land Rover I made quick preparations. On top of the folded windshield, I laid a thick blanket. I took Karen's rifle, loaded it with three rounds, put one in the firing chamber, closed the bolt, set the safety catch to SAFE, and laid it on the blanket in front of her. Then I took my own rifle, checked to see that it was loaded and with a round in the firing chamber, closed its bolt, set the safety catch, and then laid it and a five-cell flashlight on the blanket in front of me. I grabbed a black woolen sweater — courtesy of London's Army and Navy Stores and with a few years of service behind it — pulled it on and had a last quick look around the Land Rover to make sure there was nothing loose that would rattle or make a noise if we moved. I checked again to see that we had everything that we needed, pulled the brim of my Terai hat a little lower to shadow my face . . . and settled down to wait for Mr. Stripes. As I did the sullen sun behind us lowered itself into a sea of blood red strokes splashed across the western horizon and within minutes the jungle night was upon us.

For the safaris that I ran for tiger, I used several tried and true methods. They were ones that British sportsmen in India had devised over the years and, depending on circumstances and if the tiger followed predictable patterns, most of them worked, most of the time. There was "beating." This meant using villagers to "beat" a tiger out of cover to where the gun would be waiting. There was hunting from the back of domestic elephants, sometimes done in conjunction with "beaters." There was the *machan* or tree platform method, where the hopeful hunter sat over a kill and waited for the tiger to come back for a second meal, or over live bait such as a domestic buffalo. And lastly there was what I personally considered the only truly sporting method — the on foot, on the ground, in daylight method — through the proper application of which the hunter planned and hoped for a face-to-face confrontation with Mr. Stripes. In the hunting brochures that I sent to potential clients, all four methods were always clearly described. The one that was invariably chosen from the comfort and safety of an armchair in Los Angeles or Dallas or New York was the on-foot on-the-ground face-to-face confrontation. This is what the mighty hunter-to-be discussed at the pre-departure parties. What would make him hold his head a little higher and add a steely glint to his eye. What waving friends would see and admire as, in a blaze of macho glory, clothed in $500 worth of Abercrombie and Fitch safari suit, complete with imitation Terai hat and leopard skin band, he boarded the plane for Kathmandu. But it never ceased to amaze me the speed with which minds were changed on arrival at the safari camp. It usually only took one night and the rumble of a big cat from out there in the darkness. Then, instanto! there was a sudden intense interest in how a *machan* was built, how high it was possible to get one in a tree, and what it would be like to sit in one. In seventy-two jungle safaris that I ran for a total of one hundred and fifty people, I had only three clients who opted to face Mr. Stripes on foot, on the ground, and face to face.

The method that Karen and I were using now was a variation of the *machan* method. We were on the ground instead of in a tree. We were in an open Land Rover—no doors, no top, no windshield—and this was our hide, or *machan*. It was not perfect by any means. A hide is primarily built to conceal its occupants and the Land Rover hardly did this. But it was all that we could manage under the unusual circumstances of finding the tiger's kill; with the light fading and the tiger lying up close by, there was no time to do anything else. I hoped that if we kept very, very quiet and very, very still, the big cat might just show himself.

Our plan was that while Karen relaxed and stayed as still and quiet as possible, I would act as the alert system. I would listen for the tiger, or for indications from other animals of his presence and movement, and when I heard something that told me he was approaching, I would tap her once on the lower leg. As my hand and both of her legs were well below the dashboard of the Land Rover, this would be a movement concealed from anything watching us. When I sensed that the tiger was closer and possibly coming in, I would tap her leg twice. At that point she was to reach forward very slowly, pick up the rifle, bring it to a comfortable position on her shoulder and slip off the safety catch. At that point the tiger would, hopefully, appear. When it did, she was to wait again for my last signal. This would be another two taps on her leg, taps that would signal that she was to fire. With this last signal I would switch on the five cell flashlight and point its beam directly at the tiger.

The way the sounds change with the coming of the jungle night has always fascinated me. The strident humming of the diurnal insects takes on a more muted note and if one is near water, it soon includes a background of the throaty croaking of frogs. The brightly colored birds of the daylight hours go to rest and their songs fade as the winged predators of the night, the owls, take to the air. The chattering of monkeys ceases as they settle down to sleep, locked in tight-knit family groups in the tallest trees, as high as they can safely get above the reaches of their dreaded enemy, the leopard. Jungle fowl make a few last challenging calls and then with machine gun wings race for the security of their leafy abodes. Small nocturnal animals start to move and their cautious, stealthy sounds are loud in the comparative silence. The night air throbs with the heavy beating of the wings of Fruit Bats, males with a four-foot wing span. The tonking of Nightjars, those curious little terrestrial birds of the jungle floor, is a dusk-to-dawn symphony. Deer, mostly quiet in the daytime, startle the night with their alarm calls for now is the time, as Kipling called it, "of tooth and claw," and the two great predators of the Terai forests, the tiger and the leopard, are on the prowl.

We sat for an hour. I have had clients on *machan* sits, both on the ground and high in the air, who coughed. Who sneezed. Who sniffed. Who scratched and fidgeted. Who twitched and mumbled and moaned. Who groaned and sighed and talked and complained in everything from whispers to booming voices. Who fell asleep within minutes of getting into the *machan* and shattered the silences of the night with ponderous snores. Or who gave it up after as little as an hour and headed back for the comforts of the warm tent and the campfire. But Karen was very good. After an hour, with the cold damp night air slowly creeping into our clothing, I knew that she was getting chilled, that muscles were beginning to ache, and that there were joints and tendons calling out to be stretched. But she hardly moved and I was sitting quietly, subconsciously admiring this, when suddenly the silence of the night was broken by the strident call of a Barking Deer. The *Kakar*, as the native people call him, is a little russet-coated deer that stands no more than twenty inches in height at the shoulder. He is an odd fellow, with horns that shed like other deer but with horny pedicels that are permanent. In addition, making him even odder, are prehistoric, vestigial appendages, large canine teeth that protrude from his upper jaw and hang over his lower lips on either side of his mouth. He lives mostly alone in the leafy glades of the Terai forest. He is a delicate, shy, peaceful little chap and he asks of his fellow jungle dwellers only that he be left alone to live his reclusive life and to survive to breed and continue his species. In return, he has a solemn pact with the jungle folk: to warn them without fail when a big cat, a tiger or a leopard, is in the vicinity and on the prowl. Barking Deer call with a single, strident bark that to the untrained ear sounds exactly like a medium-sized dog in the first stages of alarm. The call is repeated at intervals of about five seconds and although the books say that the *Kakar* starts his call when he sees a big cat and ends it when the cat disappears from his view, this is not true. The call may begin when the cat is sighted, but more often than not it will begin when he is scented. And the little animal will continue to tell the jungle folk to watch out for minutes after the cat has disappeared from view.

The call that I was now hearing came from the deep jungle directly in front of us. I had been looking toward the left, my attention attracted by a tiny rustling sound that I thought could have been a blade of dry grass being pressed down by a paw, and now I turned my eyes in the other direction. The clearing in front of us was bright with the light of the great parade of stars marching down the Himalayan sky, but the vine-clad trees that edged it to the east formed a wall of impenetrable darkness in which nothing could be seen. Nevertheless, I watched the wall for a while for a shape, a shadow, something that would tell me where Mr. Stripes was and what he was doing. I was straining my sight against the sea of ink when suddenly I saw what looked like a single yellow eye staring directly at us. Pale yellow, unmoving, a baleful slit of an eye, the singular intentness of which slowly began to stir the hairs on the back of my neck. As I watched, it grew slowly in size and my right hand was actually beginning to creep toward the security of my rifle when I realized that what I was seeing, through that black tangle of leaf and vine, was the edge of a rising full moon coming out of the eastern sky.

Now the Barking Deer called again and a couple of Peafowl, roused out of their dreams in the top of a giant *Simul* tree, wailed an answer. The third and fourth calls of the *Kakar* told me he was moving away and then, as suddenly as he started his warnings to all who would listen, his calling ceased and he was gone. The moon rose and the night was still. I looked at my watch. Two hours had passed and I was beginning to put two and two together on the reaction of the tiger to our presence. The sum of this was, firstly, that he knew we were there and secondly, that he had made up his mind to simply stay put and not show himself or try to claim his meal until we left. Tigers are infinitely cautious animals and perennially wary of man. The books say that they fear man. They do not. They instinctively know man to be dangerous to them. How, since they do not know death, is not understood. But they view man as a constant threat and recognize his ability to harm them. The result is an unwavering suspicion of people backed by the fixed and constant wariness that is often mistaken for fear, an example of which we were now experiencing.

When building a *machan* and planning for a "sit," one of the ploys used to try and circumvent the tiger's extreme cautiousness is called the Extra Man Ploy. It works like this. In dense jungle one never knows where the tiger is. He may be a mile away. He may be lying up twenty yards away. Not knowing where he is, one always works with the premise that he is close by and all preparations for a *machan* sit are shaped around this premise. All noise is kept to a minimum and all conversations are in whispers. For if the tiger is close by then he is carefully monitoring everything that is going on, weighing it, considering it, and making his own private plans accordingly. Quiet sounds he will accept. Whispers, snapping twigs, the rustle that accompanies the building of a small tree platform are all allowable. But loud noises he will not endure, particularly human voices, and if the volume of noise climbs above his level of tolerance, he will slip away into the deep jungle and be seen no more.

The Extra Man Ploy is put into action when all the preparations for the "sit" are complete. The *machan* is finished, the clients have climbed into it with all of their gear and are frozen into silence, the rope ladder has been drawn up, and the signal is given to the men who will act out the E.M.P. Until now everyone has been very quiet and all of the conversation has been carried out in the softest of whispers. Now, for the E.M.P. men, the order of sound is reversed and, as they leave, they immediately commence a conversation clearly audible to a lurking cat. They carry this conversation with them, increasing it in volume as they draw away from the *machan*. They enhance the sound of their talking by tapping on the boles of trees with their axes or knives as they pass and the tiger, hearing them leave, presumes that all of the group have departed and that it is now safe to emerge.

With Karen, just as I had no time to build a proper hide, so also I lacked an extra man to carry out the E.M.P. And I now came to the conclusion that our tiger, having heard us arrive and heard no one depart, was not going to be persuaded to come out and show himself. I reached this conclusion as my watch showed that we had sat waiting in the Land Rover for three hours. As the dark yellow orb of the moon rose slowly in front of us, spilling a flood of saffron light into the little clearing and piercing the indigo jungle behind with translucent shafts, I made a decision. With the cold night air beginning to run little fingers of ice down my back, and with the thought that my client must be half frozen, I decided that it was time to call off the sit. I had half turned toward her to tell her this when I heard a strange sound.

The sound came from the open country to our right, where we had stopped when we first heard the Jungle Ravens. It was one that I must have heard before but for some reason this time I could not quickly identify it. It was a heavy thumping noise and sounded for all the world like someone thumping the earth with a big wooden mallet. It grew in volume and seemed to be approaching. As it did, I heard a second sound accompanying it — a strong swishing noise, like someone lashing the grass with a bunch of sticks tied together. The sound was quite close but its origin was still hidden from view by the trees when I suddenly realized what was making it. It was an elephant pulling up tufts of the thick coarse grass that grew in the *phantas* and beating them on the ground to shake off the dirt before putting them in its mouth. At the same time that this realization hit me, and with Karen giving me wide-eyed inquiring glances as to what was approaching us, an elephant appeared out of the gloom of the brush to our right, stepped into the clearing, and stopped.

The animal was a big male with short thick ivory on either side. I judged him to be a good ten feet in height, young and in prime condition. But there was something more to his appearance, something that made him look different from the many other wild elephants that I had seen from time to time in the western Terai forests and for a moment I could not quite pin it down. Then I noticed his neck, which was unusually thick and powerful, and his massive muscular build. The head itself was topped off by two very prominent forehead lobes and the animal's whole appearance projected a brooding aura of strength and power.

When he stepped into the clearing, the animal instantly scented us and just as quickly saw us and the Land Rover. In answer to the inquiring sidelong glances that Karen was giving me, I put my hand on her knee and, with a gentle pressure, indicated to her that she should remain very still. For we were now in direct confrontation with a large, wild, and potentially dangerous animal — an animal that could, with half a dozen steps, be upon us and quite easily pick up the Land Rover and toss it in the air. If he decided to do this, the only way to stop him would be to shoot and that was something that I could only bring myself to do as a last resort. Because of the very short distance that separated us, there would be no time for a deflection shot — a shot over the animal's head in an attempt to turn its charge — and my single shot would have to be a fatal one.

Elephants are curious creatures. Like most animals, their behavior for the most part follows set patterns. The Asian elephant, unlike the African, which is a much more aggressive animal, has a more or less predictable reaction when confronted with a human presence. It invariably almost immediately leaves the scene of the confrontation to seek the psychological and physical security of cover and distance. Over the years, my personal encounters with wild elephants have nearly if not quite always produced this pre-dictable reaction. But then, as can happen with all animals and cer-tainly with the big ones like tiger, buffalo, and bison, something can alter the pattern and one can find oneself suddenly and disconcert-ingly faced with the unpredictable.

This happened to me some years ago when I was a tea planter in north Bengal and it taught me an unforgettable lesson . . . that the predictable patterns of large wild animals, and particularly of elephants, as described by the books, can never be viewed as un-breakable.

In the time of the British Raj, on the tea estates of north Bengal, all kinds of private transportation were used by the white colonials. In the forties, one of the most common and certainly one of the most popular was a little British car called the Austin Seven. Austin was the name of the company that made the vehicle and the number seven indicated its horsepower. The little car, a two-door, four-seater about two thirds the size of a Volkswagen Bug, arrived into the world sometime at the end of the twenties—I remember my fa-ther had one in Dublin in 1931. It became famous when an enterpris-ing and adventurous Britisher drove one from London to Calcutta, a journey that was adventure in its truest sense in the days when there were virtually no roads east of Istanbul. Within a few years Austin Sevens, or Baby Austins as they were affectionately called, were to be seen battling the mud and the rocks and the sand from Peshawar to the Punjab, from Madras to Mandalay, from Cairo to Catmandoo.

The one that I had in those days was red, with a black canvas top. It had a wooden steering wheel, brass door handles, a radiator cap with a little gauge set in glass mounted on it, and fine big brass headlights. It was not young when I bought it and I had to rebuild the seats and fit new bumpers on it. I had a Chinese shoemaker called Fook Chung in Darjeeling do the seats for me in leather. When these proved a little hard to sit on, he fitted them with big cushions stuffed with kapok and feathers. I bumped around the dirt roads of the various tea estates where I was stationed, using the little car for work, for going to the club once a week, and of course, in those days, for hunting.

One day I set off in the Austin to look for wild boar. There was a function of some kind at the club and as the tea company's unofficial *shikari*, or hunter-provider, I was deputized to provide meat for the occasion. The tea estate where I lived at this time was set in a fine stretch of forest. A sparkling jungle river that came out of Bhutan, the Jaldaka, ran through this forest and in it were tiger, leopard, elephant, and in those days, many rhino. There was a good dirt road that ran from the estate into this forest and early one morning, with the gold-barred light of a winter sun making sword thrusts through the trees, I fired up the little Austin. Trailing a plume of dust, I set off for a grass thicket I knew about a mile into the forest, a place where a fine fat boar might well be found digging for roots.

I had gone about a mile when I came to a corner in the forest road. I could not see around the corner but I knew from previous runs that there was a short, steep incline behind it running down to a dry streambed. I slowed down as I approached, shifting the Austin into second gear. The sand and dirt of the tea estate roads had, in the previous month, worn out the brake pads on the baby's wheels and I had not yet been able to find replacements. This did not matter very much in a vehicle whose top speed was seldom in excess of fifteen miles an hour on roads where there was virtually no other traffic. A quick down-change of gear was usually enough to slow the little vehicle almost to a standstill. When I came around the corner with the car in second and still slowing, I saw two elephants coming out of the forest about fifty yards away at the bottom of the incline. One was a medium sized female, the other a big bull with a nice set of tusks. The bull reached the center of the road as I turned the corner. The cow came close behind him and a little to the side. Between the two of them they completely blocked the narrow forest road.

My problem was apparent. I was at the top of a steep incline. At the bottom, directly in my path and with no way around them, were two elephants. I was traveling at about ten miles per hour in a car that could only be slowed by the use of its gears. And at ten miles an hour in a car that was built long before the introduction of synchromeshed gears, there was no hope of getting from second into first. The answer was either to try and steer the car into the forest, to the right or left of the road and stop it by ramming it into the brush, or to bail out and let it run on down the incline. The first course seemed the better one. But a quick glance to right and left showed me deep drainage ditches on either side of the road. Any attempt to try and get over them and into the forest would almost certainly result in a capsized vehicle. The only answer was to bail out.

I grabbed my rifle from where it was propped against the passenger seat and, opening the right hand door, dived headlong into the ditch that bordered the road. I rolled a couple of times with the rifle tucked tight to my chest and then came to a halt, quite unharmed. The Austin, driverless, went on.

When the bull elephant saw the car coming down the hill toward him he froze. Behind him the cow did the same thing. With their attention centered on the little red car with its shiny brass headlights, they had not seen my hasty exit and now, as I lay in the ditch watching them, they either did not know I was there or preferred to ignore me while they centered their interest on the car.

Just before the road entered the dry streambed, it flattened out a little. Now, as the Austin entered this level area, it slowed to probably no more than five miles an hour. Nevertheless, it was still moving when it arrived in front of the bull and I could see that there was going to be a head-on collision if the bull did not move out of the way. I presumed that he would. In fact I was confident that he would. I had encountered elephants several times before this in the Austin on forest roads and they had always moved quickly out of the way, heading for the deep forest with tails up and a snort and a squeal or two. This was the reaction I now expected, one that would follow the predictable pattern of the Asian elephant. But the bull that now stood on the early morning Jaldaka forest road had decided, for reasons that the books do not cover, that the time had come to move out of his predictable pattern and into another one. This he did and the cow, following the example of her mate of the moment, decided that she would do the same.

The Austin was still rolling when the bull suddenly stepped forward, right into its oncoming path and, with the tightly curled end of a massive trunk placed firmly against the brass radiator, brought it to a halt in a cloud of dust. That done, he stepped back and stood for a moment, cocking his head to one side as if to say, "And what have we here?" Then, with slow and ponderous strides, he walked around the little car. The female followed him with quick, almost mincing steps, ears flapping.

A complete circle of the car brought both of the elephants around again to the front. Here they stopped and, side by side, stood and looked at the vehicle. What was going on in their minds I had no idea, but from the way their heads moved and from the closeness with which they stood to each other, it was obvious that there was elephantine discussion seeking a mutual resolution. Having reached a decision, the bull stepped forward again and, curling his trunk around one of the brass headlights, made a quick twisting motion, tore it out of its socket, and tossed it into the ditch at the edge of the road. The cow instantly stepped forward and, taking the other headlight in her trunk, did the same thing.

Next, the bull took hold of the brass radiator cap. He had a little trouble getting a grip on it but eventually he did and, with a twist, he tore it out of its setting and flipped it into the ditch. The cow then stepped forward and seized the front bumper. The original bumpers might have been of steel. But alas, the ones with which I had fitted the Austin were of wood. With a heavy splintering crack, the front bumper came loose from its moorings and went the way of the headlights and the radiator cap. Promptly the bull, not to be outdone by his companion, walked around to the back of the car and did the same thing with the back bumper. This done, he rejoined the female at the front of the car and once again they stood side by side and, massive heads held close together, considered further action.

From my prone position in the ditch, cuddling my rifle, I watched this very strange performance. And I considered what action I was going to take if the slow destruction of my "baby" was to continue. I did not have many alternatives. I had never shot an elephant and I was firm in my mind that I was never going to shoot one. But even if I had wanted to, the rifle that I had with me was totally inadequate for the job. Planning for wild boar, I had taken along a light .300 Mauser and the very best I might do with this would be to wound. Certainly the little projectiles that the Mauser hurled would not penetrate the honeycombed bone of the elephant's head, not even where it was thinnest above the boss of the trunk. Shooting, then, was out. The next best thing was to fire a few rounds in the air and try to drive the animals off. But partly because I was very close to the elephants and partly because I was both amazed at what I was seeing and curious as to what was going to happen next, I held my fire and did nothing.

Now, looking back at what happened next, I cannot but laugh. But at the time I think I may have uttered a moan or two at what looked like the end of my little red baby. The bull led the way for the next act. He walked around to the right hand side of the car and, after a brief examination of its interior, reached in and seized the steering wheel in a firm grasp. The Austin, reluctant to give up another vital part, resisted and for a few seconds the powerful trunk of the bull lifted the vehicle right up off the ground. Then the steering mechanism disintegrated and the steering wheel and its shaft came out in one piece. Over the bull's shoulder it went as the cow moved in from the other side. Now there was another silent meeting of minds as they both peered into the interior of the car to see what should be done next. They made a quick decision. The cushions that lay on the front seats. The bull took out one and the cow took out the other. But now, this time, instead of flinging them over their shoulders the way the rest of the baby's bits had gone, they began to beat the little car with them. Within seconds, of course, both pillows in their cotton cases burst and clouds of brown and white chicken feathers and duck down accompanied by tufts of kapok spiraled upward in the golden sunlight of the clear morning air.

When the pillows burst, the elephants decided that it was time to stop chastising the little car and perform one last act. They walked around to its rear end and together, trunks under the chassis, lifted it right up off the ground and stood it upright on its nose. Carefully, so as not to topple it over, they slid it gently to the side of the road. Then, having established a lesson about what happens to little red cars that come trundling down forest roads in the early morning to disturb the perambulations of perfectly peaceful forest folk, they turned and walked away without a backward glance.

The car that the Jaldaka elephants had soundly if somewhat destructively chastised had been empty. But the vehicle now confronted by a very large bull elephant in the dark of the forest night had two people in it. And if the bull that now stood looking at us from a distance of a few feet decided, like the elephants of Jaldaka, that he was going to step out of pattern and do something different, we were faced with a potentially dangerous situation. And this is exactly what he did, although in a way that was one hundred percent different from the broken pattern of the Jaldaka elephants. What the big bull did, instead of turning away and leaving us, instead of backing off and getting away from the danger that instinctively he would feel that we represented, was stand and stare at us. And he did this for a full five minutes with no more of a movement than the slow raising and lowering of his trunk, a movement that no doubt allowed him to gather in the strange odors, analyze them and identify them, and set each in its separate place in his mind. His reaction, being out of pattern, was disconcerting to me and, as she told me later, quite terrifying to Karen. Knowing nothing about elephants, she had absolutely no idea what the bull was doing, or what he was going to do. Among other mental scenarios, she envisioned him taking three quick steps forward, grabbing the front of the Land Rover, and tossing it up in the air, complete with human contents.

Why did the bull do this and what was he thinking as he stood and watched us? What was going on in that elephantine brain? Did he find the human scent confusing? This is possible. If it had any experience of human scent, it would have been that of local natives, and a Taru diet of rice and heavily spiced vegetables makes for a body odor quite different from that of a western person. Was the scent of the dead Axis Deer mixed with the powerful smell of the tiger troublesome? Was the sight of the dead deer, lying between him and us, part of the reason he stood there watching us? Some

elephants suffer from moriphobia and the bull may have been
afflicted this way. Two of my own hunting domestic elephants
suffered from it to a degree where a dead bird on a trail would send
them into spasms of shivering and snorting, sometimes causing a
mandatory fifty-yard diversion around the little pile of feathers.
Whatever was going on inside that massive head, it was probably
a combination of two things. One, a careful assessment of all of the
facts that told him he had stumbled on a unique and unusual situation demanding neither flight nor a defensive tactic. Two, an
arousal of the very strong streak of curiosity that many animals experience when they come across something that they do not fully
understand and which demands closer scrutiny. Whatever it was, it
took the huge tusker more than five interminable minutes to make
up his mind about what he had encountered and what he was going
to do about it. When he did, having satisfied his curiosity, he suddenly whirled without warning and in half a dozen quick steps disappeared into the night.

It was three days later and the last day of Karen's safari. She had
still not shot a tiger. In fact, the only thing she had killed was one
Axis Deer that was used for camp meat. But she was quite satisfied.
She had enjoyed the safari, loving the great experience of the jungle
and, after shooting the deer, felt that she did not want to kill anything else. We had been out since dawn and were now sitting at a
late morning campfire sipping coffee — coffee with the real taste that
only four hours of hiking in cold, clear morning air can bring — and
waiting for brunch. Suddenly I saw a movement in the trees that
fringed the campsite. I raised my binoculars to the movement and
saw, above the line of the brush, the heads of two men approaching.
Soon they came into full view and I saw that one was the *jimadhar*
or headman of a Taru village called Kalkutta that lay about twenty
miles from camp. The other was his son. As they reached the edge
of the trees and while still some distance from the campsite they
both coughed loudly. This was a courtesy to let us know that they
were coming, a custom that Tarus always apply when approaching
a camp, day or night. Then they hailed us and I got up and walked
to meet them.

The *jimadhar* of Kalkutta was an old friend of mine and one of the first men I met when I started hunting professionally in Nepal in the fifties. He was at this time about thirty years of age, five foot three—the average height of a Taru villager—with a hard brown face set off by a shock of thick black hair that had never seen a comb. A pair of twinkling brown eyes peered out from under this shaggy mop and his short, wiry body was clad in a twist of once-white loincloth, a cheap cotton shirt of faded blue, and a black waistcoat with small silver buttons. His son, about twelve at this time, was a smaller version of his father and dressed the same way.

We greeted each other and, while his son went off to the kitchen to talk with my men and get himself a cup of sweetened tea, the *jamadhar*, having placed a small log carefully on the campfire—another act of courtesy—made himself comfortable in one of my campfire chairs. When Pasang, my head camp man, brought him a mug of milky tea, thick with the coarse brown sugar that is called *ghur*, a drink all Tarus seem to love, he began to talk. Firstly, there was an assessment of the weather, its present form, the forecast for the morrow, and what the rest of the winter might bring. Then the crops and what the weather was doing or might do to them. Then his family: sons, daughters, brothers, sisters, uncles, and aunts. And, as an afterthought, his wife. Then, with a smile that revealed the gaping cavity where his two front teeth had once been—until one night, drunk, he had fallen into a fire and landed face first on a stone that some idiot had put in it—his favorite subject: the jungle and the jungle folk.

The *jimadhar* had accompanied me on several hunts and together we had enjoyed some exciting moments. Now, some of these were recapped. "The big tiger that leapt on the elephant, *Sahib*, remember that one?" The wild boar that tried to climb up a tree to get at a brother Taru and managed to get far enough to bite off his toe. The crocodile sleeping in the shallows that the *Sahib* had walked on when stepping out of the canoe. The elephant that got caught in quicksand. (One of my safari riding elephants had got into quicksand in the Sarda River and after hours of struggling, totally exhausted, had to be pulled out with a Land Rover assisted by fifty Taru men.) And then the *Sahib*'s clients. The one who wanted his *machan* to be fifty feet(!) up in a *Sal* tree. The one who got lost every

31

time he left camp. The one who was terrified of insects and spent most of his time in bed protected by mosquito net. The one who, at the sight of his first leopard, ejected all of the rounds in his rifle and then tried to fire the rifle, empty, at the bewildered cat. The rhino we did not want to shoot that chased us all over the place.

There was a pause while we had a good laugh about the enraged rhino, a brief interval during which another mug of tea magically appeared from the kitchen tent. Then he turned to me and said, "I hear, *Sahib*, that you met with Tula Hatti and had a talk with him the other night in the jungle?"

I looked at him to see if he was serious. There would be a smile on his face if he were not. But his weathered face, cocked to one side to show me he was waiting for an answer, was anything but smiling and I knew instantly that the jungle grapevine had somehow picked up the news of our encounter with the big elephant and carried it all the way to his village. I was not a little surprised at the way the news had gone so far so quickly. Twenty miles, a distance measured in milliseconds in the modern world, is a considerable stretch in country where the only communication is by word of mouth and where almost all travel is on foot. But as it would not do for a youthful P.W.H. to show surprise at everything he heard, I hid my feelings and said, "Yes, that is correct, my friend. We did meet a big elephant, a tusker, in the jungle three nights ago. But what is this name you have for him? What do you mean, Tula Hatti?"

"Tula Hatti, *Sahib*. The great elephant. The biggest of them all. The king of the elephants and the father of every little *butcha hatti* that you see running around the jungle. The one that we draw in reverence on the walls of our houses. Now you have met him and talked with him. Now he will be your friend."

That was my introduction to Tula Hatti, the Taru people's king of the elephants, and although I did not know it then, it was the beginning of something which, in time, would weave exotic threads into the tapestry of my life and the life of my family.

It is night. The small sounds of the jungle have resumed their quiet symphony. My wife and Dede and I lie awake, listening. The shadows of the big trees that shade our campsite move slowly across the canvas roof of our tent as the moon falls toward the western horizon. From the camp kitchen area, where the Sherpas have their tents, a murmuring of voices as the men, awakened by the scream of the elephant, ease back to sleep. From her sleeping bag, tucked in the corner of our big safari tent, the sound of soft breathing as Rara, our four-year-old daughter, moves happily through the world of her dreams.

We have a flask of hot coffee in the tent. I get up and pour some into an enamel mug and get back into bed to drink it. We talk, quietly, as one finds oneself doing all the time in forests that are the home of wild animals where one is privileged to be a guest. We talk about the long road that has brought us to this point, the research and effort that began nearly five years ago with the rediscovery of the great elephant and culminated with the completion of the movie about him. That started before Rara was born with half a dozen safaris leading to a photographic reconnaissance which in turn led to a season of full production with a professional film crew. A photo recce for the great elephant during which we were unable to find him and a full production run, on location, when for weeks he simply disappeared. A saga that in the end narrowed down to one goal: find the elephant and get footage of him—to prove to the world that he existed, if nothing else—or else give up and go home. This is an account of that search. It is also the story of the beautiful and little-known White Grass Plains Reserve in the southwest Terai of Nepal, of the abundant wildlife for which it provides a habitat, and of the extraordinary experiences of a family from Oregon on safari in a part of the world as yet barely touched by civilization.

2

DISCOVERY

I hunted professionally in Nepal for sixteen years and in that time, during the course of seventy-two safaris, I encountered Tula Hatti probably a dozen times. Each time I saw him he seemed to have grown another few inches and to have put on weight and muscle. The very first time that I encountered him, in 1955, my guess was that he was about fifteen years of age. He was not quite fully grown – he had another five or six years to do that – and he certainly exhibited at that time all of the robust physical qualities of a growing teenage elephant. But it was not until 1983 at which time, if my original estimate was correct, he must have been in his early forties, when I encountered him in the dense jungles that border the east side of the Bauni River in the White Grass Plains, that I realized just how enormous he had become.

With Dede, I had just finished a winter of river running in the Himalaya, culminating with a first run of what was the last of the big unexplored rivers of the mountains, the Sarda. The Sarda is the extreme western river of Nepal and it marks the border between the little kingdom's western provinces and the district of Kumaon, in India. A successful run of the river meant ending up in Kanchanpur, not far from the White Grass Plains, and so a visit to the reserve was included in our plans. We originally intended to complete the river trip in fifteen days, including getting there from Kathmandu, time on the water, and getting back. But, as so often seems to happen in Nepal, the gods frowned on our best laid plans.

We left Kathmandu hoping to drive right through to the western hill town of Dandeldhura and from there to trek the remaining fifty miles to our entry point on the river, close to its confluence with another river called the Chamlia. But two days out of Kathmandu and only halfway to the west, with our International Scout loaded with 2000 pounds of river-running equipment and three men of our Sherpa team, we found the single road that runs east to west through the lower foothills of Nepal blocked by a landslide. The slide was big and the men who were already trying to clear it told us that it would take ten days before the road would be open again. There was nothing for it but to divert through India and so we turned south, found a back road, and drove down into India's northern province of Uttar Pradesh. We spent one night there camping well off the road and deep in a forest beside a small river. We stayed away from the road because all of Uttar Pradesh, particularly its northern areas that border Nepal, has *dacoits*, or bandits, and they are a dangerous and indeed murderous lot to encounter on a lonely road in the dark of night. From there we drove west, keeping close to the border and using mostly government forest roads. Two more days of driving and three river ferry crossings brought us to the Nepal border again. Carefully fording the Mohana River, we slipped back into western Nepal close to the little Nepalese border town of Dhangarhi. Leaving the Scout there where it would be convenient for our return journey to Kathmandu, we rented space on a truck carrying rice to Dandeldhura. Perched on top of the sacks of rice with all of our river equipment, we made the forty-five-mile journey from Dhangarhi to the little hill town of Dandeldhura, grinding along at a snail's pace in the ancient and heavily overloaded truck, in one long day. We spent one night camped in a field outside Dandeldhura and the next morning, with fifteen Nepalese porters carrying our loads—two of them delighted to be getting double rate for carrying our 150-pound rafts—we set off for the Sarda. We reached our planned entry point on the river in four days. There we dismissed the porters who, after they had been paid an extra four days' wages for the return journey to Dandeldhura, happily informed us that they would make the journey in one day. After a night's rest under a giant *Simul* tree by the murmuring water of the Sarda, we launched and set off downstream.

It took us ten days to run the Sarda, to chart it for those who would come after us, and to name all of its major rapids. There were thirty rapids in all, varying on the Himalayan scale of ten from three to nine. Only two were unrunnable. One of these we named Grey-hound Rapid because it had a hole right in the center, halfway down, that could have easily swallowed a Greyhound bus. The other we named Chuka Five. It was the fifth of a set of continuous rapids that ran down past the little lower hill village of Chuka, a place famous for being the scene of one of the last great maneating tiger hunts of the legendary Jim Corbett.

On the tenth day we pulled into the east side, the Nepal side, of the river about a mile above the old British system of lock gates that controls and feeds the waters of the Sarda canal system, life's blood of the fertile fields of northern Uttar Pradesh. A runner sent to the Nepalese town of Mahendranagar brought us transportation in the form of a jeep owned by a Nepalese friend of many years, Colonel Hikmat Bisht of Mahendranagar, and within a few hours we were relaxing in his comfortable home on the Nepalgunj road, about half a mile from the center of town. We spent a pleasant night with Colonel Bisht and his charming and hospitable family and the next day saw off the other members of our group, by air from Mahen-dranagar and by train through India, back to Kathmandu. Three Sherpas stayed behind with us: our basic team.

Now, although we were running late and were more than ten days behind the schedules carefully planned in Kathmandu for the river run, a check on mail and cables forwarded to us from Kath-mandu via Colonel Bisht showed us that all was well back at the Weed Patch—as we fondly called our property in Oregon—and that there was really no need to hurry home. In fact, we thought that we could manage another six weeks in Nepal. Ideally we would spend at least four weeks of it in the pristine jungles and grasslands of the White Grass Plains Reserve, my old hunting grounds of years gone by and a place that was to us then—and still is, now—a combi-nation of spiritual sanctuary and wildlife paradise. We spent another day at Colonel Bisht's home—a day that I used to get to Dhanghari, pick up the Scout, and drive it back to Mahendranagar—and then set off on the twenty-five-mile drive south to Sukila Phanta, the White Grass Plains, home of tiger, leopard, wild boar, four species of deer including the last great herd of Swamp Deer left in Asia, one

36

species of crocodile, numerous small animals and birds, and a single herd of wild elephants that in the winter months of each year included Tula Hatti.

This was our fifth visit together to the White Grass Plains Reserve. On arrival, we made camp in a little grove of trees close to the Bauni River on the south side of the forest road that runs from the guard post at Singpur into the reserve. As with many of our campsites, this one had a name, Oriole Camp, so given because of the glorious morning birdsong that filled the trees above the tents every day, the territorial calling of Golden and Black-Headed Orioles.

It took us a couple of days to get settled in. To get the tents up, the kitchen built, the trash holes dug, and the camping equipment—shovels, tools, tarps, axes, and the kitchen utensils, pots, and pans—all stored in proper place. For big logs to be hauled in for the campfire, for the mess tent area to be cleaned and leveled, and for the men, Pasang, our worthy employee and friend of so many years, Jangbu, our cook, and Phurua, our general camp man, to build a little grass wall around their sleeping tent. And last but not least for the positioning and building of the "loo" enclosure in a place that was not too conspicuous but at the same time did not require too long a walk when nature called in the wee small hours. There are no rhino in the White Grass Plains and so no white sheets had to be hung around the camp to keep those magnificent but seemingly small brained beasts from blundering in among the cooking pots in the gray light of dawn. With a last quick brush-clearing operation—a place to park the Scout that made it comparatively safe from the attentions of curious elephants—the camp was ready for use and we were ready to begin a month of wildlife observation, of study and photography in the dark green jungles and waving brown grasslands of the White Grass Plains.

During the years that Dede and I have spent in Nepal together, our interest in wildlife has always been an all-embracing one that encompasses all kinds of animals and birds, and that includes a particular interest in certain animals like tigers, crocodiles, and the big snakes. One particular area of interest has always been the birds of the area and wherever we went we always carried at least one dog-eared copy of Robert Fleming's excellent book, *The Birds of Nepal.* In this work, which took Robert Fleming, Jr., and his father, Robert Fleming, M.D., many years of dedicated study and research to complete, some 802 species of birds are listed for Nepal's Terai jungles, middle hills, and alpine regions. Among these, the ones that most captured our interest and challenged us were those listed as rare, scarce, or status unknown, and it was with great pleasure over the years that we were able to positively identify, sometimes on more than one occasion, a number of these species. Four of them, the Great Slaty Woodpecker, the Swamp Partridge, the Common Crane, and the Spoonbill, were found in or not far from the White Grass Plains. Now, on this visit, we were concentrating on finding two more: the Black-Backed Woodpecker and the Greater Bustard. Thus it was, with bird book and binoculars in hand, a few days after we had settled in at Oriole Camp, that we set off on foot one morning into the fig tree, vine, thorn, and elephant grass jungle that shades and, in its thicker growths, even darkens the west bank of the Bauni River on the eastern side of the reserve. We were looking for birds, but what we found was something a lot larger. A giant in fact. A giant who would, within the space of a very short time, literally change the shape and direction of our lives.

Leaving camp, we walked across the little wooden bridge that carries the road from Singpur into the reserve. Stepping carefully on the thick transverse wooden planks of the bridge, I listened to them groaning and creaking underfoot and wondered how long it would be before age, wood eating insects, and the passage of an overloaded vehicle brought the bridge down. I had been under the bridge several times to check the structure and what I saw down there among the rotting beams and splitting supports had been enough to convince me that the bridge was no longer safe for vehicles. I had communicated this knowledge to the authorities, the wildlife warden and his staff at Majgaon, the reserve headquarters at the north western corner of the reserve. But it had been ignored and several times while we were there, with a degree of fatalism that my western mind found hard to comprehend, jeep loads of guards and officials had thundered across the aged and sagging structure, rattling the planks and pockmarking the dark brown surface of the

The Tribhuvan Rajpath — Nepal's first and for many years only highway, connecting Kathmandu with India — was built in the late 1950s.

The control tower, reservations office, baggage claim, and waiting room at the Mahendranagar Airport, twenty miles from the White Grass Plains Reserve.

A vegetable stall in Mahendranagar market — the main source of supply for the *Tula Hatti* film crew.

Singpur, a Taru village, on the edge of the White Grass Plains Reserve. The village was relocated some twenty miles to the east and renamed Nya Singpur (new Singpur) when the reserve expanded.

Taru lands on the edge of the White Grass Plains. The flimsy tower is where villagers spend nights during the harvest season, shouting and singing to keep wild animals out of their crops. A reserve guard stands in the foreground.

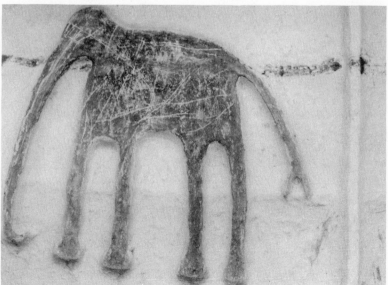

Tula Hatti pictured on the mud wall of a Taru house in the Kanchanpur district. The forked tail depicts the hair tuft found on the tails of all Asian elephants.

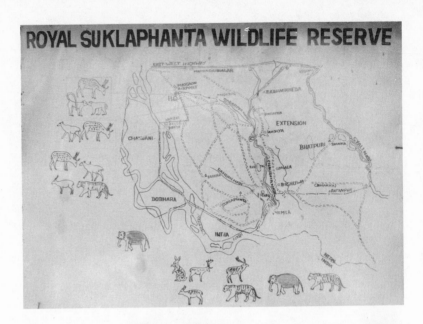

ROYAL SUKLAPHANTA WILDLIFE RESERVE

Signs at the entrance of the Sukila Phanta (White Grass Plains) Reserve. On these, located at different entrances to the reserve, the area is variously named Sukla Phanta, Suklaphanta, Sukla, and Sukila Phanta.

शाही शिकार सुरक्षित बन
ROYAL WILD LIFE RESERVE
हामी सित भेटहुन सक्छ (YOU MAY SEE US)

हात्ति	Elephant	(Elphas Maximus)
बाघ	Tiger	(Panthra Tigriris)
रतुवा	Barking deer	(Muntiacus Muntjack)
जरायो	Sambur deer	(Cervus unicolar)
वार सिंगा	Swamp deer	(Cervus Duvauceli)
चितल	Spotted deer	(Axis Axis)
लगुना	Hog deer	(Axis Porcinus)
घोड़ गधा	Blue Bull	(Boselaphus Tragocamelus)
कृष्णसागर	Black buck	(Antilope Cervicapra)
बदेल	Wild boar	(Sus Scorfa)
व्वासी	Wolf	(Canis Lupus)
स्याल	Jackal	(Canis Aureus)
चितुवा	Leapard	(Panthra Pardus)
दुम्सी	Porcopine	(Hystrix Indica)
लंगुर	Common Langur	(Presbytis Entellus)
बांदर	Monkey	(Macca Radiata)
लोखर्के	Squirrel	(Funumbulus Palamarum)
भालू	Bear	(Selena retos Thibetanus)
हुंडार	Hyana	(Hydrophasianus Chirugus)
बन कुकुर	Wild dog	(Coun Alpinus)
बन विरालो	Wild Cat	(Felis Chaus)
प्याउरो	Fox	(Vulpes Bengalensis)
खरायो	Hare	(Caprolagus Hispidus)

Hidden Phanta. A small *phanta* surrounded by dense jungle tucked into a curve of the Bauni River. A quiet, secluded place used by Tula Hatti from time to time for an afternoon siesta.

A leopard uses a fallen tree to cross a river inside the White Grass Plains Reserve. Leopards like to keep their feet dry and will seldom swim a river unless forced to. They may also be aware of the menace of crocodiles; a big crocodile will kill and eat a leopard.

The Bauni River bridge, one of two in the reserve. Both bridges have been ravaged by borer beetles, white ants, and the heat and rain of monsoons.

A big wild boar watches the approach of the *Tula Hatti* camera car on a forest road in the southern jungles of the White Grass Plains.

Peter Byrne on the middle forest Elephant Walk used by Tula Hatti and the White Grass Plains herd. The surface is beaten hard and flat by the pressure of elephants' feet.

An Axis, or *Chital*, deer stag in the White Grass Plains.

Peter Byrne in front of a wall of elephant grass. The average height of the grass is eighteen feet; single stalks can grow to twenty-five feet. Visibility in the grass is usually three feet maximum.

Bauni below with showers of splinters and rotten wood, to the consternation of the big catfish that liked to lie in the shadow of the bridge.

Leaving the bridge, we walked quietly down the road into the reserve. At this time of year—late winter—the surface of the road was, with the exception of its grass-covered center ridge, thickly coated with heavy brown dust. In the dust, clearly written for all to read every day, was the story of all the travelers of the previous night: the direction of their travel, the time of their passing, and very often the reasons behind their passage through the jungle night. Walking slowly, reading the signs, we could clearly see where a Sloth Bear had crossed the bridge and gone west. Coming in the other direction were the big, doglike imprints of a hyena. Further up the road, a little later, we found where the hyena had sensed the approach of the snuffling bear and, obeying the unwritten law of the jungle—that the smaller gives way to the larger—stepped aside to allow him to pass. Later in the night, a big male tiger had come down to the west side of the bridge. We knew this one; he lived in the dense grass of one of the islands of the swamp into which the Bauni flowed. We had been meeting him—and exchanging an occasional good morning—for many years. During the previous night he had come as far as the end of the Bauni Bridge and we guessed that he had seen the light of our campfire from there. His pugs, deep in the road dust, showed that he had stood there for a few moments before silently turning into the forest to the north of the road. The pattern of his stride showed that he was hunting and the direction that he had taken after leaving the road led us to believe that he had decided on a dinner of Axis Deer. Two small herds lived in the forest where he had gone and it was possible that one of the herds would now be minus a member that, as the laws of survival demand, would have been the slowest, or the least alert.

We stayed on the road for another hundred yards, as far as the territorial tree of our friend Mr. Stripes. We checked his scratch marks on the tree, ten feet up and torn deep into the dozens of others that he had clawed into the bark over the years. Then we turned, left the road, and in single file, moving very quietly and stopping

47

every twenty-five paces to look, listen, and smell the scents of the forest, we made our way south.

The jungle that borders the reserve road just west of the Bauni Bridge forms a long, thin rectangle about a mile in length, east to west, and three to four hundred yards in depth, north to south. Walking through this strip, we soon came to a big patch of elephant grass bordering the rectangle and after checking this carefully from the vantage point of a convenient tree—for an Elephant Walk skirts its northern edge—we entered it and walked right through to its other side. There we again entered the tree jungle. As it was much thicker, with dark patches of shade and canopy growth that shut out much of the light, we stopped for several minutes to look and listen and accustom our eyes to the gloom.

There is always a great deal of sound in the Terai forests of Nepal. It is mainly birdsong and at any one time, anywhere in the winter forests, and especially if one is near water, the air is filled with the territorial warblings and whistlings of dozens of birds. The next most constant sound is that of insects. Among these, the most incessant noisemaker of the jungle's diurnal hours is the cicada. Intermittent to this background of sounds are the noises made by animals. Probably the noisiest of these are the monkeys: the big gray Langurs that live for the most part high above the ground and the Rhesus Macaques, the smaller brown monkeys that spend as much time on the ground as they do in the trees and that are the most common monkeys of the Terai.

One of the basic ingredients of safety in jungles that contain large wild animals which, though normally inoffensive, can be dangerous if provoked, is constant alertness. One stays alert by using one's eyes and ears to their utmost capacity, by smelling the air for the distinctive body odors of the larger animals—with practice one can learn to distinguish many of them—and by analyzing sounds, particularly sounds that do not fit the constant pattern of noise. And doing this, diligently and continuously, is very important. Not so much to protect oneself from existing dangers, such as they are, but more to avoid making a mistake that might result in confrontation which will cause all wild animals, from field mice to elephants, to act defensively and perhaps aggressively. If and when this happens, situations can develop that can be fatal to the unwary, the inexperienced, or the downright foolish. To anyone, as that old master of the jungle story, Kipling, so aptly put it, who breaks the jungle law. The jungle law which, if respected and upheld, protects people from the wild things of the forest, just as in turn it protects the forest dwellers themselves. The law which, though powerful in application, is also delicate enough to be shattered by an ill-considered move.

Moving quietly in heavy jungle, breaking no twigs underfoot, rustling no dry leaves, taking advantage of the plays of light on the jungle floor to use the partial concealment of shade, being aware of the direction of the wind and where it will carry one's natural body odors make it possible to get close to most wild animals. It is equally easy, by ignoring what the sights and sounds are telling one, to get too close and to come face to face with a large wild animal. When that happens, depending on the species, one can find oneself faced with an animal that is dangerously startled, confused, or enraged. Or all three.

Standing in the gloom of the Bauni jungle, motionless and silent, we listened to the sounds. High in a tall fig tree, directly above us, a group of Alexandrine Parakeets chattered and screeched and the debris of their feeding — pieces of fruit, broken leaves, and twigs — fell softly around us. From far down in the jungle, a Peafowl called the long lonely catlike meow that gives the bird its Taru name, *Mau*. From close by came the subdued warbling of a little group of Jungle Babblers, little brown birds that, because they always seem to travel in groups of seven, are often called the Seven Sisters. From our right came the sharp piping of Coots, indicating that the edge of the swamp, with its deep pools that are the home of Coots, Purple Moorhens, and many other water birds, was close. Altogether, the air was heavy with sound. Normal sound. The sound of the afternoon jungle of a Terai winter's day. And normal scents. The scent of dry elephant grass. The odor of rotting leaves underfoot. And faint, hanging in the air, barely detectable, the sweet-sour smell of swamp water. Scenes, sights, and sounds helped us feel in tune with our surroundings and enabled us to move steadily ahead toward a group of old dead *Sal* trees that stood in the southwest corner of the

Singpur rice fields, where they bordered the Bauni jungle. It was there that we hoped to find the Black-Backed Woodpeckers.

Afterwards, we tried to remember what it was that made us, after only a few strides from our last listening and watching stop, stop again. Whatever it was, it registered on our subconscious minds in such a low range that we could not identify it. But stop we did, again. To peer through the gloom of the dense forest ahead and strain to the absolute limit of our senses, eyes and ears tuned to register the slightest sound, the tiniest deviation from the usual pattern. And the jungle told us nothing. Nothing by sight, sound, or scent. Had the giant elephant, standing motionless no more than twenty feet away from us in the gray shadows of the tree canopy above, not moved, we might well have walked right into him.

At one period in the course of a long and fascinating life in East Africa, Beryl Markham, the famed aviatrix and author of the classic work, *West with the Night*, spent some time working as a game spotter in Kenya for the White Hunter Bror Blixen. In those days, the thirties, there was much interest in trophy elephants. As a result, much of pilot Markham's time was spent looking for elephants from the air. When she first started looking for elephants, she quickly discovered that they were very difficult to find. She put this down to inexperience. Years later she realized that even with experience, it is difficult to see elephants. She reached the conclusion that elephants, by their very size, seem to create an optical illusion. It is not just their coloration, which allows them to blend so perfectly with their background, or their ability to move so silently. Or their habit of standing absolutely motionless when threatened or curious about something that needs consideration. It is their size. One simply does not expect to see something as big as what is being perceived. Thus the brain, temporarily at least, refuses to accept the message being sent to it by the eye.

Dede and I were walking in single file when we encountered the elephant. I was leading and I stopped when I saw something white in the foliage to my right about twenty feet away. It was about five feet above the ground, motionless. The instant I saw it, I was convinced that I was looking at the white headcloth of a poacher. I was also, as the wearer of the headcloth was not moving, convinced that he had detected our approach and was waiting for us to pass before moving.

Because of the importance of silence when moving in jungles that contain big game, Dede and I had created a simple set of sounds and signals for communication. The signals were minimal and usually consisted of just eye or lip movements. As these could only be used when we could see each other's faces, we enhanced them with a back-up set of whistles. We used these when we could not see each other and when we became separated, and they blended quite well, we thought, with the bird sounds with which the air was filled through all the daylight hours. There were three whistle signals. A single note meant "Be Alert," and its use indicated a situation, such as the possibility of the approach of a large animal, that required extra alertness. A double note meant "Stop, Do Not Move," and indicated a situation in which it was important to remain still and silent and, if possible, conceal the presence. The third signal, a triple note, meant "Join Up. Come Together."

In addition to the facial signals and the whistles we also disciplined ourselves to the basic common sense rules applicable to anyone walking in tandem through the habitat of large wild animals. These included walking in single file, watching the person in front for reaction to sights or sounds, following the direction of the gaze of the person leading, stopping instantly and remaining still and quiet when that person stopped. So it was that when I stopped and froze into immobility on seeing what I thought was the headcloth of a lurking poacher, Dede, walking close behind me, did the same.

I think that we stood and watched the white, still object for probably thirty seconds. While we did, all sorts of thoughts raced through my mind, all of them based on the premise that what I was seeing was indicative of a human presence. If it was a poacher, was he armed? If so, was he dangerous? Would he feel himself trapped and react violently? Was he alone or, as was more likely, was he with companions? If so where were they and what were they thinking, or planning? Were they behind us? Above us? All around us?

Thirty seconds passed and then, suddenly, silently, the white object moved. It moved in a smooth horizontal motion from right to left and just as my brain was beginning to tell me what it really was, it formed itself into the shape of a huge tusk. At the same time Dede, close behind me, whispered, "Elephant."

It took another four or five seconds for the body of the elephant, following the smooth, slow movement of the tusk, to take shape. It took even longer for us to focus. The animal was enormous and its size was of course enhanced by its proximity. In the thin sunlight coming down through the tree canopy, the tusk was a pale, creamy white. But the remainder of the vast body was steel gray in color. As the dappled light of the forest moved across it, it was almost as though a huge wall of rock had suddenly detached itself from the side of an unseen hill and set itself in motion. And it was not until the animal passed through an opening in the trees directly in front of us that we were able to see all of him and to grasp his enormous size. When we did, when I did, I suddenly realized that I was looking at the largest elephant I had ever seen in my whole life. A life that until then had included some thirty years of observing wild elephants and of intimate experience with domestic elephants of all sizes.

We were very close to the elephant — a little too close — and when he passed in front of us, slowly and incredibly silent in that thick brush, I caught a quick glimpse of his left eye, the thick black lashes curling above it, a dark pool set in the moonlike crater of his facial skin. It was an eye full of wisdom and calm, a window on a noble soul.

If the elephant saw us, he gave no sign. His stride unbroken, he moved — indeed seemed to glide, so silent was his progress — until he was directly in front of us. Then, within a few more paces, he was swallowed by the forest. As suddenly as he had appeared, he was gone.

I was carrying a small camera, a Nikon that I had had for many years. Suggesting to Dede that she climb a tree and wait for me, I started after the elephant to try and get a picture of him. Moving quickly, I came up behind him and for a few seconds briefly saw him, a drifting gray monolith, moving away from me. I tried to follow him but suddenly I found myself in thorn growth and was stopped. The growth was *Bhate*, as the Taru people call it, a dark green frond growth with wickedly sharp hooked thorns on its undersides. Along the Bauni River it grows in dense thickets to heights of twenty-five feet and it is almost impassable without a *kukri*, the machete-like knife of the Nepali people. I tried to bypass it and moved right, away from the river. But it extended too far in that direction. I moved to the left and found that it grew right up to the river bank and even hung over into the water. In the time that I spent doing this the elephant was gone. After another attempt to force my way through the thorn, I gave up and returned to where Dede was waiting, perched in the curling arms of a big Strangler Fig tree, twenty feet above the ground.

Dede climbed down and we had a whispered conference. I told her what I thought about the elephant, about his enormous size and how he was certainly the largest elephant I had ever seen. His size alone left little doubt in my mind that this elephant was none other than Tula Hatti, the great elephant of the White Grass Plains. We decided, there and then, that what we had to do was try and get a measurement on the animal. Because if he was the size that I personally suspected—well over ten feet and possibly as much as ten-six, or even ten-eight—then he was among the largest Asian elephants ever known. A unique and extraordinary animal that at the least should be, for purposes of recognition and protection, brought to the notice of the government of Nepal. We resolved to go after the elephant next day with this purpose in mind. In the meantime, for today, we would continue on down to the Singpur rice fields and look for our woodpeckers.

We spent the remainder of the day along the edge of the rice fields about a mile and a half south of Singpur village. There, in the stand of old, dead *Sal* trees that had been our destination when we had started out that morning, Dede found and identified two rare Black-Backed Woodpeckers, a male and a female. With the satisfaction of making a small ornithological achievement, a little find that would add to the knowledge of the birds of Nepal already compiled, she entered it—time, place, date, and description—in her battered bird book.

Elephants are measured at the shoulder. This, however, is not the highest or tallest part of an Asian elephant. The top of the head of

53

an Asian elephant is higher than the shoulder, as is the high point of the convex back. But the shoulder has been the traditional point of measurement since elephants first entered the service of man as domestic animals and since man first started shooting them as trophy game. Our interest and curiosity now centered on Tula Hatti's mighty shoulders. How high above the ground were they and what was his actual height? Was he well up in the ten foot range and if so how far? Would he turn out to be a new record for Nepal? Or even for all of Asia? The question was an exciting one and we viewed the prospect of getting to work on it with a keen sense of anticipation as we walked back to camp.

There are two ways to measure an elephant. One, used with domestic elephants, is to lay a two-by-four beam across its shoulders, lay a steel bubble level on top of that and, when the bubble indicates the absolute horizontal, run a tape measure from the end of the two-by-four to the ground. This of course is a method that can only be applied to elephants in captivity. With wild elephants a different method must be used. One of these is simply to wait until the animal to be measured walks past a tree, make an optical note of the place on the tree that indicates the height of his shoulders, wait until he has moved away, and then go to the tree and measure from that place to the ground. There are a number of problems with this method. One of these is making a precise determination of exactly where the animal's shoulders align with the tree, something that, unless the tree has a distinguishing mark, is not easy. One's eyes are almost certain to be drawn away from the marker point between the time that the elephant passes and when the measurement is made, either by the spectacle of the passing elephant or by the simple need to look down at the ground while approaching the tree. When this happens, if there is not a distinguishing mark of some kind at the marker point—a branch, a knob, a fracture in the trunk, or a tear in the bark—then eye contact with the marker point may be lost. An attempt to make the measurement will involve guesswork, which, for accurate records, is not acceptable.

When I was a tea planter up in North Bengal I knew a fellow planter who lived in Shillong, Assam, a man called E. P. Gee. I was introduced to him one sultry monsoon evening at the Tea Planters

Club in Tezpur, a sprawling town hard on the north bank of the mighty Bramaputra River. Finding that we had a common interest in wildlife and wanting, I think, to try and convert me to the new thinking on wildlife conservation (of which he was a pioneer), Gee invited me to come and visit him at his tea estate in Shillong, in the Khasi hills of Assam. I went there soon afterwards and my visit was the first of many during which I enjoyed the company of a man whose knowledge of wildlife was, I believe, unsurpassed in India in his time.

One day, Gee, in his sixties at this time, active, energetic, and seeming to need little rest and hardly any sleep, woke me in the gray light of dawn and asked me to come with him and measure some elephants. Over a cup of tea and a hot *chapatti* pancake, he told me that he had been keeping a record of the size and growth of elephants for many years, using a small domestic group that belonged to the Forest Department. He added that he used both the shoulder method and the foot method. I knew what the shoulder method was, but at the time I had no idea what he meant by the foot method until he explained. It was simple, he told me, and the beauty of it was that it could be used with wild elephants as easily as with domestic.

The foot method of measurement consists of taking a clear and well defined imprint of the forefoot, measuring the straight line of its diameter, and then multiplying this measurement by six. The resulting figure is always the height of the animal in question at the shoulder, to within an inch either way.

This was the method that we now planned to use on Tula Hatti. So for three days after our encounter with him, steel measuring tape in hand, we searched for his footprints. We found several old ones on the Elephant Walk that ran from the middle forest past our camp and some new ones at the ford below the bridge. But they and the others we came across were all in deep mud or sand, blurred and distorted and sometimes even doubled with a second print on top of the first. As a result they were not suitable for accurate measurement.

Then, early one morning on the fourth day, west of the Bauni

55

Bridge where the Elephant Walk crosses the road that runs into the grassland, we found a clear set of fresh prints. They were perfectly pressed into thin, brown dust on a hard mud base, a combination of surface conditions that allowed for a perfect imprint. They were no more than a few hours old. We measured the prints. Working quietly, we took the steel tape and laid it carefully across the first print, precisely in the center of the big circle. The reading, from one sharply etched rim of the flat, craterlike print to the other, was twenty-two inches. We did a quick calculation, multiplying by six. This gave us a figure of a hundred and thirty-two inches, or eleven feet. When we saw the result, we immediately suspected that we had made a mistake in our calculation. We did a second measurement and checked our figures. Was it really eleven feet? The computation and the conversion again checked out and suddenly I knew why, in that brief encounter of a few days previously, the elephant had appeared to be bigger than any elephant I had ever seen. He was. But he was more. He was bigger than any elephant ever known in the jungles of Nepal and, according to the records of elephant and game measurement meticulously kept by the English all through the years of the British Raj, bigger by six inches than anything previously recorded for the entire Indo-Nepal region.

We found another dozen prints that day and in the days following we found and measured a score more. On some of them our steel tape recorded a length of the footprint diagonal a fraction over twenty-two inches. But not more than that, so that we decided to make that figure, twenty-two inches, the official one.

As to the elephant's weight, we could only guess. As Gee pointed out to me, the footprint method of estimating height can be used with both domestic and wild elephants. But only the domestic ones can be persuaded to step on a scale and allow themselves to be weighed. We did have a comparison, however, which we used to give us a rough idea of the weight of our giant friend. This was the big male that lives in the Washington Park Zoo in Portland, Oregon. Packy, as he is called, is officially the largest Asian elephant in captivity. He stands ten foot three inches at the shoulder and weighs in excess of 14,000 pounds. Tula Hatti's weight at eleven feet? Probably 16,000 pounds and possibly as much as

18,000. Certainly he is a lot more massive in build than his domestic counterpart.

We felt a great elation as the full impact of the discovery made itself clear to us: the discovery of the largest elephant of all time alive and in residence in the White Grass Plains of western Nepal. If my friend Gee were still alive he would have shared in our elation. He was long since gone but the knowledge that he left behind and that he so generously shared with a young man many years his junior gives him, I feel, a place in the discovery.

One of the first people that we told about our discovery was the man who had brought us to Mahendranagar, Colonel Bisht. Hikmat, as he is known to his friends, is a retired military officer of the Royal Nepal Army and lives just outside the little border town of Mahendranagar. A man with an interesting background, Colonel Bisht was Military Attache to the Royal Nepal Embassy in Washington, D.C., when I first met him, back in the early sixties. Before that he had been an A.D.C. — personal assistant and companion — to the present king of Nepal, King Birendra Bir Bikram Shah, when the monarch attended Harvard University in the United States. Now retired, he devoted some of his time to a rice mill that he owned in Mahendranagar and some of it to his land holdings east of Mahendranagar. But his main interest was wildlife and it was this, together with an equally strong interest in the White Grass Plains Reserve, that drew us together over the years. While I was hunting in the fifties and sixties, he was pursuing his military and diplomatic career and so we did not see a lot of each other. Later, when he retired, he opened his home to me — a somewhat rare gesture in Nepal and one that I felt very privileged to enjoy. In return, he was a guest at my campfire many a night. With his contacts in government circles and particularly in the field of wildlife, I felt that he could be very helpful in shaping any plans that we might have for action on behalf of the great elephant. Thus it was that, the day after our discovery, Dede and I drove the twenty-five miles from Oriole Camp, across jungle roads dry and dusty in the growing heat of the oncoming summer, out of the reserve at the Majgaon guard post and through the town of Mahendranagar to his home.

Hikmat knew about the big elephant and was not too surprised when we told him of our estimate of eleven feet for its shoulder height. He had half expected it to be something close to this. He reminded us that in actual fact the elephant was bigger than eleven feet in that the point of the back, its center, was higher than the shoulder. We discussed with Hikmat how we would break the news to the Nepalese authorities, and together we conjectured on what their reaction might be. We also talked about the future of the great elephant. We began to think seriously, for the first time, about the dangers that might threaten him and what could be done to protect him. For although Tula Hatti was a mighty animal, powerful in his prime and well prepared to survive in an area that offered him all that he needed in the way of food, water, cover, and space, a number of things were a threat to him. Two of them were severe to the point that, should he encounter them, they might well prove fatal.

One of these was of course poaching, and while there is very little poaching of elephants in Nepal, it does exist. In December 1987 a fine young tusker, a member of the herd of which Tula Hatti was the leader, was shot and killed by poachers near the village of Barbatta, in Kanchanpur. This was a rare incident and in the nearly forty years that I have known the jungles of the Nepal Terai, the only one that I personally knew of where a tusker had been shot by poachers for its ivory. (In this case the poacher or poachers panicked when the tusker did not immediately fall. Believed to be Indians, they fled toward the border, leaving the elephant to die, its tusks intact.)

In Nepal, as in India, the elephant is protected by the law—a sufficient deterrent when it is enforced—and also by religion. Among the Hindus the elephant, wild or domestic, is the living embodiment of Ganesh, one of the dominant Hindu gods. Even among the Tarus of the Nepal Terai, who are not Hindus, the animal is revered as a powerful being. In many Taru villages it is depicted as such on the mud walls of houses, in drawings that are but a stone's throw away from the cave art of half a million years ago. And so the danger from poachers, while always present, is not at severe as it could be (and as it is in Africa, where the killing of elephants for ivory is driving the African elephant to the edge of extinction).

The other danger to Tula Hatti and his companions of the forests of the Terai is what is called culling. It's a word that is the official or government term for selective shooting.

In Nepal, elephants that are "guilty of disturbance" are very often condemned by government order and then shot. The practice, one that is wrongful and wasteful, originated in British India, where elephants that caused disturbances that brought them to the attention of the government were routinely proclaimed rogue elephants and shot. Minor disturbances, such as getting into villagers' crops or new forest plantations and uprooting and eating young trees, were not regarded as serious enough to warrant a rogue proclamation, so the government seldom did more than make a note of the particular animal for future reference. Nuisance offenses were also usually overlooked. A good example of this comes to mind from tea planting days.

It was 1949. I was living on a tea plantation called Tondoo, in the Jalpaiguri district of north Bengal, and the boundaries of the estate, where it met the great forests of the Jaldaka River, were demarcated with steel posts set in large cement blocks. The posts, pieces of cut railway line, weighed probably a thousand pounds each with their bases and when they were set in place it was intended that they would never be moved again. But in the Jaldaka forest lived a couple of young bull elephants who, for reasons known only to them, took exception to the positioning of the boundary markers as well as obvious satisfaction in rearranging them. They would come in the night, seize the metal uprights in their trunks, and between them pull the markers down and drag them for distances of up to a hundred yards. This happened probably fifty times while I was at Tondoo and each time it took a hundred men with dozens of thick coconut fiber ropes to drag them back into place.

Even more serious offenses, such as getting out on country roads and challenging buses or standing on railway lines and confronting oncoming trains — usually the practice of young bulls in rut — hardly warranted a rogue penalty. This, the extreme penalty, one that meant that the elephant marked and described was condemned to death and was pursued until it was destroyed, was only issued

Tula Hatti

in cases of what was officially termed "serious destruction of private property combined with threats of imminent danger to human life, or actual loss of human life." Even with loss of human life, colonial officials of British India always very carefully examined all of the alleged circumstances involved before issuing the rogue proclamation. For they realized that when a villager, desperate to protect his crops, made the mistake of running into a herd of elephants at night and was trampled to death in the ensuing panic, the fault hardly lay with his four-footed foes. Thus, at Tondoo in 1949 when a huge bull elephant from the Jaldaka forest, temporarily made savage by his state of rut, charged and trampled and killed several tea estate workers, it was only after a careful examination of all of the facts of the case — facts that suggested that the animal posed an extreme hazard to human life — that a rogue proclamation was issued and the bull was shot.

In Nepal the government shooting of elephants is very seldom practiced. In my years in the little kingdom, to the best of my knowledge only two elephants have been shot under rogue proclamation, both in the eastern Nepal Terai in the 1980s. The animals in question were charged with willful destruction of property, destruction of village crops, and, because of the unusually bold habit they developed of walking through sleeping villages at night, of being a menace to human life. Knowing of the incident in question and of the circumstances involved, my personal feeling is that the animals did not deserve to be destroyed. But nevertheless they were shot and that was the end of them. If their deaths did nothing more, they left me with a very concerned memory of the incident, one that I now applied, with Dede, to our planning for the protection of Tula Hatti.

One of the problems of being famous is the uninvited attention one receives from the general public. Having little experience of it myself, I can only guess what it must be like. But it is not difficult nowadays, if whatever one has done attracts the attention of the media, for one's name to become a household word. So it was and is with Tula Hatti. And while he has now received international attention with all of the benefits that this may carry for his protection, at the time of his discovery as the largest Asian elephant, the only people who knew him were the people of the western Terai forests. These were indigenous Tarus and a scattering of Paharias, hill people relocated to the Terai after losing their lands in the lower Himalaya to erosion. People who lived in tiny villages set deep in the Terai. People who grew rice and corn and maize and mustard and *dhal*, their basic lentil, in little clearings around their villages. They depended on these crops for their very livelihood. Crops that with their succulent growths perennially attracted wild elephants, among them Tula Hatti, the largest of them all and no doubt the one with the biggest appetite. But whereas most of the other elephants of the western Terai were unrecognizable individually to both Taru and Paharia and were simply *jungle hatti*, jungle elephants, Tula Hatti was known to all. I had seen it happening and developing over the years, particularly with the Paharias, people from the hills totally uneducated in the lore of the forest. Slowly but surely, in looking for an individual to blame for their ruined crops, their crushed rice fields, their smashed corn stacks, and their increasing fear of the silent gray phantoms of the night, they began to lay the blame on the only elephant they knew as an individual . . . Tula Hatti.

A flattened field of young rice? Tula Hatti. A devastated patch of mustard seed, from which both Taru and Paharia made their cooking oil? Tula Hatti. A grove of young banana trees stripped bare or a corn stack knocked down and partially eaten? Tula Hatti. And worse. A man, brandishing a flaming straw torch, rushing out to chase elephants from his crops and being trampled to death by a panicking herd? Tula Hatti. A young Paharia woman, late from work and running to beat the advance of night right into an elephant group and being killed? Tula Hatti. Always the big elephant. Always the only one that they were able to identify. This totally undeserved reputation was one of our first concerns in planning for the protection of the big pachyderm and one of the first things that we examined when talking with Colonel Bisht.

"He, that Tula Hatti, has killed more than forty people," the headman of one Taru village told us while his people, sitting around him, nodded in solemn agreement. Another headman, a Paharia, told us that he thought it was well over a hundred. *Sepoys*—soldiers doing guard duty and stationed at the guard posts of the White Grass Plains Reserve—agreed. Many people, fifty or more they said, had been killed, all by the big elephant. We also heard that Tula Hatti not only crushed more crops than all of the other elephants— presumably because of the size of his huge feet—but also delighted in getting into villages, knocking down houses, and terrifying the inhabitants.

It took some time to make a full examination of the various charges made against the big elephant. But we had that time available and so this was one of the first things that we did. Our findings, made over the course of three weeks of intensive investigation, talking with Taru and Paharia villagers, reserve guards, and government wildlife and forest service employees, produced a picture of the great elephant quite different from the dire one painted by those who spoke so ill of him.

We discovered that the total number of people killed by elephants in the whole district of Kanchanpur, which contains the White Grass Plains Reserve, was two within the previous ten years. One was the man who foolishly, if bravely, ran out at night to chase elephants out of his crops. The other was the young woman who had the misfortune to walk into an elephant or elephants in the dark. That both had been killed by an elephant there seemed little doubt. But on questioning, no one could state with any certainty that it was Tula Hatti that had killed them. No one had seen the elephant or elephants in question and the next day no one had seen any distinctive tracks. All that was known for certain was that an elephant was to blame. And as Tula Hatti was known to inhabit the White Grass Plains, it seemed easiest to put the blame on him. As to an elephant or elephants coming into villages at night, our conclusion was the same. Elephants certainly. Tula Hatti? Possibly. But not certainly.

Sitting with Colonel Bisht in his home on the outskirts of Mahendranagar or at the campfire at Oriole Camp on the Bauni River, we soon came to the conclusion that if the great elephant was to be protected from the dangers of poaching or frightened and hostile villagers, some kind of very special protection would have to be arranged for him. Our approach to the government would have to be designed to create awareness that in Tula Hatti they had something that was part of the national heritage of the Nepalese people. Awareness that would in turn cause them to be especially careful when examining any charges that might be made against him by nervous and imaginative villagers.

The answer, we thought, could lie in attracting international attention to the presence of the big elephant. This would help gain the attention of the Nepalese authorities just as, over the years, international interest in the status of Nepal's wildlife had helped to persuade the government to act positively in other fields of conservation and preservation.

The answer, it seemed, might lie in a film. Something that would document the story of the elephant, of its discovery and of its place as a living symbol of the wildlife of both Nepal and the world. A film that would be planned for international distribution, to reach millions of viewers all over the world. A television documentary that could be made on a moderate budget and that could be shot on location in one winter. A film that would include footage of the great elephant against the background of the rolling grasslands of the White Grass Plains. A story that would tell the world about Tula Hatti and his home, the beautiful and little known forests and grasslands of the White Grass Plains and at the same time help to make people aware of the dangers to elephants not just in Nepal but everywhere.

In Nepal, the single most obvious threat to the future of the elephant herds is destruction of their habitat. The human population of Nepal is increasing and as it does more land is needed to grow more food to feed more mouths. The government of Nepal seems to think that the place to grow that food is the Terai and when new land is opened up for cultivation it is inevitably land that is currently under forest: wildlife — elephant — habitat. Added to the population explosion is the movement of people from the mountains to the Terai under resettlement schemes. The need for these relocations begins when land is lost to erosion; geologically the Himalayan chain is young and the land that begins at the northern edge of the Terai and climbs all the way to the rim of the Tibetan plateau is subject to constant and continuous erosion and collapse. Contributing to this land loss in the mountains are other factors: bad farming practices; excessive brush and tree cutting that robs the soil of its anchors of roots; and over-grazing, particularly by goats, an environmentally insidious animal that because of the lack of teeth in the upper jaw, pulls food out of the ground rather than biting it off, thus uprooting the grasses and shrubs on which it feeds and doing immense damage to delicate ecosystems.

However, right now Nepal's elephant herds seem to be holding their own. Precise figures are not available for their numbers but my estimate for all of the wild elephants in the Terai would be in the region of two hundred and fifty. For centuries, back through the reigns of successive rulers of the kingdom, elephants have had two-way protection. The first, the stronger, is the concept of the animal as the Hindu god Ganesh. As such, among Hindus, who make up close to fifty percent of Nepal's population, the animal is never to be molested, never to be harmed in any way. The second is strong government protection. The original reason for this more-than-ordinary concern for a single species of local wildlife was that the elephant in its domestic form had many uses. Among these was as a form of transportation, both civil and military, that was unequalled by anything else available for a long time. And wild elephants were not difficult to capture and train for domestic use. Thus the elephant was a very valuable commodity and the edicts issued for its protection by the government were strong. When gentleman hunters of the old British Raj were, if reluctantly, given permission to come into the Terai to shoot, they were allowed to do so on the strict understanding that their trophies never included elephants.

As of now the elephant herds of Nepal seem to have sufficient habitat to survive well into the future. There are threats to that habitat, certainly, but Nepal's excellent policy of wildlife protection, one that is most praiseworthy for a country that is so small and at the same time has a human population problem, does seem to guarantee their future to a considerable extent. From a tradition of hunting (the ruling rajas hunted ferociously and annually ran massive hunts with hundreds of riding elephants that slaughtered literally everything that moved) the country moved in 1973 to establish its first national park. Gazetted, which means officially listed and recognized, the new park was named Chitawan, pronounced "chitaun." It lies roughly due south of Kathmandu, and originally contained an area of 210 square miles. In 1978-'79 this was increased to 310 square miles and at the time of this writing a further extension is under consideration. Three years later two more national parks were gazetted, both in the Himalaya. The larger of the two, at 660 square miles, is Langtang, an area of the upper Himalaya lying roughly northeast of Kathmandu. The other is Sagarmatha—the Nepalese name for Mount Everest—and as its name suggests, its boundaries enclose in an area of 480 square miles that magnificent peak, the highest in the world. The fourth national park, gazetted one year later, is Rara in the northwest mountains. At an average altitude of 10,000 feet, the forty-square-mile park contains the turquoise jewel Rara Lake, and as a protected area it offers sanctuary for Musk Deer, Red Panda, and the Giant Langur. The fifth national park, in what is called the transhimalayan region of the Dolpo area, is Shey. Proposed with an area of fifty-six square miles, Shey is a name known to many through the works of two highly respected writers: Peter Matthiessen, author of *The Snow Leopard*, and George Schaller, author of *Stones of Silence*.

Turning its attention to reserves, the Nepalese government eventually decided to establish three. Although work began years before, gazetting was not completed until 1976. In that year the Kosi Tappu Reserve in the eastern Terai was gazetted at twelve square miles. This was later extended to twenty-five square miles. The principal animal it was designed to protect was the wild buffalo, then and now an endangered species. (Sadly for the wild buffalo, it is not considered by the indigenous people, who hunt it for food, to be a member of the cow family. If it were, it would have the powerful protection of the Hindu religion, in which the cow is revered.) In the same year as Kosi Tappu came Bardia. Known as both the Bardia Reserve and the Karnali Reserve, in that its western boundary is the Girwa, the principal arm of the Karnali River after it enters the Terai, Bardia was gazetted at 132 square miles. Among the animals it was designed to protect is the *Susu*, or Pink Dolphin, an aquatic mammal living in the fresh waters of the Girwa and in the Karnali's other arm, the Kauriala, a thousand miles from the sea. Last but not least came Sukila Phanta, the White Grass Plains. Listed in official documents under the names of Sukila Phanta, Sukla Phanta, and Suklaphanta, the reserve, lying at the extreme western end of the Terai, was originally gazetted at 60,000 acres. This was later increased to 80,000 acres and again recently to 100,000 acres. The principal animal that the reserve was designed to protect, in line with my proposals and plans of 1968, was the tiger. As of now it has a healthy population of the big cats. It also has a great variety of wildlife, some of it quite unique, like the Red Dog, the animal that the Tarus call the *Ban Mahola*, the king of the forest, because it is an animal probably feared by all others; the Pangolin, an armor-plated ant eater that is now an endangered species; and, among the birds, such rarities as the Swamp Partridge, the Great Slaty Wood-pecker, and the Giant Hornbill. Of particular interest to conserva-tionists is the great herd of Swamp Deer that make their home in the central part of the reserve. Now close to 2000 in number, it is the last great herd of Swamp Deer left in Asia. Scattered groups are found in other parts of the Terai, in Bardia and also in the forests of north India, but nowhere is there a herd of these proportions. The herd spends much of its time in the central grasslands of the re-serve and in the fall, when the hundreds and hundreds of stags are in full horn and ready for the rut, they are a magnificent sight, a veritable sea of horns.

After three weeks talking to locals about Tula Hatti, we spent a few more days at Oriole Camp and we filled every minute of them with the enjoyment of our studies of jungle lore. Most mornings we were up in the first pale light of dawn, fending off the chill of the morning air with mugs of hot coffee while our cook, Jangbu, rattled pots and pans in the kitchen and Pasang and Phurua readied the equipment for another day's outing. Jangbu was from Kathmandu. About twenty-five years old at this time, he was small, shy, quick-moving, hard-working, dependable, and honest. Jangbu had been with us on eight expeditions that included the first running of the Sarda, the thirty-nine day exploratory run of the mighty Karnali, and the first running of the Sapt Gandaki. Married, he lived in the Phulchowk district of Kathmandu. He was the third camp cook that I had employed over the years, the other two, Injung Sherpa and Thondup Sherpa, both of Darjeeling, having long since gone into retirement. Jangbu had never been to the Terai when he first entered our employment and had never seen the jungle. It took him a while to overcome his initial and natural nervousness about conditions of which he had no experience. Once he did, he quickly proved his mastery of camp cooking by producing delightful food under all kinds of conditions — snow, rain, wind, and storm — all from a little metal grill perched on three stones over a wood fire.

Jangbu's kitchen assistant and general camp man was Phurua, another Sherpa. Phurua had been with us about four years at this time. He was a mountain man, young — about twenty-two — lean and hard, with a rather long face for a Sherpa and large brown eyes. He had the best eyesight of any man I have ever worked with, and later we used him many times as a spotter when searching for Tula Hatti. Like Jangbu, he took a little time to get used to the jungle and the beasts that lived in it. But as soon as he discovered that they left him alone if he left them alone, he became one of our most dependable men. He had done five expeditions with us by 1983 and had been one of the stalwarts of the Sarda expedition.

Pasang, Pasang Sherpa of Thammi village in Sola Khumbu, was our number one man, just as he had been my number one for the previous thirty years. In 1953, when I first opened my safari company, I wrote to Darjeeling to a man I had known from tea planting days, Tenzing Norgay of Everest. I asked him to send me three good Sherpas for permanent employment in a *shikar* or safari business. I told him to put them on a train and send them through India to western Nepal. I would reimburse him for train fares later and they would find me camped just inside the Nepal border at a place called Gauri Phanta, at the end of the old British narrrow-gauge railway line that ran up there from Palia Kalan, in Uttar Pradesh. A week later, with a thousand miles of Indian rail travel behind them, three men walked into my camp: Injung Sherpa, a cook; Tashi Kirong, a diminutive tiger of a man named after his birthplace, Kirong, in Tibet; and Pasang.

Tula Hatti

Injung retired after sixteen years of safari cooking in 1968. Tashi disappeared while on a train trip through northern Uttar Pradesh in India, lawless country where to this day gangs of bandits regularly waylay people on the highways and railways. I and his family have good reason to believe that he was robbed and then murdered while on the train. Pasang stayed on.

When I gave up hunting in 1968 and told Pasang that I was probably not going to be able to employ him any more, he did a brief stint in the Indian army. But when I came back to work with the Nepal government on the Sukila Phanta project – the making of the reserve – he left the army and rejoined me. He has been with me ever since.

Starting as a gunbearer, Pasang quickly showed unusually good common sense and versatility. He was adept with rifles and guns and quickly proved his worth as a gunbearer. He was a good all round mechanic and driver as well as handyman. At a time when I was employing twenty-two men in camp, fourteen of them tough, fractious elephant *mahouts* and elephant handler-feeders from India, he also proved his ability to handle people and quickly assumed the position of camp manager. Short, with the stocky muscular build typical of the mountain man, Pasang was probably twenty-eight when we first met. Birth records not being regarded as an important part of Sherpa village custom, he did not know his exact age. Tough, with a face as hard as a piece of Himalayan stone and eyes that looked as though they had been burned into it by the frozen winds of the mountains, Pasang nevertheless had a gentle nature and a natural sensitivity that quickly put him in tune with his surroundings in the Terai forests. Afraid of nothing, he proved his dependability as a gunbearer a dozen times in situations – usually created by careless shooting on the part of safari clients – that would have sent many another man running for cover. By 1983, in our camp on the Bauni, he had become a friend. A friend of mine and Dede's and, when she came into our lives, of Rara's as well: her strong but gentle man of the jungle.

In camp in the early mornings our routine did not vary a lot. Up early, quick mugs of coffee, a couple of Jangbu's hot *chapattis* – dry, unleavened bread straight from an iron pan — while Pasang checked the gear for the day's trip. If we were going out in the Scout, he would check the oil and gasoline and replenish it as needed. Inside the vehicle he would count and check the tools that had to go along: shovel, axe, rope, jack, repair tools, and spare parts box. If we were going out on foot he would check our personal things: binoculars, bird books, jungle knives, cameras, film, extra lenses, matches, rope, and a flask of either hot coffee or cold water, depending on how long we planned to stay out. For himself, the basic equipment of a walk with us consisted of matches, a hat, a jacket, and his faithful *kukri*, a big jungle knife that he had been carrying for many years and that had proved its usefulness in a hundred ways during our time together.

Checks completed, a last cup of coffee downed, and we were off for the day, every day. And, as always, the jungle rewarded us with its treasures, giving us in this last week another rare species of bird for our discovery list: the big, noisy Slaty Woodpecker. We found a group of six of them and, after establishing their territory, were able to view them several times. The find went into our books. We also had some delightful experiences with otters, watching their fishing tactics as they swept the dark brown waters of the Bauni in line abreast, always in perfect formation, diving and surfacing, every time with at least one big wriggling catfish between them. We listened to tigers calling at night and once to the heavy sawing of a leopard, something quite rare in the tiger ranges of the Bauni River. Tigers and leopards do not mix. They establish separate territories and live in separate ranges, and if a tiger moves into a leopard's range, the smaller cat moves out. If he does not do so then he stands the chance of a face to face encounter with Mr. Stripes, one from which the leopard, should he be bold enough or foolish enough to stand his ground, will surely emerge defeated.

A friend of mine, Jack Boyland, a tea planter in the Dooars district of North Bengal, saw and recorded such an encounter. Jack was sitting on the verandah of his bungalow one evening as the light was fading and saw a very large dog leopard moving through the shrubbery that edged his front lawns. In the same instant his eye caught the form of a tiger coming from the opposite direction. Both animals were on the same little trail that skirted the lawns and one would have to give way. Neither did and with roars of defiance they attacked each other. The battle was a fierce one and raged for several hours. When the light faded, Jack lost sight of the big cats but the roars and snarls continued into the night as the fight surged back and forth from the edge of his compound into the surrounding jungle. Toward midnight silence descended. Jack waited until dawn and then, carrying a rifle and accompanied by a couple of nervous house servants, went out to see what had happened. He found the leopard, dead, a hundred yards from the edge of his compound. Of the tiger there was no sign. The leopard had numerous bites and claw tears in its hide. But what had killed it was a single deep hole in the top of its head where one of the tiger's canines had penetrated its brain. Jack skinned the leopard and had its hide tanned. For years it decorated a settee in the living room of his house, the only trophy Jack, who was not a hunter, ever owned. Leopards do not have a very good sense of smell. But their olfactory ability is enough to detect the territorial urine markings of a tiger. When they do, with very rare exceptions, they leave for safer surroundings. For apart from man, the leopard's only real enemy, the only thing in the jungles that is a real threat to it is the tiger.

The weather warmed and as it did we made plans to close camp. From the night skies came the lonely plaintive cries of the Barheaded Geese going north, as they began the long climb that would take them over the twenty to twenty-five-thousand-foot ramparts of the Himalaya, the barrier that lay between them and their summer nesting grounds in Kashmir and the high plateau country of Tibet. Migrating at the same time as they, something that never ceased to amaze us, went the Coot, a skittering little fellow of the jungle pools, a bird that we had never seen fly more than fifty feet when it was on the water and even then with wings that flopped and flapped and barely seemed to lift it in the air. It too would climb to twenty thousand feet or more and then head for its breeding grounds in central and western Asia.

In the jungles around us the air warmed and one night, just before we planned to leave for Kathmandu, we encountered the first of the early summer storms of the June to October monsoon. It was an experience to remember.

Dede and I had been out all day and as the evening drew in we were driving back to camp. We had reached the eastern edge of the grassland when the wind, which had been gusting through the afternoon, suddenly picked up and began to blow hard. The sky darkened and the sun was soon buried in a great mass of purple tinted clouds boiling up out of the western sky. These climbed high above us and, as we watched, sheet lightning began to stab them with blue-white fingers. Thunder began to mutter behind the southwest horizon. The power of the wind increased, whipping the white tipped grasses of the *phantas* into an undulating sea. Dozens of small birds erupted out of the grass in panic and far down in the grassland the Swamp Deer began to bay in alarm. We sat on the hood of the Scout and watched in silent awe. We had been in a few storms before, both in the jungle and in the high Himalaya. Storms that had flattened our tents to the ground and thunder and lightning that had made us quail in submission to the power of the forces of nature. But this was different. Perhaps it was the extraordinary color of the sky above us. Or the calling of the deer and the darting images of the hundreds of little birds around us. Or the sight of the grass, an ocean of movement that almost made us feel as though we could sink into it. Whatever it was, we felt at that moment that we were being given a glimpse of a primeval world, our world as it was a thousand, ten thousand, a million years ago. A world known only to the most primitive of men and animals. A world now gone forever.

We sat together and let ourselves be absorbed by the unrestrained majesty of the storm until sweeping walls of cold rain, riding the wind, drove us into the Scout and sent us on our way back to camp.

We felt enormously privileged to have been given the experience of the storm. We felt, somehow, without trying to be mystical or even sentimental about it, that Tula Hatti had contributed to the experience. At the least, it was our new concern for him and our new interest in him that had caused us to be there in the grasslands and in the path of that magnificent gathering of the elements. And I think that it was about this time also that we first began to think of Tula Hatti as a symbol of all that the White Grass Plains — and indeed, the Terai as a whole — meant to us. He had become to us a living symbol of the econet, the great global web of life of which every single living thing on the planet is a part and of which the White Grass Plains were but a microcosm. The interdependence of life on earth, awareness of which was spurring more and more people to act as they learned of the threats to the oceans, to the air, and to the earth. To many, a single elephant in a far away country is just one animal, endangered or not. But to us, and in time we hoped to many, Tula Hatti could be seen as all life should be seen, from its tiniest representatives in the insect world to its most magnificent creations, elephants, the whales of the land, and whales, the elephants of the seas, each and every one a vital part of the whole, a shining strand of the great web. If this web collapses, as it surely will if we do not pay heed to the respect that each strand demands, all life on earth will end.

The next day we folded our tents and set off for Kathmandu. Storing some of our gear with the Bishts to lighten our load, the five of us rode together in the Scout and we made the run, again via India, in four days.

We did not see Tula Hatti again before we left. Just his footprints once or twice in the brown dust of the forest roads. But we knew that we had not seen the last of him. For now we had a plan to bring his name to the world, and in doing so give him the protection that he vitally needed. And we intended to execute that plan. Our only problem, when we sat down to think about it, was that although Dede and I had been involved in several films, neither of us had ever produced one before. Nor had we the foggiest idea at this time where we were going to find $100,000, the modest and minimum budget that we knew we would need for production, post-production, and international distribution of the film we had in mind.

3

ELEPHANT WALK

The three-hundred-mile run from the White Grass Plains, in the district of Kanchanpur, western Nepal, to Kathmandu took us four days. It would have been a six-hour drive on a modern highway, but our route was a little different. It included driving on buffalo cart trails, jungle roads deep in the dust of early summer, and, here and there, half-completed sections of the new East-West Highway, the only southern highway that, when completed, would link all of Nepal from east to west. We traveled via Mahendranagar, where we had a last visit with Colonel Bisht, and then drove due east, bypassing Nepalgunj and Dhanghari, border towns linked to the East-West Highway. We crossed the Karnali River on a ferry, a temporary one pending construction of a new bridge which, when completed, would carry traffic and people across the river with the second longest single span bridge in the world (the longest being over the Rhine at Dusseldorf). East of the Karnali we drove through the Bardia Wildlife Reserve, the one-time summer habitat of the White Grass Plains elephant herd, and from there over the Bhabai River into the beautiful Dang Valley. The Bhabai was still unbridged at this time and fording it meant a preliminary foot inspection of the crossing place in three to three-and-a-half feet of fast moving, cold mountain water. The Scout, fan belt disconnected to prevent water from being fanned back onto the engine, made the crossing without mishap, as it did seventy miles further on at the eastern end of the Dang Valley, when we forded another Terai river, the Rapti. From the Dang we drove to and through Butwal and from there to Narainghar, on the Sapt Gandaki River. We had crossed the Sapt Gandaki many times before on the

73

old wooden boat ferries, rowed by teams of muscular, singing hillmen. But they were gone now. A new bridge, steel and concrete, had rendered them obsolete. The old ferry boats now lay rotting on the grey sand beaches of the Sapt Gandaki at Narainghar, skeletal remains that would soon disappear under the onslaught of the monsoon rain and the burning sun of the Terai summers.

From Nepalgunj we drove up what is called the New Chinese Road—because it was designed by the Chinese and constructed by Chinese engineers using Chinese money—to Kathmandu. Four days after leaving Oriole Camp—four days without a shower and with the dirt and dust of 300 miles of cross-country driving on our skin, hair, and clothes—we booked into a suite at the Shangri La Hotel in the Lazimpat district of the city. The Shangri La is a medium-sized and fairly new hotel that, with its formal gardens, European cuisine, and first class staff, has an old world ambiance and charm sadly lacking in so many international hotels these days. We have made it our Kathmandu watering hole for many years.

In Kathmandu we spent some time talking with officials of the National Parks and Wildlife Service about our find and about the need for some official protection for the great elephant. Response was muted at best. The discovery was perhaps too new to be immediately acceptable and we could see that it was going to take more than just a tale from the woods to convince the bureaucracy of the need for action.

When we talked about the film that we planned, there was some enthusiasm, but it was quickly pointed out that no money would be available from His Majesty's Government of Nepal. While they would offer help and cooperation with licensing and permits—something for which we would be grateful in that permits for films by foreigners in Nepal can be difficult to obtain—that would be the limit of their help.

In Kathmandu we said goodbye to our Sherpas, telling them that we would be back at the end of the year to make a film about Tula Hatti and that once again, if they were available, we would like to have them work with us. We paid all three of them. Phurua set off for his mountain village, a four-day walk from the end of the bus line at Jiri, east of Kathmandu. Pasang and Jangbu returned to their homes in Phulchowk, not far from my old Kathmandu home of the hunting years, Julia Cottage in Jawalakhel, over the Bagmati River in the eastern part of the city. We stored the Scout at the home of an associate in the city, had a last round of visits with friends, and then boarded a Thai International flight at Kathmandu International Airport, bound for Seattle and Portland via Bangkok.

Kathmandu International. A comparatively modern airport now, it has a strip built to take big jets, a glass-walled control tower, and seething throngs of tourists from all over the world. But it used to be called Gaucher, which means "cow field," from which it was converted to an airstrip not long after I came to Nepal. (The conversion consisted of putting a wooden fence around it and employing two men to run up and down and chase the cows and goats off it whenever a plane was due.)

When we took off, dark, pre-monsoon clouds were building in the southwest, harbingers of the summer heat just a few weeks away. With the powerful engines of the Thai 747 thrusting us toward cruising altitude, we crossed the nine-thousand-foot walls of the valley of Kathmandu within minutes and then swung south and east over the Terai. Looking down, I was able to recognize towns and rivers where the hills swept down to the border and the plains of India. Then, as we gained height, the images of places where we had spent many a delightful winter's day — river valleys, dark green stretches of jungle, little border towns that had supplied us with our basic needs — blurred and faded into the haze. Soon the flat and monotonous plains of India edged in beneath us and as they did our interest in what lay below waned. But that last glimpse of the Terai formed pictures in our minds of what, though we could no longer see it, lay behind us. The mountain rivers that come surging through the foothills and then, as though released from bondage, open out and flood across the gentle slopes of the Terai. The great reserve of Chitawan, home of the One-Horned Asian Rhino, an armor-plated creature that is bigger than either of its African cousins, the Black or the Wate. The curling reaches of the Sapt Gandaki River, snaking down around the eastern reaches of Chitawan through islands that are the homes of tigers, leopards, wild boar, and deer, a true jungle river and one that we have enjoyed, in quiet

75

rafting runs, several times. Westward, the lovely Dang Valley and its quiet pastoral lands flanking the Rapti River. And west again to the deep forests of Bardia, the eastern limit of the extraordinary system of elephant trails that run from there to the White Grass Plains and that, at one time, before they were destroyed by the ever growing millions of people of India and their insatiable demands for more land to grow more and more food, may have extended all the way to Corbett National Park in Uttar Pradesh.

The trails that elephants use are called Elephant Walks. They are used to travel from one feeding area to another or, on a seasonal basis, for purposes of migration to summer and winter habitats. Whatever their purpose, they always take advantage of cover— shade against the hot sun that elephants prefer to avoid—and the availability of food and water. Walking the trails, one notices that there is always water available at frequent intervals, as well as cover against the sun. Nobody knows the age of the Walks of western Nepal but they may well be thousands of years old. Certainly, in places, where the mighty pressure of huge feet has imprinted the earth hundreds of thousands of times, the trails indicate centuries of usage that should, if uninterrupted, continue for hundreds more years.

For animals as large as elephants, the Walks are quite narrow. In most places they are no more than three feet in width on the ground. But this is all that an elephant needs for the placement of its feet. Above the Walks, in the thick foliage that shades and encloses them, there often appears to be no opening, no mark of the passage of huge animals. This is because the streamlined bodies of the elephants do not break the foliage, but rather open it and then allow it to close again as the animals pass through.

The main Elephant Walks in western Nepal lie between the Bardia, or Karnali Reserve, an area of land bordering the Karnali River on its east side in the district of Bardia and, to the west, passing through the provinces of Kailali and Kanchanpur, the White Grass Plains Reserve. In Bardia, one Elephant Walk skirts the Bhabai River, the river that marks the eastern boundary of the Karnali Reserve. It crosses into the reserve close to the Bagora Phanta grassland. Another runs through the center of the reserve north to the edge of the hill, and a fourth, linked to this, runs westward out of the reserve. Leaving the reserve, this fourth Walk bends south of where the Karnali comes out of the hills. It probably did this originally to avoid the now abandoned village of Cheesapani, a tiny collection of huts on the eastern bank of the Karnali close to its exit gorge from the mountains. But once across the two tributaries into which the Karnali divides at this point, the Girwa and the Kauriala, it quickly bends north again. Hugging the edge of the first escarpments of the mountains, it runs through a narrow strip known as the Bhabar that runs east to west along the edge of the hills, in the northern part of the Terai. Never having walked out all of the trail from the Karnali to the White Grass Plains, I do not know how many twists and turns it makes through the Bhabar and thus cannot with accuracy estimate its length, but its entire route probably extended a hundred miles. This was the age-old Walk, no longer used, of the western herds between these two areas.

Entering Sukila Phanta, the Walk breaks up into a number of branches. Two of these run right across the northern part of the reserve to the Sarda River. One skirts the village of Haria—abandoned when the reserve was extended in recent years—and winds around the lovely jungle lake known as Rani Tal. Near the village of Singpur—also relocated with the new extensions—the Rani Tal Walk joins one that goes west to the Bauni River. This one in turn meets another coming down from the north through the middle forest of the reserve and joins it close to the Bauni River Bridge, crossing that dark brown, slow moving jungle river not on the bridge—for no sensible elephant will ever cross a man-made structure like a bridge—but a hundred yards below it. Here the river shallows into a sandy bottomed ford, hard sand that, for many years before the bridge was built, allowed the passage of my safari vehicles and, for many years before that, the passage of elephants.

From the Bauni crossing, the Walk runs through a small patch of jungle before joining the main reserve inspection road running west, a road that was built with little thought for the needs and rights of the elephants, on top of the Walk. Entering the reserve, the Walk runs right across its central grasslands, south of the giant *Pee-*

77

pul tree that marks the north center of the grassland. (On many a moonlit safari night, when I was far from camp and not too sure of my bearings, that tree, seen against the dark blue bowl of the sky, served as a navigation point to guide me back to my campfire.) Leaving the grasslands, the Walk cuts into the forest that lies between the open country and the Sarda River and is then lost in the white sand bars and numerous little islands of the delta-like reaches of the Sarda. Twice, over the years, I have tried to follow the Walk in the sandy reaches of the Sarda to wherever it went and twice I have been defeated in my searches. The first time, in the hunting years, I took Pasang with me and we spent a day tracking the trail right across the grasslands. We were halfway through the forest between the grassland and the Sarda when we ran into Indian poachers. They were four in number and they were foolish enough to speak to one another in low, murmuring voices, a sound that we were easily able to detect from a hundred yards away. We stalked them and found them setting steel, serrated-toothed traps for deer. We had a brief chat with them, confiscated their traps, and then sent them on their way, across the open white sands of the Sarda, to their homes in India. They left on the run and to the accompaniment of the booming of my .375 H&H rifle.

The second time, Pasang and I made an attempt accompanied by the headman of Kalkutta village and four of his Taru villagers. This time we planned to kill two birds with one stone, so to speak: to find the end of the Elephant Walk and to look for a historical British stone marker which, the headman had been telling me for years, had a brass plaque on it with writing. "You can take a photo of it, *Sahib*," he said, smiling his gap-toothed smile.

The marker, which I had also heard about from others over the years, demarcated the western boundary between Nepal and India and had been placed there after the British happily seized two thirds of the original kingdom of Nepal in return for not being allowed by the ruling Maharaja of the period to include all of it among the British colonies. The brass plaque, the headman thought, told the story. It was in English which, he added with a wry grin, he could not read.

Once again we walked the four and a half miles to the western end of the grasslands. Once again we plunged into the Sarda forests.

Once again, for various reasons, it was afternoon when we reached them. The sun arced down across the sky overhead, the sun by which the Tarus, most of whom had never seen a watch, marked the time of day and, most important, the approach of night. And once again we encountered something that brought our search to a sudden halt. This time it was not poachers. Or even tigers or elephants. This time it was hornets and, as I was leading the little expedition, it was I who suffered the full fury of their attack. An attack on someone stupid enough to walk into a big nest of them, glaringly visible in a little tree no more than five feet off the ground. I could not understand, at first, why the headman and the Tarus were all running away from me so fast, all in different directions. Good enough jungle men, they would freeze at the sound of something that might threaten them, such as tiger or elephant. Or poachers. Freeze and not run. But when the first three-inch long, yellow-jacketed demon landed on me and, in the instant of landing, jabbed his quarter-inch stinger into me, I knew why. I got four bites. Two in the face and two in the neck. Then I was down, rolling in the grass and as quickly as they had attacked me the whining little black and yellow demons let me be. I got up, staggered off vaguely in the direction that the Tarus had taken and then sat down again, dazed by the pain and the toxic fluids coursing through my veins. Then the Tarus joined me, laughing. I could not believe it at first. But they laughed. Stood around and laughed. Laughed at the silly young man foolish enough to walk into a jungle hornet's nest without seeing it. After a while I felt a bit better and I laughed with them. I got up and we reassembled for the search. But by then the night was beginning to reach long dark fingers toward us out of the east. The Nightjars were beginning to call. And the long sad moan of a hunting tiger followed by the wail of a peafowl told us it was time to go home and leave the search for the end of the Elephant Walk and the long-lost — and still lost — memorial of the British Raj to another day.

The group that uses the Elephant Walks of the White Grass Plains currently numbers twenty-one animals. Leader of the group is Tula Hatti, and when he is absent the leadership falls to a *mukna*, a

Tula Hatti

large tuskless male.* *Muknas* are something of a phenomenon. No one seems to know why some male elephants do not have tusks, but when they do not, as though to compensate, they grow much larger than average. (Only some females grow tusks; when this happens the tusks are usually small. Six to eight inches is average.) Thus the largest bulls in a herd may be *muknas* and because of their great size, even without tusks, they often gain leadership of the group. In Assam, in the northeast corner of India, trying to photograph a group of elephants in the sixties, I was defeated several times by the attentions of a huge *mukna*. The young bulls of the herd took due note of what I was doing, but allowed me to get close to the herd on several occasions. The single *mukna* in the herd, though, a huge animal that must have been the dominant bull, took exception to my presence and eventually, with a couple of demonstration charges, sent me scurrying.

The White Grass Plains herd has in addition to Tula Hatti and the single *mukna*, seven adult females, five adult bulls, and seven sub-adult males and females ranging from three to seven years of age. The area that the herd now uses totals 100,000 acres. This area, with its forest, grassland, and water supply from two jungle rivers, the Bauni and the Chaundari, as well as numerous smaller streams, offers ample area and sustenance for the present elephant group— provided that their numbers do not increase too much and provided that another herd does not find its way into the same area. As of now the White Grass Plains herd contains the only elephants in the whole area and, because of the closing of the Elephant Walk with Bardia to the east, they now have no contact with other herds. (In the long run, because of this confinement, there may be adverse genetic consequences to the herd due to inbreeding.) If the present herd were to increase significantly, it could face problems because

---

* The generally accepted opinion among scientists is that in Asia and Africa female elephants lead the herds. My studies — the occasional studies of a fieldman only, not a scientist — suggest that males are the herd leaders. Certainly all of the herds that I have seen in both Nepal and India appear to have been led either by mature tusked bulls or by large *muknas*. Certainly it has been these animals that have challenged me when I approached too close to the groups.

80

the White Grass Plains Reserve represents only half of its original habitat and feeding area. Until recently, the territory included, in addition to their present homelands, the forests that lie between the Karnali and the Bhabai Rivers, what is now called the Karnali or Bardia Reserve. This is the land that lies on the eastern end of the main Kailali–Kanchanpur Elephant Walk and for eons this has been the herd's summer home. Now, for a number of reasons, they no longer use it, just as they have abandoned the Elephant Walk that connects the area with the White Grass Plains.

The principal reason for this change in the migration pattern and in habitat is the cutting of the forests that lie across the northern lands of the districts of Kailali and Kanchanpur, close to the first escarpments of the foothills. Through these forests wound the main routes of the Sukila Phanta to Bardia Elephant Walk. Though the forests have not been completely cleared, the remaining corridor through the center of which the Elephant Walk used to run is too narrow to provide the cover that the herd needs and too sparse in vegetation to provide them with food.

In addition, close to this narrow strip, resettlement has taken place and hill people, their lands lost to erosion and over-grazing in the middle hills of the Himalaya, have been relocated here. These relocation tracts are carefully demarcated by the government and village boundaries end where the forest begins. But as the main source of fuel for both cooking and heating is wood, and as the new tracts are completely denuded of trees within days of occupation by the new arrivals, fuel must be gathered within the forest, in this case the thin remaining strip that contains the east-west Elephant Walk. The law says that villagers are not allowed to cut trees in government forests. But the law is one thing; enforcing it is another. The result is further thinning of the surviving forests as well as considerable disturbance by bands of hill people, something to which the herd would be very sensitive and to which it would react with unease and avoidance. In addition, new surroundings would make these hill people more disruptive than usual. Being new to the Terai forests they would be fearful of its larger animals and would no doubt make as much noise as possible, banging on trees and shouting back and forth in loud voices, to keep them away.

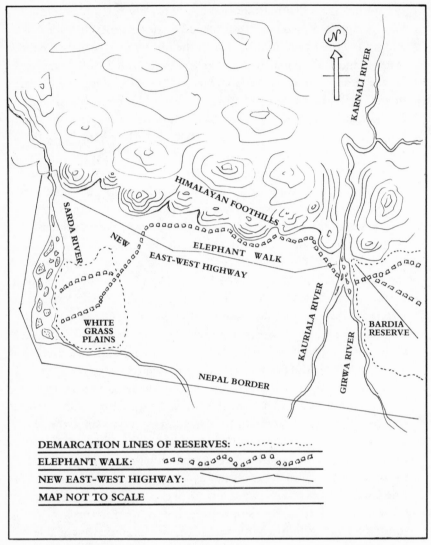

DEMARCATION LINES OF RESERVES: ⋯⋯⋯⋯⋯

ELEPHANT WALK: ▭▭▭ ▭▭▭▭▭▭▭▭ ▭▭▭▭

NEW EAST-WEST HIGHWAY: ⟋⟍⟋

MAP NOT TO SCALE

Sukila Phanta to Bardia Reserves Elephant Walk

Another factor detrimental to the elephants' use of the ancient Walk is the new East-West Highway. The Ghastly Gash, as we call it, is a major highway planned for completion in 1991. A great gash in some places three hundred feet in width — for an eventual single-lane hardtop highway of only fifteen feet in width — the road's flanks are strewn with a million wantonly destroyed trees. For the most part it is fifteen to twenty miles south of the Elephant Walk. But it cuts the ancient Walk where it bends south and west to enter the White Grass Plains and it cuts it again where it runs up to the Karnali River ferry crossing. The ferry is temporary, but it is placed at the site of the new bridge and so the road alignment in this area is permanent. That the elephants had little to say in the matter of the alignment of the Ghastly Gash is obvious. If they had, they would probably have been given as little attention as the original surveyors who, led by hydrologist Basil Bell of East Africa, made the strongest recommendations for a southern alignment. That alignment would have meant considerable saving of forest land and would have kept the road, with its noise and traffic, far from the Elephant Walk. It would also have meant that in the Bardia area the road would have cut across the delta of the Kauriala and Girwa Rivers and not right through the middle of the Bardia Reserve. Now it looks like the work of some monstrous steam roller as it winds its way for miles on the crushed debris of the raped forest. One wonders what the elephants must think when they come across that awful scar through their ancestral jungles. Since much of their Elephant Walk movement, especially during the seasonal migrations, takes place at night, they are probably spared part of the awful spectacle. Nevertheless, with a little imagination one can see them coming out of the forest into that awful slash of devastation and hurrying through it with quickened pace and averted eyes.

The name Elephant Walk conjures up pictures of stately animals moving majestically in single file through the sylvan glades of the forest. Whereas mental pictures are often quite the opposite of reality, elephants moving through forest really do travel in single file. The leader of the group, whether it be a *mukna* or a tusked bull or, in the absence of either, a mature female, will usually be in the front. If not in the lead, he or she will be close to the head of the column.

Immediately behind will be a mixture of cows and bulls and, locked in between them, always close to a mother or a protective aunt, the *butchas*, the little ones. All move as quietly as mice. Under normal circumstances and if there is no cause for alarm or panic, there is no vocalization. No whistling, no screaming, and no trunk thumping. Silence is the order of the day when the herd is on the move and one has to have been close to a group of elephants in motion to realize just how extraordinarily silent they can be. The soles of their feet are thick and calloused, but they are soft in comparison with the hard-packed dirt and thus are able to absorb and cushion objects like dry roots and twigs, preventing them from breaking and making noise. The Walks themselves are mostly clean of debris and this allows for noiseless placement of the feet. If there are branches, tree trunks, or debris of any kind in the pathway, the lead elephant will pick them up in his or her truck and quietly put them aside. If the object is too heavy for one animal to lift then a second will come immediately to the aid of the first. Working together, two mature Asian elephants can pick up objects in excess of four tons and soundlessly relocate them. While this is being done, the line of elephants behind will halt and wait quietly until the way is clear.

Their silence is just that to the human ear but, as was only recently discovered, to elephants it is filled with the sound of their communication. The sounds are subsonic. The discovery of elephants' abilities in this area was made only recently by a young woman named Katharine Payne studying the great animals at the Washington Park Zoo in Portland, Oregon. It was followed up by a research program in Africa during which it was determined that African elephants, using sounds inaudible to humans, can communicate with each other over great distances.

Sometimes elephants will stop to feed when using one of their Walks. But my experience is that they eat very little when travelling. One reason may be that when they feed there is unavoidable noise. The tearing sounds of bark being ripped from trees. The crash of branches being pulled down and crunched between giant molars. The crack of small trees as they are snapped off. The elephants' reluctance to eat on a Walk may be to avoid drawing at-

84

tention to the Walk itself. The Walks are vital passageways between feeding areas as well as essential routes for seasonal migrations and the less others—especially man—know about them, the better.

Through the years I have had several experiences with the silence of elephants. Each one, each time, has added to the respect that I have for something of their size being able to move so soundlessly. One sees it in small animals and even in larger ones like the big cats. But there one expects to see it. We have a saying in the Terai: as silent as the footfall of a tiger. There is little that is more silent. But for an animal that may weigh in excess of 12,000 pounds and as much as 17,000 or even 18,000 pounds, which is what we think Tula Hatti may be, to be able to move with almost no sound other than the softest hissing—the sound of branches and leaves running along the flanks in combination with the swishing of grass against the feet—has always been almost uncanny to me.

One experience comes to mind, one that brings back memories of the burning heat of the Terai, the real heat that comes during the weeks before the arrival of the monsoon. The month was late April. The place was Oriole Camp on the Bauni River in Kanchanpur. The year, 1987.

With Dede and Rara, I had spent three months in the Terai. We had arrived in the country later than usual and so stayed on into the warming months of early summer. When day temperatures began to climb above the hundred mark, Dede decided to take Rara up to Kathmandu and wait for me there while I wrapped up the work of a photo reconnaissance for the movie, our main reason for being in the Terai at this time. We contacted Colonel Bisht who made bookings for us on the weekly Royal Nepal Airlines flight to Kathmandu. On a Thursday morning, the day of the weekly flight, accompanied by Pasang and Jangbu, we drove to Mahendranagar airport, a wire fence-enclosed—to keep cattle and goats out—grass field just big enough to take Royal Nepal Air Corporation's cross-country workhorse, the Canadian-built nineteen seater Twin Otter. We arrived on time, had our reservations checked by a smiling little man who was Airport Manager, Ticket Sales Manager, Reservations Clerk, Flight Controller, Baggage Check In, and in charge of keeping cattle and goats off the airstrip. Then we settled down to wait in the little grass-roofed hut that was the combination Ticket Sales, Reservation Desk, and Control Tower. We waited for seven or eight hours and when the plane did not come, shrugged our shoulders with the rest of the waiting passengers and left. We spent the night with Colonel Bisht at his home and had a delightful dinner—hot curried chicken washed down with copious draughts of cold Nepalese Star beer—and next morning, early (in case the plane arrived and then departed an hour or so before its scheduled time, which sometimes happened with the R.N.A.C.) were back at the airport again. We waited all day. The plane did not come. We spent another night with Hikmat and his wife in Mahendranagar and on the Saturday made another attempt to get on the plane. This time, after no more than five hours waiting, the plane arrived. It landed. It taxied up to the little grass hut. The pilot and the co-pilot got out, stretched their legs, and nodded and smiled to us. The baggage was given a couple of kicks by two sleepy security guards and loaded on the plane. Dede and Rara and seventeen other passengers climbed aboard. The pilot and the co-pilot got back into the cockpit and started the engines. Everybody waved and the plane took off. Nobody, not the Airport Manager, the security guards, the passengers who did not manage to get a seat, or the numerous others who came down to see the weekly plane arrive remarked on the plane being two days late. In Nepal a day late or two days or once, for me, seven days—at the nine-thousand-foot mountain airfield of Lukla in the Everest region—is taken for granted. Nepal is a country fast moving into the twentieth century. But some twentieth-century things do not seem to matter too much and time is one of them.

I said goodbye to Colonel Bisht, told him that I hoped that he could visit me before I closed camp, and drove back into the reserve, the eastern gates of which actually lie no more than half a mile from the airport. I planned to spend another week and then get up to Kathmandu to join Dede and Rara. From there we would fly home. I spent another six days in the reserve. The weather was still tolerable for the most part and nights were still cool and delightful under the spreading canopy of trees that shaded Oriole Camp. But when the sun rose in the mornings it did so with a summer glare. From the cool of night the thermometer raced upwards through the mornings, climbing fifty degrees Fahrenheit by midday and then another fifteen to twenty degrees into mid afternoon. This was the beginning of the kind of weather that drove one out of the jungle and if it did not, then another factor would: the emergence from its winter dormancy of the Anopheles Mosquito. The female of this species carries malaria and the Terai has several types of malaria of which one, falciparum malaria, is often fatal. All of us, including the Sherpas, had been taking a protective medication, Chloroquine, all winter. But recent medical findings had suggested that even this, the best known prophylactic against malaria, may fail in the face of the deadly falciparum variety of the disease. So it was that a few days after Dede and Rara left for Kathmandu, I started closing down the camp. We had had quite a big camp all winter, with extra safari tents for visitors, and I had set aside two full days for the work of packing and cleaning up the camp site. It was one day before I was due to leave, with all of the tents down except mine, the Scout and its utility trailer partially loaded, the burnable garbage burned, the biodegradable garbage buried, and the remainder, mainly plastic and metal, packed and ready to be hauled to Mahendranagar, that the elephants arrived.

We had worked through the heat of the morning. About midday I told the Sherpas to take a break and brew up some tea. Jangbu brought me a mug of tea with a slice of lemon in it and then he joined Pasang and Phurua in the kitchen. I took the tea into the tent and set it on a box beside my bed to cool. I hoped it would cool. The thermometer on a tree outside the tent registered 112 degrees Farenheit and inside the tent, though the awnings were all open and tied back, it was probably ten degrees hotter. The metal of my cot burned my arm when I touched it and when I drank some of the tea sweat poured down my body, soaking my shirt. I took off the shirt, put a towel down on the bare canvas of the cot, and lay down on it to rest. The packing could wait. It was too damned hot to work and the Sherpas would also be glad of a break. Mountain men, they liked the heat as little as I did.

I lay on the camp cot for about ten minutes. I may have dozed. The sun glared through the mosquito netting of the big safari tent and even though I had hung a tarpaulin above it to keep the direct heat of the sun off its roof, I could still feel the waves of hot air radiating downwards. Outside, apart from the incessant shrilling of the cicadas, the jungle was silent. From the kitchen lean-to where the Sherpas sat drinking their tea came the low murmur of their voices. I had taught them to speak softly when in the forest and over the years they had become very good at keeping their voices low and minimizing the sounds of their work in camp as much as possible. Suddenly through my drowsiness, faint but imprinting itself on my sub-conscious mind as something different, apart from the shrilling of the cicadas and the muttering voices of the men, I heard a strange sound. The decidious forest sheds its leaves at this time of year and behind the tent was a thick carpet of dried brown leaves. I used to think of it at night as my security system because nothing could move through it without making some sort of sound. Often awakened suddenly from the light sleep that I enjoy in the jungle night, I found that I was able to interpret the sounds and quickly identify what was moving past the tent in the wee small hours: big cat, small cat, porcupine, snake, or even mouse. The sound that I heard now was different. It was mouselike, a faint rustling, at first. But then, slowly, it grew in volume and within minutes what had begun as the small sounds of one or two mice suddenly began to sound like a small army of the little creatures. I sat up, jolted out of my half sleep. Something was wrong. Sounds like this in the middle of the night were acceptable. But in the diurnal hours? And in this heat? No. What I was hearing sounded like mice. A lot of mice. But it had to be something else and what now brought me fully awake was the realization that I was hearing something that I could not identify or interpret.

I grabbed my binoculars off the bedside box. They were hot to the touch. I slipped out through the open tent flaps and whistled to the men in the kitchen, thirty feet away. When they looked up I made a signal to them to stop talking and to be quiet. Then I walked around to the back of my tent and looked down at the leaves. Quickly, the noise, still growing in volume and now sounding like the advance of hundreds of mice leaping and diving and burrowing their way through the dry leaves, gave me an audible focal point.

It was not coming from the leaves down at my feet at all, but from the green wall of the jungle, three or four hundred feet away. I fixed my gaze on what seemed to be the source of the strange sounds and as I did so the huge, gray shape of an elephant appeared, walking with a swinging and rapid stride down the Elephant Walk that ran behind the camp toward the Bauni River. The shape was immediately followed by another and then another and another. As I watched, eighteen elephants emerged from the green curtain of the forest and strode in single file, massive heads nodding to the rhythm of their stride, paying not the slightest attention to me, the tents, our campsite, or the open-mouthed Sherpas. The only sound they made, the only sound that I heard from all eighteen of them – adult females, bulls with gleaming tusks, and half a dozen little ones trotting to keep up the rapid pace being imposed by the herd leader, a huge *mukna* – was the soft rustling of the leaves against their feet.

Within minutes of my first hearing them the herd was gone. The forest to the immediate south of Oriole Camp is open and thin, with single huge trees wrapped in giant creepers thicker than a man's body. But where the Elephant Walk comes to the Bauni there is a dense wall of *Bhate*, a green frondlike growth that climbs to a height of thirty feet and is armed with viciously sharp, hooked thorns. The Elephant Walk cuts through this to the Bauni ford – the shallows that the elephants have used for years to cross at this point – and it swallowed them within seconds. I heard them splashing across the river. They paused to drink and then climbed the bank on the west side and disappeared into the forest that borders the Sukila Phanta swamp. Soon the only sounds were once again the shrilling of the cicadas and the clatter and bang of equipment as we resumed our packing. The Sherpas worked willingly. They were anxious to get away, out of the heat of the forest and back to the cool of the valley of Kathmandu, the hills, and the families they had not seen for three months. But my thoughts were on the silence of elephants and our extraordinary experience when eighteen of them – perhaps thirty tons of animals – had walked within a few feet of my camp making no more noise than a flight of small birds. I have no doubt that had the floor of the forest not had its seasonal coverage of dry leaves I might well have dozed through their passing.

Tula Hatti

Little is known about the White Grass Plains herd and almost nothing is known about its individual members. No one has ever studied them and my own knowledge of them is gleaned, I have to admit, from chance encounters, from what the Elephant Walks tell me about their patterns of travel, and from secondary observation of their footprints. True, I have seen them on and off over the years, in the middle forest of the reserve, in the grasslands, and out on the sandy reaches of the Sarda. But for the most part I have never had them in view for more than ten minutes at a time. I presume that they live the ordinary life of ordinary elephants, much the same as they must have done for countless years in the comparative isolation of the White Grass Plains, untouched and undisturbed by outside influences, eating, sleeping, and drinking where and when they want.

There has always been enough food for the small group that composes the White Grass Plains herd. The herd is particularly fortunate as far as food is concerned, for with the resettlement of whole Taru villages in line with the expansion plans for the reserve, areas that were formerly rice fields now offer them hundreds of extra acres of succulent grasses. Two of these areas, where the villages of Haria and Singpur used to be, are now completely covered with dense reaches of fifteen- to twenty-foot-tall grass that is an excellent source of food for the herd and provides the cover that is one of their essential needs. Elephants do not like hot sun and in the afternoon, the hottest part of the jungle day, nearly always seek cover and shade.

The herd uses both of these areas as food sources; it is from these lush grasses that the adults of the herd take the 700 to 800 pounds of green fodder that each of them needs on a daily basis.

For water the herd seems to concentrate on two sources. One is the Bauni River, the principal river of the reserve which, regardless of seasons, contains a steady flow of comparatively clean water. The word comparatively is not used as a suggestion that the water might be polluted. It is just that I have never seen the Bauni other than dark in color, often brown with mud after rain, slow and sluggish in movement. It is a typical jungle river that, in spite of its coloration and its taste, provides the White Grass Plains herd with as much water as it needs to bathe, frolic, and drink (adults need forty-five to fifty gallons each per day, summer and winter).

The second source of water for the herd is the lake of Rani Tal, near Singpur. This is shallow, probably no more than three feet at the most, and the herd does not hesitate to enter it with young calves, something it will not do at another place which actually offers more and cleaner water, the Sukila Phanta swamp. All elephants can swim and I think that they can even swim from an early age. But they can also get bogged down in mud or soft sand—and certainly in quicksand—so the herd, accompanied as it usually is by young calves, stays out of the four- to five-foot-deep waters of the swamp. I have seen single adult elephants in the swamp, lone *muknas*, and I know that Tula Hatti goes in there from time to time. But elephant parents know that its muddy bottom is hazardous to their young and as a family group all stay away from it.

Like all animals elephants need sleep and in my experience the White Grass Plains herd sleeps mainly at night. I have encountered them standing together in the dark of the *Sal* forest, in those small hours before the dawn when, for a short time, many animals seem to rest. On the brief occasions when I have seen them like this only the calves were actually lying down. The remainder of the herd stood quietly and if elephants really sleep standing up, as is believed, then this is what they were doing. I have also encountered the herd drowsing in the early afternoon, again with calves lying down on the ground and adults all standing, still and silent. Adults will sometimes lie down; once I watched Tula Hatti stand in the grass for half an hour in the afternoon sun and then, as though giving it due consideration, sink slowly down and stretch out on his side. He lay like that for only ten minutes. Then suddenly, after a quick inspection of the air currents with his proboscis, he was up and away.

It is the elephant's trunk, its proboscis, that gives this order of mammals its name, *Proboscidea*. At one time in Asia the order included seven species of elephant and eight mastodons. Today the single Asian survivor of the fifteen species, *elephas maximus*, is a direct if somewhat deviated descendant of the common ancestor of all of them: a hairy, three-and-a-half-foot-tall creature of the Eocene named Moeritherium. From this diminutive mammal with four legs, five toes on each foot, and a complete set of incisor, molar, and canine teeth, all the elephants of the world are descended. The proboscis is what the elephant uses to eat and drink. It is such an important part of the elephant's anatomy that one of the first things that it will do when threatened is curl the trunk up tight under its chin to protect it. If an elephant's trunk is damaged to the extent that it cannot be used to pick up food or drink, then the elephant will die.

Today the elephant is the largest terrestrial mammal on the face of the earth. (African elephants tend to be larger than Asian.) It is well adapted to all kinds of terrain and conditions of climate and, in the Indo-Nepal-Burma region of Asia, altitude. In Nepal elephants have been seen in hill forests as high as 5000 feet. In Burma they graze at all seasons in bamboo forest to elevations of 10,000 feet and in Sikkim, immediately east of Nepal, their tracks have been found in snow at 12,000 feet.

Elephant herds vary in number. Consisting of single family groups that seldom mix, herds may number from ten to fifty animals. Young females and males may leave the herd to join another, but on the whole separate herds stay together. If food is scarce or if there is insufficient food in an area for all of the animals in the herd to eat together, it may break up into small groups, to rejoin later. Single mature bulls will often leave the herd to lead solitary lives, joining the herd for only brief periods when the urge to mate arises. Their size allows them to shoulder aside any protests that might be made by younger bulls about their amorous intentions when they rejoin the herd. The breeding season in the wild is not clearly known; it is probably during the heat of the monsoon period. This, with a gestation period of about nineteen months, would allow for calves to be dropped in the fall, in the cool of the year. The usual delivery is one calf. Twins are not very common and triplets even less so. In 1988 the White Grass Plains had five calves, each about five years of age. A new one was born to the herd while we were in the White Grass Plains in the late winter of 1988–'89. As of late summer of 1990 the numbers of the herd had increased from eighteen in 1988 to twenty-one animals. Eighteen was the number that I was able to count when that silent and stately procession of animals emerged from the forest and walked past my camp to the Bauni in the searing heat of that pre-monsoon day.

(At the time of this writing there are supposed to be — the official figure — 35,000 Asian elephants left in the world, 11,000 of which are in captivity. I think that the figure for those left in the wild is somewhat exaggerated. We still have much to learn about elephants in the wild. Let us hope there is time.)

When we flew home from Nepal at the end of our 1983 visit with our discovery of Tula Hatti fresh in our minds and plans for the movie, embryonic as they were, taking shape, we carried with us another thought. This was about the Elephant Walks and their importance to the future of Tula Hatti and the herd that makes its home in the White Grass Plains. The system of Walks within the White Grass Plains was, we felt, reasonably secure. As were the Walks within the Bardia Reserve. But the link between the two reserves that carried the elephants back and forth in their seasonal migration was now cut, confining the Sukila Phanta herd to the west and whatever elephants remained in Bardia to the east of the Karnali River. Nursing this thought, we decided to include within our film story of Tula Hatti and our plea for his protection additional material on the vital need to preserve the ancient Elephant Walks of Bardia and Sukila Phanta.

In addition, we could not help but think of the actual status of the lands of the reserves themselves. By Nepalese law, while the establishment of a national park is permanent and fixed for all time, reserves are subject to a mixed set of rulings that in the end render them temporary in nature. Also, unlike national parks, reserves may also be opened for hunting. Since they were created several hunts have been carried out in both reserves, mainly by members of the royal family of Nepal. Our film about Tula Hatti could be a tremendous achievement for conservation if its messages included the need to name both Bardia and the White Grass Plains reserves as national parks, thus protecting Tula Hatti and his herd as well as preserving the ancient Elephant Walks for as long as the elephants and their descendants survive.

4

RECONNAISSANCE

Arriving back in the United States in the spring of 1983, Dede and I set about making plans for the film about the great elephant. We spent some time studying the formats of similar films and then decided that what would give the story the most exposure would be a televised release. A series seemed too ambitious so we decided on a single one-hour film. We gave it the name *Tula Hatti: The Last Great Elephant*, and wrote an outline of the story. We contacted several teams of professional photographers to estimate what their services might cost us. This would be the major budget item. The best offer we could get was $30,000 for a team of two people, one a cameraman, and the other a sound technician, for one month. Building on this with my own experience of expedition and safari costs, I eventually came up with a figure of $75,000 as a reasonable budget. But, knowing from experience what the ever-lurking gremlin of the unforeseen contingency can do to the best laid plans of expedition budgets, I added another $25,000 to this, bringing the total to $100,000. Then we set out to look for financial backing.

Nick Webster, the film director with whom I made the film *Monsters and Myths* — the story of the twin phenomena of the Yeti of the Himalaya and the Bigfoot of the Pacific Northwest — told me that when he taught filmmaking and sent students out to get footage of various subjects, he had one piece of advice for them. If they came back with the footage, well and good. If for some reason they did not, then he did not want to know why. The wording on the blackboard, his wording, for all to see and note was, NOBODY WANTS TO HEAR YOUR SAD STORY.

It has been some years since Nick shared his axiom with me, sitting in a cave in the high Himalaya trying to warm his frozen fingers and toes after a chill wind had caught him in the open at 14,000 feet. But I have never forgotten it. And now, tempted as I am to write about the frustrations, anguish, and near despair of two people who had never made a film before trying in vain to find $100,000 to make a movie about a wild elephant that lived—probably still lived, as it was pointed out to us—in the far-flung jungles of a little country locked in the mountains of the Himalaya, I put the temptation aside. Suffice it to say that it was a long haul and that it was not until late 1987 after another four winters of safaris spent in Nepal—during which, at the least, we were able to keep an eye on Tula Hatti and reassure ourselves that he was still living there—that we managed to find the backing that we needed from private sponsors and were able to make a definite plan for production of the film.

When the funding came, it arrived in two parts. We received about half of it to start, with a pledge of the remainder later. Later meant too late to carry out full production on location in the winter of '87–'88. And the winter season, the northern hemisphere winter, is the only time of the year that the Terai jungles allow freedom of operation and freedom of movement for something like a film production team. Winter in the Terai is November to March. April and May can be hot, very hot, and June brings the monsoon with high winds, storms, and from 300 to 350 inches of rain in five months, to about mid-October. The jungle at this time turns into a veritable swamp. Trails and roads disappear and even the smallest of the rivers that have their sources in the middle Himalaya can rise a much as twenty feet in twenty-four hours, becoming impassable barriers and severing communication with the outside world. So we thought the best thing to do in the limited time we had available within the '87–'88 Nepal winter season would be to perform a photographic reconnaissance in the southwest Terai—the home ranges of the elephant—establish film locations, arrange the licenses and permits needed for the movie, ship out and store equipment for the following winter's production, and generally do as much advance preparation as time allowed.

Late in 1987 we entered into a frantic period of choosing, listing, assembling, and packing stores and equipment. A number of U.S. companies offered assistance in the form of equipment and services. Principal among them was the Coleman Company of Wichita, Kansas, who gave us carte blanche on their catalogue of excellent outdoor equipment in return for a simple credit in the film when it appeared. In the end, ninety percent of our equipment was from Coleman. The only thing we did not use was camping and safari tentage. Our only reason was that for years we had been buying tents, from high mountain ultra-lights to big safari tents, from the Eureka Tent Company in Binghamton, New York. In our experience Eureka makes the best tentage in the world and we wanted to stay with them. Which is how we now feel about Coleman camping products, having really field tested them under often tough conditions through two winters in the Terai jungles of Nepal.

Christmas day, 1987, saw us working in two feet of snow trying to get boxes and bales and bags of tents, folding chairs, sleeping bags, writing tables, writing materials, portable toilets, kitchen utensils, notebooks, journals, clipboards, axes, saws, shovels, cable, rope, tools, and warm clothing packed and loaded inside a big, steel-bodied utility trailer — one of two donated by the Wells Cargo Company of Ogden, Utah — or inside our International Scout which, as an old faithful and keeping in mind that our budget was not as fat as it seemed, we decided to contribute to the expedition. A second vehicle, a Suzuki Samurai, was purchased to accompany the Scout. Our plan was that while the Scout would be used for heavy hauling and pulling the trailer, the Suzuki, its canvas top stripped off, would be used as a camera car.

Early in January I drove the Scout and the trailer to Portland. Dede followed in the Suzuki and after a minimum of paperwork and formalities we handed both over to the agents of American President Lines, the shipping company that would carry them to India. We had used APL once before and found them to be an excellent company with which to do business. Later, they donated part of the service of getting the two vehicles to and from India as a contribution to the film.

Since Nepal is landlocked, an Indian port must be used for access by sea to the country. We saw the vehicles and the trailer container-ized, gave the agents a check for $6000, the cost of shipping them from Seattle to Bombay, and then had a friend pick us up and drive us back to Mount Hood. We were given an estimate of six weeks for arrival of the vehicles in Bombay. I added to this a week for clearance of the container in Bombay, plus another seven days for the drive from Bombay to Kathmandu. We would keep track of the passage of the ship—in this case the American President Lines' President Jackson—through their agents in Portland. They would monitor the progress of the ship and give us a precise date for its arrival in Bombay.

We spent the remainder of the six-week waiting period working on the story for the movie and, by correspondence with Nepal, set-ting up arrangements for the reconnaissance. We wrote to Pasang and told him to be ready to meet me in Bombay and accompany me on the drive to Nepal. We wrote to a friend in Bombay, Jimmy Modi, whose father, Sir Homi Modi, had been a friend of mine since the end of World War II, to ask him to arrange for some pri-vate garaging for the vehicles when I got them off the ship and for a second driver to take the Suzuki to Nepal. And we wrote to Jangbu, culinary magician of a thousand camps, to ask him to stand by for another season's work and to alert Phurua—who lived up in the mountains and was sometimes hard to find—to come to Kath-mandu as soon as he could. We also contacted our financial sponsors to advise them of the schedule of arrival for the ship, around which we would build a definite plan for setting up a base camp in the southwestern jungles, where they hoped to spend a couple of weeks with us on safari.

At the end of January 1988 we received a call from the APL ship-ping agents giving us a definite arrival date for the President Jackson in Bombay. We made immediate preparations for departure. I had received no reply from Pasang in Kathmandu to my letters but I presumed that he had received them and now I sent him a cable—he and Jangbu shared a post office box in the city—asking him to meet me at the airport and to be prepared to leave for Bombay immedi-ately. I called our travel agents and asked them to have our tickets made ready and a few days later I climbed on board a Thai Interna-

97

Tula Hatti

tional flight in Seattle and flew to Kathmandu. Dede and Rara would follow me. Their arrival in Kathmandu was planned to coincide with my arrival by road from Bombay. This would be three-year-old Rara's second expedition. A seasoned traveller, she had already been with us on an expedition to the Cocos Keeling Islands in the Indian Ocean in 1986 at the age of two.

Pasang was not at the airport in Kathmandu when I arrived. After checking in through customs and immigration I waited around to see if he might turn up. I met several other old friends but Pasang did not appear so I took a cab to what has now been our base in Kathmandu for more than a decade, the familiar Shangri La Hotel. I checked into the hotel, made a few phone calls, and then set out to look for Pasang. I eventually found him, ill in bed in his tiny ground floor apartment in the Phulchock district. We had a talk and the upshot of it was that he was too ill to come to Bombay with me. He thought he might be better later. In the meantime he suggested that I take Jangbu and Phurua with me. He would meet with me when I got back to Kathmandu and then come down to the Terai with us.

A few days later I flew with Jangbu and Phurua to Bombay. I arrived on a Saturday, when customs and most other offices are closed. The ship had arrived but I had to wait until Monday to start the work of clearing the vehicles. I checked into the Astor, a relic of British India in the Colaba district, where on many a night at the end of World War II, I and a stalwart bunch of survivors had wined, dined, and danced away the midnight hours. On the following Monday, bright and early, I set off to attack the problem of getting the vehicles and equipment through the veritable maze of rules and regulations that the Indian government imposes on anyone who tries to import something into the subcontinent. I started with the shipping agents for APL and that part of the procedure was fairly easy. I simply paid them a landing fee and collected the shipping papers. Then I contacted a clearing agent. Armed with a sheaf of documents and information as to the exact amount of gratuities that had to be paid to various officials, we entered the docks and threw ourselves into the work of getting the vehicles off the ship, out of

98

the container, into customs storage, through customs, and out of the docks in the seven days I had set aside for the work.

Fourteen days later I cleared the vehicles and equipment from the Bombay docks and, with an Indian driver hired for the run to Nepal, drove them over for garaging at the Astor. Once again Nick Webster's high Himalaya axiom come to mind. Nobody wants to hear your sad story. But briefly, for fourteen days I spent all day every day battling the unbelievably complex and totally ridiculous system of regulations that governs importations into India of everything from ball-point pens to tractors. Each morning I got up and took a taxi to the docks. At the dock gates I met my agent, Vispy Patel, without whom I would probably still be in Bombay haggling with officialdom. Together, each day armed with more and more documents, we entered the fray. Each day some customs official would inform us that today would be the day, without fail, that the consignment would be cleared. Each day, without fail, some new impediment arose to bar our clearances. One day it would be a strike. Another day an official needed for a signature on a document would not be available. Then a public holiday (India seems to have at least three hundred of these a year) would intervene and all the offices would be closed. Then came something called "end of fiscal term" during which, for several days, everything moves at an even slower pace than usual. On weekends of course nothing could be done, and all senior officials — without whose signatures half a dozen times in triplicate on each of the dozens of forms that we carried around with us everything came to a stop — leave early on Fridays, or simply do not come in at all.

I am a patient man and my patience is born of years of experience with, among other facets of the mysterious east, Indian bureaucracy at its worst. I once spent six weeks in Calcutta trying to clear some camera equipment through airport customs. I have long since learned that time, so important to us westerners, matters not a whit in that vast and teeming subcontinent. And so it was that when I eventually saw the last document signed, the last ink-stained stamp descend on the last piece of paper, the last gratuity handed over — to two guards who would not open the dock gates to let us out until they had been paid — I did not rant and rave and tear out my hair the way many a foreigner would. I just accepted the way things were for the way they are, the way they have been in India since the end of the Raj, the way they will probably be in that incredible country forever. My only real disappointment was that the carefully laid plans of our film backers to meet with us in Nepal and enjoy a safari with us would, because of the delay, now have to be abandoned. Sadly, I informed them of this in a long cable and, as cables emanating from India have a habit of being delivered anywhere from Greenland to Terra Del Fuego, I backed it up with a telephone call to Dede, telling her what had happened and asking her to make sure that our guests-to-be were advised.

The drive to Nepal took nine days. It should have taken seven. It is eleven hundred miles from Bombay to Kathmandu. In spite of the condition of the narrow, one-lane highways — potholes that could swallow a buffalo and that twice smashed springs on the Scout, waves in the pavement that can throw a vehicle a foot in the air if driven over at anything more than ten miles an hour, and miles of corrugation that rattle the teeth in the head and threaten to shake loose every nut and bolt in the body of a vehicle — and in spite of the endless lines of slow moving buffalo carts, cows, sheep, goats, rickshaws, handcarts, bicycles, and pedestrians walking by the hundreds down the center of the road or sometimes simply lying in the middle of it, eating, sleeping or just sitting around aimlessly, and the thousands of trucks that thunder up and down with the greatest of glee, driving one off the single lane into the ditch a hundred times a day, still it is possible, driving from the crack of dawn to early evening, to average about one hundred fifty miles a day. But the long delay in Bombay had moved my carefully planned itinerary into a period when no sane traveller will brave the roads of towns or cities in India, the three day Hindu holiday called the Kali Puja that has, over the years, become an opportunity for the lawless, under the cloak of religion, to break the law without fear of police retaliation. The Kali Puja lasts for three days, three days that in north India are given over to drunkenness, violence, and destruction. Nowadays, because of the value of the tourist trade to India, certain aspects of its culture are, when possible, swept under the carpet and left there. Thus the origin of the Kali Puja, the ancient practice of the annual deflowering of young virgins by the Hindu priests, is no longer a subject of discussion, especially in the presence of tourists. But the red dye that people throw on one another during this time was originally human blood and the present day *puja* is a memento of those grim ceremonies when the blood of young girls was smeared on all who attended them.

The first signs of the *puja* began soon after we had left Varanasi, the old Hindu city that used to be called Benares. Groups of young men, many of them drunk, paraded on the roads carrying plastic buckets of red dye which they hurled on anything that moved. No women were to be seen anywhere, only men. As we passed through several small towns, the crowds grew. In addition to the red dye, which was splattered on the vehicles and the trailer, we were also hit with rocks and handfuls of cow manure. The crowds thickened in each town. In places, if they saw us approaching, they tried to run in front of the vehicles. We kept going, determined to let nothing stop us. I told Jangbu, who was driving with me, and Phurua, who rode with the Indian driver in the Suzuki, to keep the doors locked at all times. I also gave each of them wads of one-rupee and two-rupee notes. In a ploy that enabled us to get through several encircling mobs of wild-eyed drunks, pounding on the hood and the doors and screaming obscenities, they opened the windows a crack and pushed out bills as fast as they could. Each time they did this, my rearview mirror showed tumbling piles of men fighting and scrambling for the money.

The first day of the *puja*, we managed to get through many small towns and villages without mishap. We spent the night far from the highway in a lonely grove of mango trees. The second day was bad and at the end of it, with the cars covered with red, yellow, and blue dye, cow manure, sand, gravel, and small stones — some larger ones had bounced off the Scout without doing too much harm — we found a small canal a mile from the highway, washed off both vehicles, and camped for the night.

It took us another seven days to reach Nepal and with the experiences of the first few days firmly impressed on our minds we bypassed, whenever we could, all major cities. One, Allahabad, was too large for us to go around and we had a most unpleasant and dangerous time getting through it. At night we always camped as far away from human habitation as possible. In India, with its one thousand million people, this is not easy. No matter how much we tried, there always seemed to be the lights of a small town and the sounds of people in the distance. We slept fitfully and we all took turns standing guard, two men at a time. During the day the Sherpas slept while I and the Indian driver did the driving, he consoled with the thought of the extra wages I would be paying him for "guard duty" and I with a vision of the peaceful hills of Nepal that lay ahead: the cold, clean air of the mountains and the people of the little kingdom who, at the least, could be depended on not to stand around throwing rocks at passing cars. And so we came to the ninth day and, with a thousand miles of road behind us, arrived at the border of Nepal.

As we crossed the Indo-Nepal border I made a solemn resolution that this would be my last drive across India. I had done the Bombay run five times over the years as well as one to Madras and each time the hazards imposed by people and traffic seemed to grow more pronounced. After the first trip, years ago, I never wanted to do another. But the problem at the time was that if one needed a good serviceable vehicle in Nepal, one had to import one's own. Reliable transportation is essential to any kind of work or travel in the mountains or the Terai, where service facilities and spare parts are non-existent. The only vehicles available on often dubious rental arrangements were twenty- to thirty-year-old Land Rovers and Jeeps, some of them W.W. II leftovers. Recently some importation of four-wheel-drive vehicles has been allowed and reasonable rentals are more readily available.

We crossed the Nepal border at Sonauli and from there drove due north to the Nepalese city of Butwal. There I left the trailer and the Suzuki with friends and, accompanied by Jangbu and Phurua, drove right through to Kathmandu in one long day, pulling into the Shangri La as the evening sun threw long shadows across the gray flagstones of the big courtyard and sank slowly behind the western hills that rim the valley.

I sent the Sherpas home in a cab. (Phurua would stay with Jangbu at Phulchowk until we were ready to leave.) Then I handed a couple of bags to a smiling attendant, asked him to take them up to my suite, grabbed a handful of mail and cables from the reception desk, left word for the hotel's general manager, Utpal Sengupta, an old friend and the heartbeat of the Shangri La, that I was in residence, and went straight to the Pagoda bar where the barman had already poured a very tall, very cold Nepalese Star beer in a giant pewter tankard.

Sitting in the Pagoda, letting the ambiance of the Shangri La — assisted by a little alcohol — loosen up the physical and mental knots tied by the long haul from Bombay, I opened and read through the cables. One was from Rara, written with a little assistance and addressed to Peter Byrne, F.R.O.G.S, Shangri La Hotel, Captain Doo, Nepal, giving me her arrival date. Another was from old friends in Concord, New Hampshire, Bob and Carol Rines and their son Justice, saying that they were on a round-the-world trip and would be coming through Kathmandu and asking if they could join us on safari some time in the coming month. The cable had arrived three days before and needed an immediate reply, so I had hotel reception send a cable off at once saying that we would be delighted to have them join us and recommending the Shangri La as an excellent place to stay and as a contact point through which they could confirm arrival dates and schedules.

Two days later Dede and Rara arrived in Captain Doo. With Jangbu, Phurua, and Pasang, who was now feeling better and planned to come with us to the Terai, we spent another couple of days in last minute preparations for the reconnaissance. Just before we left we got a cable from the Rineses saying that they would join us. Then, early one morning, before the warming spring sun had flooded the formal gardens and gray-stoned courtyard of the Shangri La, with blue-gray mist still holding the chill air of night, we loaded up the Scout and chained and hooked on the big utility trailer. Using the roof rack of the Scout to its fullest, we managed to make seating for just five inside. Phurua went ahead to Butwal by bus and the rest of us, Rara happily cushioned between Pasang and Jangbu in the back, rode in the Scout. A last minute call at a cold storage shop in Kichipokri district for bread, a couple of frozen chickens, a smoked ham, and a giant wheel of hard Tibetan cheese and we were off. Ahead of us lay a journey of three hundred miles, most of it—with the exception of some parts of the new East-West Highway which were now hard top or gravel—over forest roads of dirt and sand or on Taru village-to-village buffalo cart trails with deep ruts and high centers. Fifty rivers would have to be crossed, some of them major ones. Many, still unbridged, would have to be forded. Our first stop, apart from overnights along the way, would be the Bardia Reserve on the Karnali River, some two hundred miles away. But the weather was good and road surfaces would generally be hard and we estimated three days to Bardia and another two to the White Grass Plains, which proved to be accurate.

We stopped in Butwal to pick up the Suzuki and Phurua. The Indian driver was paid and sent home to Bombay so Dede took over the driving of the Suzuki. She was accompanied by Jangbu and from time to time, as her childish moods suited her, by Rara. We travelled in tandem, I in the lead with the Scout and the trailer, and we had a simple signal—a flash or two of the Suzuki headlights for me to stop—to prevent us getting separated. This was important, for once we were off the main highway from Kathmandu to Narainghar there was little traffic—no one to send a message up or down the road in the case of emergency—and as a result no communication at all if we got separated. So I drove with one eye on the rearview mirror all of the time. When Dede stopped, as she did fairly frequently to allow Jangbu to pick up fresh fruit or vegetables—hard to find in many places and to be pounced upon once seen—I pulled in and waited for her.

We had three overnight camps between Kathmandu and Bardia. In some of the little towns through which we passed there were small hotels. But although the people who ran them were always pleasant and hospitable, hygiene is not yet a priority of the typical wayside inn in Nepal and we preferred to cook, eat, and sleep under the more controlled conditions of our own campsites. In one of these, a forest of tall straight *Sal* trees not far from Butwal, we had one of those rare and beautiful experiences that nature will sometimes bestow on one as a gift.

It was evening and for more than an hour we had been looking for a place to camp. The sun, falling rapidly into the western horizon, was an angry red eye that peered straight down the road into our faces, reminding us that it was time to make camp while the daylight lasted. Suddenly we saw a little stream off to the right, coming out of the forest. I hand signalled to Dede behind me and we slowed down and stopped. Pasang and I got out and walked into the forest to look for a campsite. We quickly found what we needed: a clearing, flat and clean, with access to the water of the little stream, a space big enough to allow us to get the vehicles in and out without having to back and turn — difficult with the Scout and its heavy trailer — and far enough from the road for our campfire to be hidden from the gaze of nocturnal travellers. We drove the vehicles in, unloaded what we needed for the night, and put up a couple of our small Eureka Aurora tents, one for Dede and Rara and me and the other for the men. Within minutes we had a couple of campfires going, one for light and warmth and atmosphere — the heart of a camp without which a camp is not a camp — and the other for cooking.

Now the light was fading. Dede and I sat at the fire with a couple of glasses of scotch and Rara, already bosom buddies with the Sherpas, joined the men at the cooking fire. It was quiet now with the daytime birds gone and only a few Nightjars beginning to call. So the little scratching noises that we heard from a tree just outside the rim of the campsite quickly attracted our attention. When the sound continued, our curiosity was aroused and, drinks in hand, we left the fire and walked a few paces toward it. As we did, from out of the trees directly ahead of and above us a small shape came flying through the air, aimed straight at us. We both ducked and as we straightened up another one followed it. Both shapes soared past us within inches of our heads and then shot up into the trees behind us, where they slapped against the trunks and hung there, peering around at us. It took us a few seconds to realize that they were the beautiful little animals known as Flying Squirrels, what the Taru people for some reason call *Pacheri Musa* (backward mice) — actually not flying but gliding animals. While we whispered to each other about what they were, the two little animals were joined by another, whereupon all three launched themselves straight at us again, gliding down in graceful swooping flight, passing within a foot of our heads and then, using the momentum of their downward glide, soft furred skin membrane tight between outstretched legs, soaring upwards to regain height for another foray. The game — and this, or a very strong streak of curiosity that helped them to overcome their natural shyness, is what we believed their unusual behavior to be — lasted for another several minutes. Then, as suddenly as they had appeared, they were gone into the growing darkness of the trees, leaving us to the quiet of our little roadside camp. Hikmat's Hill, the campsite next to Oriole Camp on the Bauni River in the White Grass Plains Reserve, has Flying Squirrels living in the trees above it. We have heard them there in the night, listened to their childlike cries in the darkness, seen their eyes glow red in the light of a flashlight. But the little gliders there have always stayed high above us and we have never had a repetition of that enchanting encounter in the *Sal* forest of the Butwal road. We probably never will.

In the afternoon of the third day we drove into the headquarters of the Bardia Reserve at Gularia. There we met and talked with the warden, Mr. Krishna Man Shrestha, an old friend. We asked him if he or any of his people had heard anything about Tula Hatti or seen any sign. He told us that the only news they had of the big elephant was from Sukila Phanta and, as far as he was aware, Tula Hatti had not visited Bardia for some time. This information helped to confirm my theory that Tula Hatti and his herd were no longer visiting Bardia across the ancient Elephant Walk but were now staying, summer and winter, within the confines of the White Grass Plains. Mr. Shrestha told us that a young rhino had been born in his reserve within the last few days of a mother that had been transplanted there with eight others from the Chitawan National Park. He asked us to keep a watch for rhino and to report to him if we saw any. We promised to do this, keeping in mind that as there were now rhinos in the Bardia Reserve, we would have to take extra precautions when walking in the forest. Rhinos are cantankerous animals, short-tempered and easily provoked. With the *Mugger* crocodile, they are one of the only two really dangerous animals of the Terai. Rara, at an age where all animals are Disney creatures to be walked up to and kissed on the nose, would have to be carefully watched all the time we were in Bardia.

We thanked the warden for his information, asked him to come and have dinner with us in camp, and left for our destination on the Karnali River, twenty miles north of Gularia, at a place called Naka Tal. Naka Tal means Crocodile Lake, or pool in this case, and for many years we had camped there on a high bank above a river eddy that forms the pool, a favourite eating place of the Karnali *Muggers*.

We arrived there in the late afternoon, with russet-winged Braiminy Ducks calling plaintively from the broad reaches of the river and flights of Cormorants wheeling across white sand bars that gleamed pale in the weak winter sun. We immediately set about building the camp. Apart from the fact that we wanted to use every day available to us for research, the Rineses were due to arrive the next day. By dark we had tents up for the Sherpas and ourselves and after a light dinner we all slept. Guest tents, kitchen tents, mess tent, and those other facilities that contribute to a comfortable camp — showers and toilets — could wait until the next day.

Next morning I was up at dawn. With Rara still in the land of dreams and Dede sleepily drinking a cup of coffee, I left with Pasang for Nepalgunj Airport to meet the Rineses and bring them back to Naka Tal. The day was the twenty-fourth of March, Rara's fourth birthday. It was also the day the weather decided to change.

The distance from our campsite at Naka Tal to Nepalgunj — in Nepal but close to the Indian border — is forty-five miles. By using some old Taru village roads that I knew from my hunting days I hoped to made the journey in the Scout, unloaded and travelling lightly with no trailer, in two hours. But, as sometimes happens when one fails to take into account the whims of the gods of jungle and mountain, a little change in the weather soon dashed that hope. It started to rain soon after we left Naka Tal. Within an hour the Taru backroads that I had chosen to use through Gularia and then south and east to Nepalgunj turned into a river of mud. Within another hour I was up to the axles in a sea of thick brown chocolate clay and struggling to winch the Scout out of morass after morass every quarter mile. As luck would have it, the Rineses' plane arrived on time, at nine thirty A.M. It was three in the afternoon, nine chocolate hours after leaving Naka Tal, at which point the Rineses were beginning to wonder if P.B. was really going to turn up, that I got to the airport.

Tula Hatti

The Rineses were good humored about their six-hour wait at Nepalgunj's rather bleak little airport. But it was now mid-afternoon and a decision had to be made as to whether we should overnight in Nepalgunj or chance what was obviously going to be a night run back across the rain-soaked roads to the reserve. Might we not get bogged down somewhere in the middle of the jungle? Or mired in a giant mud hole with the prospect of a cold and food-less night? Should we not consider the alternative: a night in one of Nepalgunj's little wayside hostels and an early morning start when the roads were drier?

We decided to toss a coin on the decision. I made the call on the coin and as it was a special two-headed one that I keep for occasions just like this, and as it was tails for an overnight in Nepalgunj and heads for a return to camp, the decision to take a chance on the run to Naka Tal was made for us, so to speak, in the air.

We loaded up and headed out of the airport. My guests, now that the decision to head for our jungle camp had been made, were ex-cited at the prospect of getting there. Only Justice, with the en-thusiasm of youth, murmured something about how interesting it might have been to try one of the little bordertown hotels. I made no comment. Had I done so, I might have said that try as I might, I was just never able to get on friendly terms with Nepalese border-town hotel fleas, mosquitos, lice, bedbugs, and hot and cold run-ning cockroaches.

I expected trouble on the return journey but the rain had stopped and the roads had dried out to some degree, so the forty-five miles took us only five hours. We arrived in the dark and homed in on the campfire glittering in the trees to find that Dede and the Sherpas had worked all day to get the camp completely built and all ready for our guests.

Robert Rines and his wife Carol have been friends of ours for many years. Bob is a patent attorney by profession and a man of varied interests that include the Loch Ness Monster mystery, the Bigfoot phenomenon of the Pacific Northwest, organic fungicides in fruit culture, fish farming, and wildlife conservation and preser-vation. He is Dean of the Franklin Pierce Law School of Concord, New Hampshire, and President of the Academy of Applied Science of Boston, of which I have the honor to be a member. Academy participation in the program about Tula Hatti and the making of the film were the reasons for his joining us in the Bardia Reserve. Carol Rines has interests as varied as her husband and thirteen-year-old Justice was given time out from school to develop a special project about wildlife. Years ago, when Bob and Carol first came with us river-running and camping in the Himalaya, Bob asked me what was the most important thing they could bring with them on a safari. I told them a good sense of humor. In all of the times that we have spent together, this visit included, they never let it get away from them. Which was particularly appropriate when a violent pre-monsoon storm hit our camp above the Naka Tal three days after their arrival and nearly blew it, and them, into the river.

In the months prior to the monsoon the weather in the Nepal Terai mostly comes out of the southwest. When, early one afternoon, I saw a dark line of clouds gathering far down on the southwest horizon, I kept my eye on them. Pasang also noticed them. When the dark line thickened and began to climb up the sky toward us, I suspected we were in for a storm. Everyone in camp began to lash down tents and put away anything that might get picked up by the wind. Our camp faced west on its high bank above the river. We had dense forest behind us which would protect us from any wind from the rear, but nothing in front, where the storm would come from. When the sky really began to darken and the wind started to whip the tops of the trees above us, I sensed that the storm might be a really violent one and applied extra precautions. I brought both vehicles into camp. I parked the Scout right in front of the Rineses' big safari tent, a 15 x 20 Eureka Riverside, and using lots of nylon rope lashed the tent down to its wheels. I lashed the mess tent to the Suzuki and tied other smaller tents with extra lines to trees. Dede had put our tent between three small but strong trees and these were used to rope it down.

The storm struck in full force as the light died. Wind howled, thunder roared, lightning turned the sky into daylight, and rain came racing in on the wind in sheets. In the forest behind us we heard branches snapping and in the glare of the lightning we saw showers of leaves and small debris hurtling through the air in horizontal flight. The roar of the wind grew stronger. Looking through the slit in our tent door, I could see in the glare of lightning the Rineses crouched in their tent, the roof of which was forced down by the wind from its nine foot height to no more than four. Seeing me watching them, they waved and shouted something. The roar of the wind drowned out whatever it was that they said but their cheery wave indicated to us that they were all right and ready to brave it out. Which they did until, at about ten that evening, the wind suddenly died. As it did the rain stopped and within minutes the clouds had rolled away and the stars appeared. Soon we had a campfire going. When I asked Bob and Carol if they would like to join us there for a scotch, they told me that their only complaint about the storm was that the scotch had been in my tent and not theirs. As for Rara and our fears that the storm would frighten her, her comment was, "When can we have another one? That was fun."

Although the game warden of Bardia had told us that there was no evidence of Tula Hatti being in the reserve and although I believed him, in the course of our film location reconnaissances we kept a sharp eye out for any sign of the big elephant. With Bob and Carol accompanying us we travelled the length and breadth of the reserve and talked with anyone we met. There were few enough people and those that we met were mostly travellers passing through the area. Most were connected with the work on the new bridge over the Karnali and knew very little about the wildlife of the reserve. Like the warden, Mr. Shrestha, we deplored the new bridge as much as we did the dreadful gash of the East-West Highway that cut its way through the heart of the reserve to feed it. But the decisions for both had been made at levels far beyond him or us, and deplore was about all that we could do now.

We found elephant tracks in several places. They were usually the prints of medium-sized adults, having diameter spans of fifteen to eighteen inches. But nowhere did we find the huge twenty-two-inch footprints that might indicate the presence of our friend. And sadly we felt that with the abandonment of the east-west Elephant Walk across Kailali and into Kanchanpur, the Bardia Reserve may well have seen the last of Tula Hatti and his family.

The Rineses stayed with us for ten days. Justice and I took some walks in the jungle together during which I shared with him some of the jungle lore that I had gathered over the years; from those pleasant little outings he eventually wrote his paper. Bob and Carol were, as always, wonderful campfire companions. Together one day, returning from Gularia in the stripped down Suzuki— windshield down, canvas top off—we had an exciting encounter with a big dog leopard on a jungle road. The leopard: a vicious animal with cold, lifeless eyes ready to head for the nearest village, eat a native child, and walk up and down roaring his triumph? A slinking, treacherous cat with yellow fangs ready to bury themselves in the throat of anyone foolish enough to get near him? An appropriate description of the average jungle leopard, also known as the panther? This description is, incredible as it may seem, that of a well-known American sports writer, writing as an authority on big game and big game hunting about a leopard encountered in the Indian jungles during a hunting safari. (Needless to say, the vicious beast had to be promptly shot.)

The big leopard that we encountered on the road with the Rineses behaved as all leopards do when they meet with man. He simply turned and walked away. He did give us a bemused and rather curious look, and twice while walking away he stopped to look back at us, golden yellow eyes gleaming in the dappled light of the mid-afternoon jungle, the rosettes of his ochroid coat blending perfectly with the light and shade of the trees as he glided between them on silent feet. When he had gone about fifty feet and established a little territorial space, he sat down and looked back at us again: me sitting at the wheel of the Suzuki, Carol clicking away with her camera, and Bob trying to zoom in on him with his video. After a while, when Carol's clicking stopped and he felt he had enough footage, Bob turned to me and whispered, "What do you think. Are they really as dangerous as people say? Would he really attack if we were to get out of the car?"

In reply to his question I jumped out of the Suzuki and walked toward the leopard. As soon as he saw me coming he raised himself to all fours and lowered his head a little, looking directly at me. As I got closer he slowly turned his body away from me but kept his head toward me, his eyes watchful and wary. He let me get to within twenty feet and then with a woof of alarm he went bounding off into the peaceable kingdom of the forest, a kingdom of which he is one of the most peaceful subjects. Like many of the larger animals, the leopard is much maligned by Hollywood and mis- guided writers of stories that are more fiction than fact, who point to him — especially in his melanistic or black version — as the epit- ome of evil. In fact — and I speak from experience — when I stepped out of the car to show the Rineses just how shy an animal the leop- ard really is there was no bravery involved; I knew exactly what the leopard would do when I approached him: retreat at once. And this is what he did.

Their safari at an end, I drove the Rineses to Nepalgunj for the flight to Kathmandu and put them on the plane there. At the airport I said goodbye to them as they went onto the aircraft, pushing my way through a somewhat larger than normal crowd of wide-eyed youngsters who stood staring at Justice for nearly half an hour be- fore they left. Young foreigners like Justice are not a common sight in a place like Mahendranagar and so it was quite natural for him to be something of a curiosity. But those who followed him almost to the door of the plane before they were shooed away by a security man were oddly silent, as though they were in awe. As the plane taxied and then took off, they still stood there, staring and whisper- ing. I walked over to them and asked what they were whispering about, what was so odd about a young American travelling with his parents and getting on a plane in Mahendranagar. They were silent for a moment and then one of them, a little bolder than the rest, said, "*Chandi ka dart, Sahib, chandi ka dart.*"

Chandi ka dart, I thought? Silver teeth? Then I got it. Justice, like many an American boy of his day and age, had braces on his teeth. His audience had never seen braces; however, they had seen, from time to time, in the mouth of a senior Nepalese official or a wealthy landlord, the status symbol of a single silver tooth, or perhaps two at most. Now here, in a boy no older than any of them, was a whole mouthful of *chandi ka dart*, and they were awestruck.

We stayed on at Naka Tal for another week, then drove on west to the White Grass Plains. On the way, breaking our journey, we spent a night at the home of our friends the Bishts. As soon as we arrived we asked about Tula Hatti. Was he in the reserve? Had he been seen lately? What news?

Hikmat Bisht's son was visiting him. The two of them had recently entertained guests in the reserve under the banner of Silent Safaris, Hikmat's safari company through which he takes paying guests on driving and walking tours in the White Grass Plains. It is the only company in Nepal offering this service. Working out of his base camp at Hikmat's Hill—a little hill named after him close to the Bauni River just a few yards north of the bridge—Hikmat had been operating at this time for about two years. I personally knew that he offered, at rates that were a tenth of normal safari fees, a comfortable camp, good food, and the genial and warm atmosphere that only an experienced and mature safari guide can give. I also knew from talking to his guests that his knowledge of jungle lore made their safaris unique. Like the hunting season for safaris that I used to run in the area, his season was and is the winter months. During these months, whenever Dede and I have been in the White Grass Plains, he has always been of great assistance to us. His network of family friends and business and bureaucratic contacts have proved invaluable to our studies of Tula Hatti. In the summer months, when we are at home in the U.S., he has kept in close contact with us by mail, forming our single and vital link to the White Grass Plains and the great elephant that makes them his home. Moreover, with the recent establishment of a satellite system for Nepal's international telephone service, Hikmat's home telephone in Mahendranagar can actually be reached from the U.S.—or probably anywhere in the world—with a minimum of delay. As a result, we have been able to keep in touch with the movements of the big elephant whenever they are known—which is a great deal of the time—to the Bisht family.

Because of Hikmat's interest in Tula Hatti and his ability to keep track of him most of the time, we expected to have promising news of the animal's whereabouts on arrival at Mahendranagar. But this was not to be. In two recent days spent in the reserve, Hikmat and his son had seen no sign of the tusker. None of the contacts with whom he had recently talked seemed to know where he might be. The reserve, at this time eighty thousand acres, bordered onto another fifty thousand acres of government forest containing a few scattered villages and this offered many places where the elephant could remain undetected. (Consideration was under way with the government of Nepal to allot more of these forests to the reserve. But bureaucratic wheels grind as slowly in Nepal as in any other country and this had not yet been done.)

One of the places where the big elephant could go and remain unseen for probably weeks at a time was the Sukila Phanta swamp. The swamp, a near perfect retreat for an animal wishing for isolation and seclusion, contained about 450 acres of dense, eighteen-foot-high elephant grass and four- to five-foot-deep cold, clear water in which were set a dozen or so small islands covered with lush growth. The deep water and the thick, high elephant grass offered an almost impenetrable barrier to anyone trying to get into it. Once, years before, Dede and I had tried to paddle into it in an eight-foot inflatable raft. We found the water in the swamp to be crystal clear. It was very cold but alive with life of all kinds. Huge catfish darted off at our approach and a brilliantly marked young python flopped out of the grass and into the dinghy with us; he swam away most gracefully when we put him back in the water. Birds of all kinds fed in the weeds or hunted for insects in the tall yellow grass, among them Purple Gallinules, White-Breasted Waterhens, Coots, Brown Crakes, and Ruddy Crakes, to name but a few.

But try as we might we were unable to get beyond the outer fringes of the main body of the swamp. The twenty-foot-tall elephant grass, its roots amply supplied with water, was incredibly thick; the many small channels through which we tried to find a way into the heart of the area all proved to be dead ends. There were no big trees and therefore nothing to climb for a vantage point; the center of the swamp, a place where I knew at least one big tiger had been living for years, remained beyond our view. To this day, after hunting around it and probing its barriers for thirty years, its center still remains a mystery to me. This is a center that is big enough to hide a half dozen elephants the size of Tula Hatti, a center that right now might well be hiding him and, with its lush grasses, clear water, and dense cover, amply supplying him with all of his basic needs.

We enjoyed the warm hospitality of the Bisht home for one night and then motored down into the reserve. We set up camp once again at Oriole Camp. Since our time was now getting short, with the hot weather just around the corner and the days growing warmer, we started searching for the big elephant at once. As we did at Bardia, we stripped the windshield and the canvas top off the Suzuki and used it as our search vehicle. We went out each morning and spent long days in the reserve and its surrounding forests. The swamp frustrated us and I wished we had a small plane that we could use to search it from the air. At this time of year, early April, the jungle was at its thinnest. During and after the rains and some years, depending on the intensity of the monsoon, right through to late December, it is almost impossible to see anything from the air in the twenty-foot-high grass, including elephants; now, with the grass burned and thinned, a small plane would have been invaluable. But a plane not being available, there was nothing to do but slog it out on the ground on foot and by Suzuki four-wheel-drive. I did most of the driving and Dede, for the little bit of extra elevation that it gave her, stood on the passenger seat, binoculars at the ready and one arm hooked around the roll bar. Rara, with Pasang keeping a watchful eye on her, came with us, sitting or standing in the back of the little vehicle surrounded by what we called our survival gear: an assortment of equipment carried against breakdowns on the trail, bog-downs in sand or mud, or a night out in the open. The gear, compiled from experience, included a box of tools, a box of spare parts, a big Kenya five-ton jack, a couple of three-cell metal-cased flashlights, two 750,000-candle-power twelve-volt cigar lighter plug-in searchlights, an axe, a shovel, a coil of nylon rope, a bag of parachute cord, two Stanley stainless steel unbreakable thermos flasks: one with hot coffee and one with cold water, jackets, woolen hats, gloves, a sleeping bag for Rara in case we had to spend a night out, a spare wheel, wheel wrench, and a twelve-volt dashboard plug-in tire inflator. The unwelcome prospect of a night in the open or a long walk back to camp was the main reason for all of the extra gear, equipment without which we never left camp. We had found from experience that ten or fifteen miles bounced over in a four-wheel-drive vehicle is an entirely different kettle of fish when one has to hike it all the way back to camp for the shovel that was left behind, or the wheel wrench, or the jack. Once bitten twice shy is the watchword. One has only to spend a night out in the winter jungles of the Terai in a pair of shorts and a short-sleeved cotton shirt, watching the grass crystallize with frost through the wee small hours, wondering whose fault it was that the spare wheel, flat as a *chapatti*, was not checked before leaving camp, that the tire inflator was left behind, or that no one thought about bringing any matches for a fire, to develop an unforgettable reluctance for a repeat performance. By the time the dawn wind begins to blow and one realizes that the faint sound of machine gun fire that rattles through the trees is nothing but the chattering of one's teeth, it really does not matter whose fault it was. What matters is that it must not happen again. Which is why, every time we left camp in the little Suzuki, the reading of the equipment checklist was part of the essential ritual. In fact, the rear of the vehicle was so well packed with equipment that anything more than one and a half people, Pasang and Rara, meant that someone had to sit on it.

One morning we drove to the village of Jillmillia, just outside the southeastern corner of the reserve. There we talked with several Paharia villagers and asked them about Tula Hatti. While they knew about him — oh yes, they all knew about the big dangerous elephant, the one that killed people — they had no idea where he might be other than in the jungle. One man did say that he might be in the swamp. When I asked him why he thought this, he said he was not sure, but he had heard an elephant call from the swamp a few days before. The Bauni River comes out of the swamp close to Jillmillia and, just below the village, loses its dark brown waters in the broad expanse of the Sarda. The Sarda is wide here, more than a mile across, and the single channel of water, meandering back and forth across the expanse, may change course from year to year. The men of Jillmillia were farmers and hill people, so their knowledge of jungle lore was slim to the point where I knew I could not depend on them for useful information. Resettled from the hills when their own villages were lost to erosion, they had been in the Terai barely a year.

While we were at Jillmillia, Hikmat drove down in his Jeep with two of his men to join us. Together we questioned the guards at the Jillmillia Guard Post, one of five such posts in the reserve, about Tula Hatti. (The other posts, at Singpur, Majgaon, Mangalserai, and Barcola, were, like the Jillmillia Guard Post, part of the security system that protected the reserve from poachers and enforced the laws that prohibited cattle grazing, unlicensed fishing, and grass and timber cutting.) Like the Paharias of Jillmillia the guards were poorly versed in the ways of the jungle. Some of them were hillmen and even city men from places like Nepalgunj or Dhanghari, enlisted in the Nepal army for military duty and, possibly to their surprise and even disappointment, posted in the depths of the Terai jungle on game reserve guard duty. For the most part they knew nothing about the wildlife of the forests they were supposed to guard and none of them seemed to have had even minimal instruction in natural history. As a retired military officer, Hikmat commanded a certain amount of respect with them and thus was able to get better responses than I. Nevertheless their ignorance made extracting information from them about animals and their movements in the reserve very difficult. Part of the problem was that things that they might have heard or seen while they were out on patrol, such as elephants calling or fresh elephant tracks, were of no significance to them and were either ignored or promptly forgotten. On this occasion, with Hikmat asking the questions, we eventually learned that some elephants, number and gender unknown, had passed by the guard post a few days previously. They had come from the north on the east side of the Bauni and had gone toward the Sarda River, just south of the post and the village.

After talking to the guards and thanking them for the information they gave us, we asked them, through their *havildar*, the noncommissioned officer in charge, to come to our camp and tell us if they saw any more elephants. If they did there would be tea for them and whether they came on foot or on a bicycle, one of us would run them back to the post by car without delay. They agreed to do this as long as they were not expected to come at night. With very few exceptions most of them were frightened of the jungle at night and after the sun went down nothing short of an invasion would get them out of the post.

Leaving the guard post, Hikmat and I walked across to where we had parked our vehicles. It was a bright cool day with some cloud cover taking the heat out of the early summer sun. While Rara played with some children from the village and Hikmat's two men stood by, we had a talk about what the guards had seen and how we could act on it to our advantage. All that they had told us was that some elephants had been seen. Obviously these were part of the Sukila Phanta herd. They seemed to think there had been only four or five elephants which suggested that the herd had temporarily split up, as it did from time to time. The question was, was Tula Hatti with them? The answer was to go and look for footprints. If the group had been going toward the Sarda, it was possible their footprints were still out there in the sand of the dry parts of the river bed. Hikmat promptly volunteered to go out on the river bed and do a search. For my part I thought that I would try and backtrack from the place where the elephants had been seen, up the Bauni. The ground was getting hard now in the growing heat of the summer sun and tracks would be hard to find. But here and there, on the east side of the Bauni, there were damp areas where small springs fed water into the little jungle river. In one of these I might find some prints. The distance from Jillmillia to our camp on the Bauni was about four miles by road. The river route, which I would follow on foot, lay throughout the jungles on the east side of the Bauni. It was more of a direct line and in length about three and a half miles. Moving slowly and stopping to search for tracks, I estimated that I could do it in about five hours. It was agreed that Pasang would come with me and Dede would go back to Oriole Camp with Rara.

I took a flashlight from the Suzuki and made sure that I had binoculars, matches, and a knife with me. Pasang took an extra flashlight and, tucking his big *kukri* into his belt, told me he was ready to go. We checked the time with Dede, waved to Hikmat as he set off for the Sarda with his men, told Dede to expect us about dark, and left for our search.

The big patches of elephant grass that border the eastern edge of the White Grass Plains and run from the now abandoned village of Singpur all the way down to Jillmillia had been burned off and a sea of yellow and black stalks greeted Pasang and me as we started north from the Jillmillia guard post. Most of the elephant grass of the Terai burns like this every year. Some of the burning is natural, the result of lightning. A small fire started in a storm can quickly spread in the bone dry grass of the late winter months and burn for miles. Some of the burning is done by villagers, who want the new green grass that comes soon after the fires for their cattle. In Sukila Phanta, however, where cattle grazing has been forbidden for some years, the fires are now started by guards. When questioned as to why they start the fires, their answer is that the thinner grass, after the burning, makes their patrolling easier.

Grass fires, started in the open and primarily aimed at burning the dead elephant grass, also burn into the evergreen forest. But here the fires burn slower, with none of the huge conflagration of the dense twenty-foot grass of the open country. It is not uncommon to see fires in the forest itself creeping along in thin, slow-burning lines, consuming only the dead leaves and stick debris of the dry winter season and leaving the trees undamaged. Since there are no birds nesting on the ground at this time of year and the fires move very slowly — as I was able to show Rara when once we walked out to look at one — animals, even small ones, remain unharmed by the creeping lines of flame.

With Pasang following close behind me I moved quickly out of the wasteland of the burned grass stalks and into the green forest that edges the Bauni. Within a few minutes we had picked up the Elephant Walk that the White Grass Plains herd uses when it is passing through here. Moving cautiously, checking for prints of the big elephant, we made our way north up the Walk.

The jungles of the lower Bauni River hold a great variety of wildlife. The area, a narrow rectangular strip running from north to south, follows the line of the river as it runs south to join the Sarda. Hemmed in as it was by the swamp on one side and the grassland that has taken over the former rice fields of Singpur on the other, at its widest it measures no more than a quarter of a mile. The vegetation varies from canopy forest that controls the light and keeps the ground growth down to a few feet to scrub and mixed growth. Along the edge of the river, no doubt because of its need for water, grows the huge *Bhate*, a plant that grows to heights of thirty feet or more and has dark green frondlike growth barbed with the most wicked thorn. The thorn is needle sharp and hooked. One has only to get close to *Bhate* a couple of times to feel that it almost seems to reach out to snag you with those vicious little wait-a-bit hooks. Creeper growth entwines many of the trees, and vines thicker than a man's body climb like huge constrictor snakes all the way into the upper branches. Eventually the sheer weight of the creeper will bring the tree down; once in a while one comes across a huge tree which has fallen to the ground and buried itself in masses of the parasitic growth. Giant trees grow close to the water, some with boles fifteen feet in diameter. Many carry the scratch marks of the claws of the Sloth Bear. Here and there are Strangler Figs, parasitic trees that start as small vinelike growths at the base of host trees. As they commence to climb they spread and begin to embrace and enclose the tree. Slowly, across the space of years, they envelop the host tree until in time the victim completely disappears, strangled to death deep in the heart of the parasitic fig. Strangler Fig trees grow very large. With their huge spreading branches, they have offered a comfortable perch for us from which to view wildlife on many an occasion. Along the edge of the Bauni strip, close to the open on both sides, grow two species of strikingly beautiful flowering trees. One is the *Simul*, or kapok cotton tree, the other the Flame of the Forest. Both have brilliantly colored flowers in season: the Simul is bright orange, and the Flame of the Forest is a dark glowing red. Both are food sources for the flower-eating parakeets that live in these jungles, the principal of which is an iridescent green chap with a long tail called the Alexandrine.

In the Bauni forests there is constant sound and it is important to stop from time to time to try and interpret its messages. The background of the sound is of course bird song. The veritable cacophony of sound, from muted, melodious notes to strident whistling to continuous screeching, emanates from, among others, Alexandrine Parakeets, Golden and Black-Headed Orioles, Three-Toed Golden Back Woodpeckers, Scarlet Minivets, Pied and Jungle Minas. In addition to the bird sound there is, much of the time, the chattering of the two species of monkey that live in the forest, the Rhesus Macaque and the Langur, a big gray, black-faced simian that lives in groups of up to fifty or more and feeds noisily. His habit of ripping dry bark off the trees or tearing open rotten limbs with his powerful little arms makes him one of the noisiest of the forest creatures to the extent that the sounds of his feeding activity are often mistaken for those of elephants. Close to the river itself a variety of other noises contributes to the symphony. From the water comes the splash and gurgle of giant catfish thrashing the surface to take down a fat insect fallen from a tree above and, seconds later, fleeing in panic from a bank-to-bank line of otters hunting upstream. Frogs croak, cicadas sing their staccato serenades, and a thousand other insects made the air vibrate with their humming. The forest is alive with life and to me and others who have enjoyed its songs and its messages, spiritually as well as physically exhilarating.

It took us five hours to hike up the Elephant Walk from the Bauni-Sarda confluence to camp. On the way, we diverted into Hidden Phanta, a little clearing in the forest embraced by an arm of the Bauni, with a small stream, almost dry now, that had some big fig trees along its edge. We climbed into one of these and sat quietly for a while. I have always enjoyed climbing trees in the forest; some of my friends have made fun of me for it. But there are reasons for my seemingly odd interest. In the forest, as well as in open country like the grassland of Sukila Phanta, elevation contributes much to viewing. In addition most animals, and probably all large animals that have nothing to fear from arboreal predators, do not look up. In a tree, if one is above the line of sight of a large animal and if one remains perfectly still and silent, then chances are that one will not be noticed, not even by something as wary as one of the big cats. There is still of course the problem of being detected by scent and animals that use their olfactory senses to detect an entity dangerous to them, such as a deer scenting a tiger, will still pick up human scent from a tree no matter how high one climbs and sits. The disadvantages of being detected by scent while above the ground are, however, far outweighed by the advantages that a little elevation provides.

We spent forty-five minutes watching the forest edges and the elephant grass of Hidden Phanta for movement. A leopard walked under us while we watched and I marvelled at how he placed his feet with such infinite care between the big, dry leaves that lay scattered on the ground. He touched not even the edge of a single one and his progress beneath us, for the eight or ten seconds that we watched him, was absolutely silent.

When the wailing of peafowl and the low, fast flight of parakeets started to call in the evening, we made our way back to camp. We reached there just after dark and found Hikmat and his men waiting for us, back from their search on the Sarda. They had walked five or six miles up one side of the river and then zigzagged across the center on the way back. They told me there were lots of tiger pug marks in the soft white river sand, as well as hoof-prints of Axis Deer, Hog Deer, and Swamp Deer. They found tracks of some small elephants, possibly the ones that the guards at Jillmillia had seen a few days previously. But of Tula Hatti there was no sign. Even though they had driven over to another village on the way back and spoken to the headman there, a man who kept his eye on things happening in the jungle around him, no information was forthcoming as to where Mr. T.H. might be. Once again the swamp was mentioned and once again I had a feeling that he might be in there, trumpeting the old tiger out of his way from time to time and making the big *Muggers* give ground as he waded ponderously from island to island, feeding on the lush grasses that grew in its green heart.

Our season was coming to an end. Delays in the beginning had cut down on the amount of time that we could give to the reconnaissance and now time was running out. In addition, the weather was beginning to grow uncomfortably warm. As the great heat of the monsoon months began to creep into the jungles, the Brain Fever Bird warned us with his summer songs that it was time to leave. Soon, and who knows, perhaps sooner than expected, the dreaded Anopheles Mosquito might be coming out of dormancy, carrying with it the deadly threat of falciparum malaria. All of us were on a weekly dosage of Chloroquine, started two weeks before we left home and to be continued for six weeks after we got back. But even with the protection of the best prophylactic that science could provide, falciparum malaria was something not worth risking and so we began to make plans to leave. Dede and Rara would go ahead to Kathmandu and I would follow in a day or so.

Thus followed the closing down of our safari camp of '87–'88 which included my extraordinary personal experience with the Sukila Phanta herd. With the Sherpas I stayed on for a few days after Dede and Rara got off to the cool of Kathmandu, then in the burning heat of the first days of the oncoming summer drove up to Mahendranagar to have a last visit with Colonel Bisht, arrange for the storage of all of our equipment with him—including the Scout, the Suzuki, and the utility trailer—and catch a flight to Kathmandu.

The Kathmandu flight did not come in for three days. I stayed with the Bisht family while I was waiting. Each day, Hikmat drove me to the airport to wait for the plane and, when it did not come after we waited five or six hours in the sweltering heat of the grass hut ticket office, control tower, etc., he drove me back again. The delay was a nuisance. But it was a Royal Nepal Airlines delay and as such quite acceptable and quite to be expected. If nothing else we got a great laugh out of the various excuses that arrived each day at the main office in Mahendranagar by phone from Royal Nepal's headquarters in Kathmandu, detailing the reasons why there was no flight. High Winds was a good one. Approaching Storms was fun. Fog (in early summer?) was better. Pilot Unavailable was better still. But Hikmat and I agreed Low Ceiling was the best of all, causing us to cast a wary eye at the sky when coming out of the little grass oven of the waiting room—the only shade in the whole airport—prepared to duck in case of a low flying cloud.

The delay, at the least, enabled me to have some end-of-season talks with Hikmat centering around the elephant and our plans for him for the coming season. We had not found the elephant and that fact worried me. The following winter, if all things went as planned, we would be coming back with a photographic team for film production that was going to cost us a great deal of money and could be hired for only a limited period of time. Where would the elephant be at that time? Would we be able to find him? For that matter, with his elusiveness and his shyness, something of which I was now gaining more experience, would we be able to get cameras and sound equipment close enough to him to get him on film or

videotape? What if we did not find him? What then of the money
the sponsors had put up to make the film? What about the cost of
the photographic team? Who would be responsible? Would suppor-
tive monies have to be returned? What were the moral, not to say
legal, ramifications?

Hikmat and I tossed these questions about, back and forth, and
in the end we decided that we could only do our best and leave the
rest to the fates. Or, as Hikmat was more inclined to consider, to
the gods of the jungle, in particular to the divine Ban Devi, the Taru
goddess who ruled the green mansions of the forest and whose every whim was law. To whom, Hikmat pointed out, we had made
no offerings on this last visit and because of which, at least two of
his Taru acquaintances had pointed out, we had not found the elephant. This was something that would have to be immediately rec-
tified on arrival the coming winter, he told me with a twinkle in his
eye. The twinkle moderated what he was saying about native su-
perstitions. Without trying to analyze his real feelings and beliefs on
the subject, suffice to say that like me, Hikmat was not a supersti-
tious man, but after half a century of living among people whose
gods were elephants, peacocks, monkeys, snakes, and creatures as
ephemeral as Ban Devi, phantom of the forest, he had, like me, at
the very least a healthy respect for all of it.

When the R.N.A.C. plane actually arrived and when I actually
managed to get on it, Hikmat sent me off with a heartwarming
word. "Don't worry," he said, with the twinkle beaming even
brighter than before. "If you can't find that big chap and if your cre-
ditors start making it tough for you, you can always come down
to Sukila Phanta and hide in there somewhere. Maybe the middle
of the swamp. Silent Safaris will make sure that you are well supplied with scotch and other essentials. They'll never find you in
there."

5

THE SEARCH

It was November 25th, 1988 and we were standing on the airstrip of the Royal Nepal Army in Kathmandu. We were waiting to board a military aircraft to take us down to the southwest Terai. We were on our way to start production, on location, of *Tula Hatti: The Last Great Elephant*.

It was nine in the morning and the air was cool. The light was bright, almost dazzling, and the dark blue bowl of the Himalayan sky above us was cloudless from horizon to horizon. Off the end of the flat black tarmac of the airstrip, the humpbacked ranges of the Jugal and Lang Tang Himal marched across the northern sky. Their crystalline coats glistened from seventy miles away and twenty-five thousand feet up in the sky; they seemed close enough to touch. This illusion was created and sustained by the void that lay between them and us, the stepping stones of the middle hills, invisible in the haze of smoke from burning wood and cow dung, the fuel of thousands of cooking fires.

There were eleven of us waiting for the army charter flight: Pasang, our old hand of many years; Jangbu, our great field cook; and his friend Phurua, down from the hills for another season with us. With them, also part of the camp staff, were two extra men: Lahpka from Kathmandu and Jangbu from Namche Bazaar. (To avoid confusion with our first Jangbu, we called him Jangbu Two.) Like the others, the two extra men were Sherpas and they had been recruited to work with the video team; theirs would be the job of carrying the heavy video gear.

The video team was composed of two people: Dick Fisher from New York would be director of photography for the movie. His wife, Teresa Powlovsky, would handle the sound and recording gear. Both were professionals in their field and they had taken a month off from their work with Fox Television Stations in New York to shoot and record our movie. The eighth person in the group was a Nepalese named Madhab Bhattarai, the Liaison Officer that the Nepalese government requires for all foreign movie-making in Nepal. Dede, Rara, and I completed the team.

Far down the airstrip, lines of soldiers marched back and forth. As the sun gathered strength a heat haze, rising off the blacktop of the strip, created a mirage and the soldiers appeared to be floating in the air. Standing around with us were a number of military officers one of whom, a full colonel in the Royal Nepal Army, was the pilot of the plane. A hundred yards from us, near a hangar, a group of mechanics worked energetically on a plane called a Flying Boxcar. Built in Ireland, it was a two-engined freight plane. In it we hoped to be able to get all of our gear—about one thousand pounds of it—and the eleven of us for the flight to the southwest.

The sun climbed a little higher and the activity around the Flying Boxcar increased, with mechanics jumping in and out of the plane, shouting and waving at one another. Then, quite suddenly, all activity ceased. Something was wrong; when all of the mechanics gathered in a group and stood looking at us, I sensed that we were about to be given bad news. I watched them. There was a hurried exchange of words and then one of them, delegated no doubt by the others, left the group and walked rapidly to where we stood. He came to attention in front of the colonel, saluted, and then whispered his message. "Sir, there is a problem."

"Yes," replied the colonel, "And what is the problem?"

"Sir, the engines. They will not start."

"Oh, and why will the engines not start?"

"Sir, a mouse has eaten the wires."

I do not think that the good colonel knew that I could speak and understand Nepalese, the language of his conversation with the technician. Now he turned to me and said with a grave look, "Mr. Byrne, I am afraid that we have a serious technical problem with the Boxcar. However, you are in luck. We have another aircraft, a bigger one, that I think we can get ready for you fairly quickly. If you do not mind a short delay."

We told the colonel that we did not mind at all and rather miraculously for Nepal's tiny air force which (though the information is strictly classified) has at the most, I believe, three or four planes in all, a nearby hangar quickly produced another aircraft. This was rolled out and pushed up to where we were standing. It was an Argus, another twin-prop plane. The colonel climbed in, started one of the engines, revved it up to make sure that it sounded all right, started the second engine, did the same thing, stopped the engine on the door side, and waved to us to start loading. We leapt into action and had all of our stuff in the aircraft within minutes. We climbed on board, strapped ourselves in, and, twenty minutes after the Argus had appeared from its hangar, we were climbing out over the green mountain walls of the valley of Kathmandu.

An hour and a half later we arrived at Dhanghari, a little border town about forty miles east of the White Grass Plains Reserve in the district of Kailali. We landed, rolled to a stop, and opened the doors to be greeted by the welcome sight of Colonel Bisht with a big blue and white bus that he had rented to take us to Mahendranagar. We removed our gear from the aircraft, thanked the pilot for his services, and watched the Argus take off to return to Kathmandu. We loaded the bus and climbed aboard, Rara in the front seat with the driver and delighted to be allowed to assist in the driving, to bump and grind our way over the hollows and wallows of what passes for a road from Dhanghari to Mahendranagar.

We spent the night there with Hikmat and his wife and family. Next day we pulled the tarps off the Scout, the Suzuki, and the utility trailer—all three dry and in good shape after five months of monsoon rain and heat—and loaded them with the gear we had brought with us. We drove them into Mahendranagar and at that quaint little city's only gasoline station—two broken down hand pumps and a stack of leaking, rusty forty-gallon drums—filled both vehicles and all of our extra gasoline cans with Indian gasoline. At $3 a gallon the bill came to $175.

Fueled up, we set off for Sukila Phanta. Hikmat came with us to help set up camp. This time, because of our larger crew and because his safari company, Silent Safaris, had no clients booked and had no need of it, he allowed us the use of his bigger campsite, Hikmat's Hill, on the Bauni River just a couple of hundred yards from Oriole Camp. Twenty-four hours after leaving Kathmandu, with a dark red sun sinking over the slow moving waters of the Bauni, with peacocks wailing from the high *Simuls* at the edge of the reserve and Swamp Deer braying tiger alarms down in the grassland, we were in camp, tents up, feet to a warming campfire holding back the chilling air of the winter evening. With good-smelling things bubbling in pots in the kitchen, bodies relaxed in canvas chairs in the flickering light of the flames, we raised our glasses to Tula Hatti, to each and every one of us, and to the success of our venture. The date was November 26th.

At one time in Nepal the only government service that dealt with the forest and wildlife was H. M. Department of Forests. As the emphasis of this service was on the forest rather than on the game that it contained, it was eventually conceded that a second service was needed to regulate wildlife. This service eventually came into operation and was called the Department of National Parks and Wildlife. Its first Director — and as of 1990 he is still its able administrator and guiding light — was Mr. B. N. Upreti. Soon however, with the winds of international interest in wildlife conservation blowing strong across the globe, it became apparent that yet another body was needed, not so much to manage Nepal's wildlife as to conserve and preserve it for the future. The result was the King Mahendra Trust for Nature Conservation, a government recognized but privately funded body with a broad span of concerns that embraced the entire spectrum of the econet in Nepal. A brother of the king of Nepal, Prince Gyanendra, was appointed as Chairman of the Trust; a personal friend of ours of many years, Dr. Hemanta Raj Mishra, recipient of the J. Paul Getty Award for conservation in 1987, was appointed its Executive Secretary.

Among the many functions of the Trust, carried out from its new offices at Nya Baneshwar not far from the airport in Kathmandu, is assistance in the licensing of films connected with wildlife. Thus, it was to the K.M.T. that we turned for all of the sometimes quite complicated matters of licenses and permits for our film. Three bright

young men from the K.M.T. staff, R. K. Shrestha, Administrative
Office, Arup Rajouria, Conservation Education Officer, and B. P.
Malla, Public Relations Officer, not only waded through all of the
paperwork required by the government when foreigners shoot films
in Nepal, but also smoothed our way through a dozen other
bureaucratic tangles with customs and importation matters. It was
through the K.M.T. also, working with the assistance of a retired
military officer, Lt. Colonel Mukunda Khatry, that we managed to
arrange the army charter flight to the Terai. (With our tight schedule
and our video team costing us a thousand dollars a day, in addition
to other costs, this was one time that we felt we would find ourselves
a little intolerant of a three- to five-day wait for a "scheduled"
R.N.A.C. flight.)

All of their able and willing assistance was rounded off when the
Secretary, Dr. Mishra, appointed his Chief Officer with the
K.M.T., Madhab Bhattarai, as Liaison Officer to accompany us in
the field. We had known Madhab for some time and were delighted
to have him with us in camp. As it turned out—as it so often seems
to in Nepal—Madhab knew the Bisht family quite well; he and the
husband of Hikmat's only daughter, Sungita, were close friends
from school days. On safari with us for a month, Madhab applied
a calm efficiency to his work with both the National Parks and
Wildlife Service and the military personnel in charge of guarding
the reserve: areas of sometimes delicate interaction where his clear
thinking and diplomatic touch solved many a problem before it became in any way serious. In addition, although somewhat unac-
customed to safari life and the company of foreigners, he blended
quickly into the group at camp and within the short space of a
month became a firm friend.

The plan for the film, designed during the photo reconnaissance
the previous winter and honed and polished during the summer
months of 1988, was to tell the story of the great elephant as simply
but as fully as possible: his beginnings somewhere in the forests of
either Bardia or the White Grass Plains and his life with the Sukila
Phanta herd across the years. It would include our discovery of his
exceptional size, discussion of his present status, and a strong plea
for the protection of the elephant and the exceptionally beautiful

and little known area—the White Grass Plains— that was his habi-tat. The film would also include as many of the elephant's compan-ions of the forest as we could manage to find and film in the time available to us, as well as stories of the Taru people among whom he lived.

Just as in the previous year, when we had come out for the photo recce, the first thing that we did on arrival in the White Grass Plains was to ask everyone we met about Tula Hatti. This meant the guards at Singpur who sometimes walked past our camp on their way to patrol duty in the reserve, the occasional official passing on the road, and a villager or two. Had anyone seen him recently? Had any tracks been seen? Did anyone know where he might be now? And just as at the time of the photo reconnaissance, no one had any positive information to give us. Hikmat had been in and out of the reserve during the early summer, the last time with clients in May. (His clients had been two Germans. He had warned them about the furnace-like heat of the Terai sun in May and having been warned, they had come anyway. But temperatures in the one hundred and fifteen range, making metal objects even inside a safari tent too hot to touch, rather took them by surprise.) In that merry month he had seen Tula Hatti twice: once in the western part of the reserve and once in the north end of the jungles of the lower Bauni. But since then, nothing. No word. No village alarms. No tracks reported to him through his Taru contacts, many of whom had worked on his family lands for many years, living close to the jungle and listening to its songs and its messages. Nothing now for eight months.

We were faced with a problem. Where was Tula Hatti? Was he in the reserve and if so, which part of it? Was he with the herd and if so, where were they? Perhaps he was in the Sukila Phanta swamp or in the Sarda wetlands, enjoying those lush grasses and the deep warm water. The water would be cold but, at this time of year at least, through the hours of darkness, warmer than the cold winter air of the forests. I envisioned him standing silently in the swirling dawn mists, vapors that are created when the water warms and con-denses in the air immediately above it.

Once, walking quietly down the bank of the upper Chaundhari, the second little jungle river of Kanchanpur that ran through the reserve until it changed its course in recent years, I had seen a whole herd of Axis Deer standing belly deep in the early morning mists of the river, perfectly still in the comfort of water warmer than the air around them. The banks on which I walked glistened with frost and I moved away without disturbing them. And Tula Hatti? Elephants have very sensitive skin and are known to be susceptible to heat and cold, physical factors that might well have him in the swamp now, or in the Sarda wetlands, as winter temperatures crept into the forest.

Unless they live in a contained area, one that allows access to all of its parts, elephants are not easy to find. What weighs against the searcher, mainly, is their habit, except when they are sleeping, of almost continuous movement in search of food. This movement may continue through the hours of darkness. They do leave footprints though, and these, combined with the debris of their feeding, can be followed by anyone with some experience of tracking. Single elephants are of course a little more difficult to track than herds. There are fewer footprints and there is a lot less debris. With both, however, it is the speed factor that determines if one is going to be able to successfully track and catch up with one's quarry. What it comes down to is, can the tracker travel at a speed in excess of the object of his pursuit in spite of the difficulty of tracking? If he can then slowly but surely he will gain on the track maker or makers. Unless the hours of darkness intervene, during which no one in his right mind should be out tracking elephants, he will catch up. If, however, the tracker runs into difficulties in his pursuit—stony creek beds where the tracks disappear or where an elephant may backtrack, or dry grass where the single set he is following have been trampled out by other elephants—then the object of his pursuit will gain ground on him and slowly move further and further away from him. Speed then, is essential in tracking and closing in on elephants. If one is doing it on foot (and many parts of the White Grass Plains will not allow the use of even a four-wheel-drive vehicle) then in the intervals between stopping to interpret individual tracks or untangle them from the tracks of other animals, one must be prepared to walk fast, trot, or even run. Our problem with Tula Hatti at this point was not tracking him and catching up with him though. Our problem was finding tracks to start with. While I personally was prepared to walk, trot, or run the length of the reserve to catch up with him, I did not have even a single track with which to start.

Find the elephant. We did not have a sign hanging up in camp that stated this, nevertheless it was foremost on everyone's mind. Finding Tula Hatti and then getting footage of him were the prime objects of the production, ones to which we knew we must give the major part of our time, ones around which we now proceeded to build a master plan.

In 1957 I had taken the first American reconnaissance expedition to search for the Abominable Snowman into the northeastern Himalaya. With a couple of undauntable companions, N. D. (Andy) Bachkheti of New Delhi and Tom Slick of San Antonio, Texas, and a team of valiant Sherpas, I spent three months on foot searching the snows of the 15,000-foot levels for the elusive Yeti. We found footprints twice but after three months walked back to Kathmandu without having seen one of the mysterious snowmen. When we went back again the following year to spend nine months in the mountains in the longest search ever projected for the mysterious primates, with an understanding of the near futility of very small groups of people searching a vast area for something that was probably moving all the time, we quickly designed and put into action a different plan. This involved, very simply, using the people of the mountains, the people who were already there, who knew the mountains and understood them, to do our searching for us. It included, again quite simply, enlisting their services, paying for said services, and offering rewards for finds that were verifiable as authentic. The plan worked. Although the mountain people never actually led us to a Yeti, they responded energetically to the challenge, bringing us hair, bone, and feces for examination and showing us the location of caves where Yeti had lived and streams where, it was believed, the big primates regularly hunted for frogs.

Now, more than thirty years later, we would do the same thing with the great elephant. We would, of course, search for him our-

selves; Pasang and I would make a special effort, using our experience and knowledge of the White Grass Plains gained from our
hunting years. Everyone in camp would also keep an ear to the
ground, so to speak. The photo team of Dick, Teresa, and their as-
sistants, who would be out every day getting stock footage including the Tarus, their art, their villages, the jungle, the grasslands, the
birds and the animals of the reserve, would also keep a sharp eye out
for tracks or other elephant signs. But our main body of searchers
would be the jungle people, the Tarus, whose little villages lay scattered around the reserve and who, although few if any of them came
into the reserve any more, often seemed to know a great deal of
what was happening in the forests that walled in their homes. In addition, we would assemble a team of Taru searchers and send them
out in pairs throughout the reserve to look for tracks, feeding signs,
or the elephant himself. We would top off the plan by offering a reward to anyone who brought in news of the big elephant that enabled us to see and identify him. The reward would be one thousand
Nepalese rupees, a sum that at this time and on the prevailing rate
of exchange amounted to about fifty U.S. dollars. A small sum in
U.S. money but, to a Taru, the equivalent of giving a middle income
American a tax free gift of $50,000.

We sent messages to the headmen of two villages. One was my
old friend, the *jimadhar* of Kalkutta. I hoped that within a day or so
of sending for him we would see him riding into camp on his ancient and rusty bicycle, grinning his gap-toothed grin and telling us
how happy he was to see us. But he never appeared; though the jungle grapevine told me that he was alive and well when we left at the
end of the winter, we still had not seen him. The other man was the
headman of Radhapur. The day after we sent for him he walked into
camp with a couple of his villagers. He was a small bronze-faced
man with a shock of thick black hair, barefooted, wearing old khaki
shorts and wrapped in a brown woolen shawl. We invited him to
sit with us at the campfire, gave him and his men tea with milk and
sugar in big enamel mugs, and told him about our need to find the
big elephant.

At the mention of the reward he nodded quietly, indicating that
he thought that it would be a good enticement for someone to come

forth with information. We added that if anyone came to our camp during the day, we would make sure that he was returned home by vehicle no matter how far his village was, especially if it were late in the day and darkness threatened for the return journey. This was important because the Tarus will not travel on foot in the dark of the jungle night. They would not come to our camp no matter what the reward if they thought that doing so would mean having to travel back to their village in the dark. In the daytime, they could see and hear anything that might threaten them; analyze it; and take appropriate action. But the night held too many unknowns, not the least of which was the possibility of walking into a big animal and surprising it. Large animals like bears, elephants, rhinos, and buffalo do not like to be surprised and if surprised may quite suddenly and without warning become extremely dangerous.

We asked our guest if he would be able to supply us with some men for searching. We told him that we would like to have about thirty, if that could be managed. He nodded at this and said that he would see what he could do. He asked us when they were needed and I told him immediately, tomorrow morning and for a week if that would be possible. We talked more about the plan and agreed on a wage for each man (twenty-five rupees a day — about one dollar). After another mug of tea the headman left, promising to spread the word about the reward and to return next day with the men for the search. Madhab, doing his bit as Liaison Officer, promised to arrange the permission needed for the searchers to come into the reserve. Had he not done this, they would have been stopped by the army guards at the gates. If found in the reserve without permission, they could have been arrested.

The headman's visit ended when Dede drove him and his men back to their village in the Suzuki. Madhab accompanied them. After dropping them at the village, he and Dede would drive right through to Majgaon, the reserve headquarters. There Madhab would advise the major in charge of the military guard force of our intention to bring Taru searchers into the reserve and he in turn would advise his *sepoys*.

Dede took Rara with her for the drive to Radhapur and then to Majgoan. Dick and Teresa had gone out with Hikmat and while the camp was quiet Pasang and I sat down and talked about how to find the elephant. Pasang thought, as I did, that if we went down the lower Bauni we might find some tall trees, climb to the top, and see into the swamp. He also reminded me that the reserve now had a new employee, a game scout who supposedly had training in wild-life management and who was based from time to time at Singpur, the guard station near our camp. He could be useful to the search. I resolved to meet with him and asked Phurua to walk up to Singpur to request that the new man come down to camp to see me the fol-lowing day. Then, telling Jangbu that Pasang and I were going down the Bauni for an hour or so and planning to return before dark, I left with Pasang and headed for the lower Bauni forests.

We spent the afternoon in the dense jungle on the east side of the river and managed to find and climb a couple of trees that over-looked the swamp. But we saw and heard nothing of elephants; even though the vantage point of the trees that we climbed enabled us to see all the way to the western side of the swamp, the elephant grass, averaging twenty feet in height, was incredibly dense and could easily have been hiding the big pachyderm. We agreed that the whole herd could be in there for that matter and, if motionless, remain unseen and unheard.

We walked back to camp as the shadows lengthened through the jungle and racing flights of Alexandrine Parakeets, their feathers iridescent in the soft glow of the dying sun, streaked for their roosts in the high *Sal* trees that grew to the south along the edge of the Sarda. When we got back, Dede and Madhab had returned from Majgaon. They had news of a find for us. Before either of them could get a word in edgeways, Rara, obviously having caught the excitement of the discovery and jumping up and down with the news, told us that they had found elephant tracks on the road. Her eyes wide with the wonder of it, and nodding her head for empha-sis, she said, "*Hatti* tracks. Big *hatti* footprints. And I saw them first!"

Dede told us that they had found elephant tracks on the Singpur to Majgaon road in the middle of the forest. They were the tracks of several small elephants that had crossed the road from west to east. They were probably, Dede thought, heading for the grasslands of the abandoned village of Haria. When Dick and Teresa returned, we told them about the find and made an immediate plan to go to the area first thing in the morning. I would go first and see if there were elephants in the grassland there. Dede would come with me in the Suzuki and if I found any she would race back and pick up Dick and Teresa and the video gear. With plans expanding in our minds we spent a quiet evening together. We had dinner around the campfire and by nine, pleasantly tired from the activity of the first day of production—and of the search for Tula Hatti—we were all under canvas and in the land of dreams. The date was November 28th.

Next morning Dede and I left camp in the first light of dawn and drove down the road to Singpur. Teresa had kindly offered to keep an ear open for Rara and Jangbu, now a friend for life of the happy four-year-old, would stand by to get her some breakfast when she woke up. At Singpur we stopped for a moment to talk with a couple of the guards and to ask if they had heard any elephant activity in the night. They told us they had heard nothing. Leaving the guard post we turned immediately north onto the old road to Majgaon via the beautiful little lake of Rani Tal, a shallow, weedy jungle lake alive with fish and birds about two miles from Singpur. A body of water probably thirty acres in area and surrounded by a solid wall of elephant grass on two sides and by the forest on all of its northern and western sides, the little lake always has hundreds of birds feeding on it and is, for us, a source of delight with its activity, sounds, and color. It was at Rani Tal in 1985 that we added another rare bird to our lists: the Spoonbill. A flight of forty had come in while we were sitting watching for crocodile and they had stayed long enough for us to count and photograph them.

We bypassed Rani Tal within ten minutes of leaving Singpur. When we were about a quarter of a mile north of the lake, Dede estimated that we were probably in line with the place on the main Singpur to Majgaon road—which lay west of us and paralleled our road—where she and Madhab had found the elephant prints the previous evening. Now, if we found prints on our road and if they crossed it and went east, this would mean that the group that made them was heading for the Haria Phanta, the grasslands that covered the one-time rice fields of Haria. We stopped and made quick preparations for a search of the road. Dede got out and moved to the hood of the Suzuki where she sat, legs dangling over the radiator. From there, leaning forward, she could see the road immediately in front of us very clearly. Pasang stood up in the back. His job was to watch the jungle on either side. I took the road ahead and, through the rearview mirror, behind. A watch of the rearview mirror when driving a jungle road can produce interesting results and over the years I have spotted quite a few animals in this way, animals that hid and waited for a vehicle to pass before crossing.

We had gone about three quarters of a mile beyond Rani Tal when Dede spotted tracks on the road. They were clear enough in the thick winter dust and indicated the passage of six medium-sized adult elephants and three sub-adults from left to right, west to east, and going in the direction of the Haria Phanta. We immediately stopped, drove the Suzuki into the grass on the side of the road and, leaving it there, set off to follow the tracks on foot.

The prints wound into the forest in a fairly straight line east, only once diverting around a deep *nullah*, or ravine, with ten-foot-high, almost vertical sides. Elephants do not like deep, sharp-sided ravines. They do not like getting into them, a laborious task for such a heavy animal and one that may mean sliding down with the forefeet fully extended and the rear legs folded. And they do not like getting out of them, a task which may mean having to find a convenient tree for leverage. In particular, females with young calves will avoid them, just as they will avoid deep water.

We followed the tracks for about half a mile. Then we came to the edge of the forest and the beginning of the Haria Phanta, an area of probably a thousand acres that had once been the rice fields of the village. Haria was abandoned when the reserve was expanded; the villagers were relocated and the jungle, in this case in the form of dense elephant grass, had quickly reclaimed the whole area. Into this the elephants had made their way the previous evening and we guessed that they were still somewhere inside.

Leaving Dede to watch the surrounding jungles and the edge of the grassland with her binoculars as well as she could from her low elevation, Pasang and I quickly climbed a tall tree at the edge of the grass. Perched in the top we could see all the way across the *phanta* to where the rim of the Kalkutta forest was a dim line more than a mile away. But we could not actually see into the ocean of grass beneath us and we had to admit that if there were elephants in there, as long as they stayed motionless and made no sound, they would remain hidden from us. The sea of grass had swallowed them completely.

Pasang and I stayed in the tree for about half an hour, hoping that if there were elephants moving below we might see them. But in the cold air of the winter morning the grass was still. The only movement that we saw was a couple of Crow Pheasants swooping from grass-top to grass-top in search of food. We climbed down and the three of us drove back to camp. There, warming up with coffee at the campfire, while the slow winter sun tried to burn off a blue-gray mist that hung in the trees, we told Dick and Teresa what we had found and what we had not found. We all agreed that we would check the area again in the hope that where there were elephants there might also be Tula Hatti. The best thing for them to do would be to continue shooting stock footage for the movie while the rest of us concentrated on the search.

We breakfasted on eggs, canned Australian bacon, fresh baked bread hot from Jangbu's Dutch oven, and a couple of dozen more cups of coffee. Then Dede, after an equipment check of the Suzuki, set off for the day with Dick and Teresa. Pasang and one of the new Sherpas, Lakpha, went along to handle the gear. Pasang was the best jungle man that I had and if possible I liked to have him in the vehicle with Dede when she went off for the day. Lakpha was probably a tough, reliable man if it came to a pinch. But he had no knowledge of jungle lore at all, unlike Pasang who was also fluent in English and could converse with Dick and Teresa (who knew no Nepali or Taru). I kept Rara with me although she very much wanted to go in the camera car with Dede and Pasang. She had been out already in the camera car and it had proved a bit of a disaster. Several times the crew had stopped to shoot, Teresa working her ultrasensitive gear from the rear of the Suzuki and Dick shooting from the big tripod that we had set up in the open rear section of the vehicle. And whereas the remainder of us had quickly trained ourselves to stay absolutely still and remain completely silent when our professional crew was working, trying to get a healthy, super-active four-year-old to do the same was, we quickly learned, quite impossible. So, except on rare occasions, Rara was not allowed in the camera car any time shooting was being done or was expected. On this day she would stay with me and, while in camp, divide her time among me, Jangbu, Phurua, and Jangbu Two.

Soon after Dede left camp with the crew, I heard voices in the trees coming from the direction of Singpur. Within a few minutes the headman of Radhapur arrived, walking briskly and followed by sixteen men. He greeted us and I invited him to sit down. Madhab joined us and the men sat around in a circle while we talked.

Sixteen men was the best that he could do, the headman told us. But he vouched for them and said that if anyone could find the elephant it was they. I looked at the men. They seemed a bit young and timid to me and I wondered how actively they would pursue a search for tracks in the deep jungle. I also wondered if they could be depended on to break up into pairs and spread out for the searching. For the moment, however, I kept my thoughts to myself.

We discussed wages again and agreed that these could be paid to the headman in a lump sum for distribution to the men. We also agreed that if any member of the group personally found the elephant and became due for the reward all would benefit from it. While we were talking Madhab listed the names of all of the men and then gave each a slip of paper with his name on it. He had prepared the slips himself and each one stated that the bearer had the right to enter the reserve and was working for the film team camped at Hikmat's Hill on the Bauni. Should any of our searchers meet with reserve guards they were to show the slips and they would be allowed passage.

While Madhab was giving the men their papers I saw another man slip quietly into camp from the edge of the jungle. He did not come to the campfire to join us but went straight to the kitchen area where he talked with Jangbu. I watched him sit down and I saw Jangbu bring him a mug of tea. I noticed that he was dressed in a pair of light brown trousers, a matching shirt with sleeves rolled up, and green, high-sided canvas boots. His clothing looked like some kind of uniform.

One last thing we did before the search party left was to give each man a piece of string. Each piece measured about two-and-a-half feet in length and on it were two knots. The distance between the knots was twenty-two inches and this is what they were to use to measure any elephant prints they found. Anything smaller than twenty-two inches would be ignored. The location of anything close to twenty-two inches, or even larger, allowing for distortion in mud or sand, would be marked so that they could find it again and lead us to it if we wanted to see it.

All of the agreements between us and the search party having been discussed and understood, the Radhapur headman and his men stood up and filed out of camp. They would leave at once for the reserve and, at the suggestion of the headman, they would start their search in the small islands and thick jungle of the Sarda River. This was an area a good three-and-a-half miles from camp toward the western border of the reserve. As it was an area that saw very few people (even the reserve guards seldom went there), it was agreed that it might well produce some evidence of the big elephant. As the men were leaving, all of them together in single file, I again reminded the headman, in words that I made sure they overheard, that it was most important for the group to break up and work in twos. In this way a much larger area would be covered, with a better possibility of finding tracks. All, including the headman, nodded their heads in agreement. Then they left, each man carrying a blanket, a small cooking pot, and a cloth bag of rice and chilies. For their first search they would walk across the reserve to the Sarda, search the river bed, the islands, and the jungles that covered its banks, spend the night there and return on the morrow at which time we would select a second search area.

When the headman and his companions left I waved to Jangbu, out in the kitchen area with the man I had noticed earlier. He came over and I asked him who the visitor was. He told me that the man was one of the new game scouts of the reserve—specially trained men whose principal task was animal counts—and that he wanted to speak to me. He added that the man had not wanted to disturb the meeting with the headman of Radhapur and so had waited in the kitchen. I told him that he could send the man over and he did so.

The man who walked over to join Madhab and me at the campfire was tall for a Taru, with a sun-bronzed face and neatly cropped hair. He had dark, intelligent eyes and a quick smile that showed even white teeth under a small black moustache. He greeted us in the traditional Taru way, raising both hands in front of him palms together, and I bade him be seated with us. He ignored the chair out of politeness, I believe, and instead squatted quickly at the edge of the fire, into which he tossed a few small sticks.

I asked him if he knew about Tula Hatti and the very first thing that he said rather took me by surprise. "Yes," he said, "I know about him. It was his brother that the poacher killed last year."

I knew about an elephant that had been shot by poachers in December 1987, in Kanchanpur. But until now I had never heard of it in relation to Tula Hatti. I asked the man to explain, but it was as though he suddenly realized that he had said too much already and he was reluctant to elaborate. I let the matter drop, but two things stuck in my mind. One was that he thought that the elephant that had been killed, a big elephant, had been a brother of Tula Hatti. The other was his use of the singular in describing the killer; until that time, talking with Tarus and guards and even with the Bisht family about the tragic incident, I had always been told that the killing was the work of poachers, not a poacher. I resolved to keep the information in my mind. Later, I thought, when we had time to look into the matter, the pursuit of a single poacher might be a lot easier than trying to find a group. (As of 1990, in spite of extensive inquiries, the culprit or culprits had not been apprehended.)

The man stayed with us for an hour, during which time he impressed me with his knowledge of jungle lore. It was, as I thought then and as I found out later, by no means perfect. But for one who had never had access to books and whose experience was therefore gained solely from fieldwork—unlike mine, which was the result of a combination of both books and fieldwork—it was unusually good and I thought he could be useful in the search for the elephant. I asked him if he could work for us for a while. He replied that he would have to get permission from the warden but that he would go to Majgaon, reserve headquarters, to seek it that day, if we wished. He had a bicycle and said he could make the thirty-five-mile journey there and back within the day if we let him go at once. I agreed to this and the man stood up, touched his hands in front of his chest in the traditional gesture of departure, then hesitated. "I heard, sir, that a reward would be paid to the man who finds the big elephant and leads you to him. Is this true and if so, who will pay it?"

"It is true," I told him. "I will pay it and this gentleman here, this government officer," pointing to Madhab, "is a witness that I am responsible for the reward."

The man bowed again and then walked out of camp. I watched him go to the tree where he had left his bicycle, stand it up, wheel it toward the road, mount it, and ride off into the forest. Later he told me that his name was Pant and that he lived in a small village just off the western boundary of the White Grass Plains Reserve, close to the Hatti Sar, the place where the government domestic elephants were kept.

That evening, with all of us back in camp and sitting at the camp fire, I heard above the sounds of our talking and Rara's laughter with the Sherpas, coming from the kitchen, the rattle of a bicycle coming down the road from Singpur. The sounds ceased as the rider dismounted and our visitor of the morning, his trousers and shirt gray-brown with the dust of the forest road, walked into the firelight. He greeted us and smiled. Yes, he had been given permission by his office to work with us. Yes, he would be happy to start immediately. He would come back first thing in the morning.

I got up and walked to the edge of the camp with him, to where he had set his bicycle. It was dark now away from the flickering light of the campfire. The only lights that we used in camp were small battery-powered lamps in the living tents, the mess tent, and the kitchen. Once away from them the shadows thickened quickly. Under the band of starlight that roofed the little road that ran into the campsite the trees were dark shapes in the darkening jungle. Somewhat surprised that the man, a Taru, was about to set off into the night alone, I said to him, "It is night. Are you not worried about leaving now and travelling on the jungle road in the dark?"

"No," he replied, "the night does not frighten me. You see, sir, I understand the animals and because of that I think that they understand me." Saying this he mounted his bicycle and rode off toward Singpur and the guardpost, where he would spend the night, and where a hut had been allotted to him by the military guard for his personal use while he was on duty in the reserve. The date was November 29th.

Next morning we all awoke with a sense of real purpose. At an early breakfast in the big Eureka mess tent, with Phurua scurrying back and forth with hot *chapattis*, oatmeal, eggs, sauteed tomatoes, and flasks of hot coffee and tea, we discussed our search plan and our general production plan. The overall production plan was fairly straightforward. Dick and Teresa would spend each day compiling footage of everything we thought would contribute to the film. They would stand by to leap into action the minute Tula Hatti was found and when he was found — and at this point we were confident that we would find him within a few days — everything would be dropped while as much footage of him as possible was obtained. Dede and I would take turns accompanying the video team, driving them either in the Suzuki or the Scout. Already tried and tested, the Suzuki was proving to be an excellent little camera car. With its short wheel base and its four-wheel-drive capability, it was providing excellent service. We preferred it to the Scout for much of the camera work in the forest. The Scout, bigger and heavier — some 6000 pounds to the Suzuki's 1500 — and equipped with an 8000-pound Warn winch, could four-wheel-drive it through mud and deep sand that would defeat the smaller vehicle. But, being a lot heavier, it needed more careful handling and Dede, who did most of the jungle driving for Dick and Teresa, liked the smaller car. In addition to this the Scout, with its powerful V8 engine, was, we had to admit, a bit of a gas guzzler at ten miles to the gallon. The Suzuki, on the other hand, gave us something between twenty and twenty-five miles per gallon most of the time. Gasoline at three dollars a gallon was probably the most expensive item among the costs of running the camp. But of more concern than its cost were its availability and the problems of hauling it from Mahendranagar. As in other parts of Nepal all gasoline in the area came from India, and when supplies ran short in India one of the first areas to suffer was Nepal. Since this seemed to happen on a regular basis, it was not at all uncommon for us to drive to Mahendranagar to find the piles of rusting and dented drums that served as the local gas station as dry as bones.

In addition to the daily shooting on the part of the video team, we now had a three-pronged search team under way for Tula Hatti: the sixteen-man Taru team out in the field, the game scout, and Pasang and me. The Taru team would stay out on a twenty-four hour basis. The game scout would be allowed free rein to search independently and come and go as he pleased. Pasang and I would get out on foot into some of the more difficult areas: thickets of dense *Bhate*; places which might require wading in deep, cold water; jungles that the Tarus might be reluctant to get into and that the game scout, who would use his bicycle as much as possible, might miss. Madhab would help out in whatever way he could, sometimes going with Dede in the Suzuki, sometimes remaining in camp, and all the time working his expertise with whatever officialdom we might encounter along the way. Hikmat would visit us to impart information gleaned from his Taru contacts, lend us the use of his aging Jeep, and apply his knowledge of jungle lore to the search. The Sherpa team, apart from Pasang, would divide its work between the camp and the field. In camp, with Jangbu in charge and assisted by Phurua, they would attend to camp matters and generally hold the fort pending the arrival of people back from field sorties. The two extra men, Lakpha and Jangbu Two, would go with Dick and Teresa whenever they were needed; this was usually if walking was envisioned, footwork that meant backpacking the heavy video gear. As basic coordinator of the search, I would accompany Pasang in the field on an almost daily basis, and also vary the application of my own time and energy in whatever way seemed to make the best contribution to the search.

Acting on this variation I now decided, on this bright clear morning, with the bowl of the Himalayan sky showing a robin's-egg blue through the green tracery of the trees, with the air a pleasant sixty-five degrees and a light breeze energizing a group of Rhesus Macaques in the tree canopy above us, to accompany Dick and Teresa in the camera car on a sortie to the western end of the reserve. I had not been there for some time and felt that some searching of the grassland there would be worthwhile. Also, the Taru search team was out in that area and we might bump into one or two of them while driving the ring road that circled the reserve and, if they had any useful information to give us, act on it at once. Dede, in keeping with the general plan, would take the Scout and, accompanied by Madhab, Rara, and one of the Sherpas, go down to the villages of Jillmillia and Chicksua and ask if anyone had seen or heard anything of the elephant. She would also check the Singpur and Jillmillia guard posts and, on the way back, spend some time at Rani Tal, where the authorities had recently constructed a viewing tower on the northwest corner of the lake. The tower allowed a view of the whole lake. Using binoculars she and Madhab would be able to glass most of it for any sign of elephants.

Dede left in the Scout with Madhab, Rara—"I'm going to find Tula Hatti today"—and Phurua. Dick and Teresa and Pasang and I delayed our departure while we waited for the game scout to arrive. It was now eight thirty and a little late, I thought, for a field man in his first morning on the job. But just as we were talking about going without him, he walked into camp carrying his bicycle—obviously the reason why he was late—under his arm. He had carried it the two miles from Singpur. He greeted us with a solemn look, put the bicycle down, pointed to it and said, "Sir, the air escaped from the tube through the hole made by the thorn. I have closed up the hole but I am not able to persuade the air to go back in. Do you kindly have a pump?" We told him that we most certainly had a pump, pulled out the Coleman tire inflator, fitted the bicycle valve nozzle to its hose, plugged it into the dashboard lighter in the Suzuki, and in less than a minute the escaped air was returned to the tire. The game scout, to whom an electric tire inflator was as foreign as a computer, was delighted. He thumped the tire a couple of times to make sure that the air was truly back inside and then saluted, thanked us, and said that he would be off. He would come back that evening if he had anything to report. Or sooner if he found any sign of the big elephant. He would start by searching the Rani Tal area where, he said, there was sweet grass that the elephants liked. From there he would go north to the Haria Phanta and then he would return via the Majgaon to Singpur Road. If we wished to find him later that evening he would be at Singpur, at the guard post where they had given him a bed in the guard barracks. He saluted again, thanked us again for persuading the air to go back into his tire, and departed.

An hour later, driving slowly with the slap-slap-slap of dried grass stalks entwined around the drive shaft of the Suzuki making a constant sound as they beat against the underparts of the vehicle, Pasang, Dick, Teresa, and I made our way slowly west on the southern ring road of the reserve. To our right the golden grassland stretched all the way to the green and brown wall of the forest that enclosed it to the north. Beyond the forest, brooding down on it, the escarpments that edged the foothills and marked the northern line of the Terai ran east to west to where they disappeared in the distance. Behind their three-to five-thousand-foot barrier, now but faintly seen in the soft blue haze of the middle hills, the Himal gleamed softly. To many of the people of the jungle those frozen rims of the frontiers of Tibet marked the edge of the world. The Taru people call the white stuff that covers the mountains *burraph*. From the sound of the word one feels that they have some distant understanding of the cold of those icy pinnacles floating in the sky so far away and so high above them.

We had stopped to listen to Swamp Deer calling when I heard voices. Soon a group of men appeared coming toward us. They hesitated when they saw us and then came on. When they got nearer to the vehicle, I saw that they were some of our Taru searchers. I greeted them and they returned the greeting. I asked them if they had seen anything of the big elephant. They said no. Noticing that there were eight of them in the group I asked them when they had joined up, and why. They looked at me in some surprise.

"Joined up, *Sahib*? What do you mean joined up?" I explained: they were sent out in sets of two and were to search in sets of two in different areas.

"Sets of two, *Sahib*?"

"Yes, two. Two men together. One with the other. No more

than two. Searching different areas. This is what you have been doing, yes?"

"Two, *Sahib*?"

"Yes," I replied. "Two at a time. Two together. No more than
that."

They looked at one another. There was a hurried and subdued
conversation that I could not catch. Then one of them, in a bright
blue shirt and holding his cooking pot and blanket tucked tightly
under his arm, said, "Oh no, *Sahib*. Two is as we were leaving camp.
Two together. But not here. Not in the jungle which, as you know,
is," eyeing us sitting in the Suzuki, "most dangerous for anyone on
foot. Only leaving the camp were we two. Now," and this with a
contented smile and wave of his hand, "we are all together, as you
can see." The wave of his hand more or less encompassed the remainder of the sixteen-man search party, the other eight of which
at that moment walked up and joined the group.

"And so, you have been together ever since you left camp?"

"Oh yes, *Sahib*, all together."

"And you spent the night together?"

"Oh yes, *Sahib*. On the riverbank. Under a very nice tree. All together."

"And you stayed together when you searched? All searching the
one area?"

"Oh yes, *Sahib*. Most certainly."

"And you found nothing?"

"Oh yes, *Sahib*. Nothing. Nothing at all."

When I explained the conversation (which had been in Taru) to
Dick and Teresa, they looked somewhat disgusted. It was difficult
for them to understand why these seemingly honest villagers would
do what they had done, which was take our money as wages, agree
to perform a certain function, and then do something quite the opposite. It was equally difficult for me to explain that in their minds,
to the detriment of our search plan of course, they had done what
we had paid them to do to the limits of their ability. That was as
they saw it, in all good conscience. An agreement to them did not
mean that they had to live up to each and every part of it. They had
fulfilled the agreement by going out into the jungle and doing some

searching. They had not, as the agreement demanded, split up into twos. They had not done so because this was not a fair thing to ask them to do. It was fair of them to agree to do it, but as it was not a fair thing to ask them to do, they did not have to do it. So they had not done it. And they were not going to do it. And later, when I talked with the headman of Radhapur and asked him if there was any possibility of their changing their minds, perhaps for extra wages, he simply shrugged his shoulders and said, "No, I don't think so, *Sahib*. They are good men. But they are shy in the jungle. They are afraid of the animals and the only way that they will go into the jungle, especially where there may be elephants, is like this. In big groups. This is mainly why I got sixteen men for you, *Sahib*."

"Why you got sixteen? What do you mean?"

"Any less than that, *Sahib*, and they would not have gone in the jungle at all. You, *Sahib*," giving me something of a reproachful look, "having known the Taru for so long, should surely have known that."

The Radhapur headman was right. In the back of my mind I had suspected that the Taru search plan would not work. I should have known better, from experience. I had encountered the same kind of problem many times over the years when I had tried to use some of them in areas of work that were foreign to them, or that made them nervous, or, in the jungle, that downright frightened them. In every Taru village there is usually one man who is something of a *shikari*, a hunter. In larger villages there may be two or three. But the Taru by nature, odd though it may seem for people who live so close to nature at the edge of the jungle, are not generally good naturalists. They may be good farmers, but the wall of the jungle is just that, a wall that encloses not just their villages, but also to a certain extent their minds. Beyond that wall live large dangerous beasts, beasts that have been known to kill and eat people. Beasts that are a threat to them and their children. That is enough for the Taru. They are generally content to live by the maxim, "I'll leave you alone if you leave me alone." For the animals, that means staying in the jungle where they belong. For the Taru it means staying out of the jungle or, if they must go into it, doing so only in the safe company of large groups of companions.

Scratch one Taru search team. On to squares two, three, and four: Dede and the video team; P.B. and Pasang; the game scout. We discussed it over dinner that night and while we felt that the loss of the Taru team (under terms of gentle understanding with their headman, I had dismissed them that afternoon) put a dent in the scope of our search, with the time that we had available and with the efforts the remainder of us could put into searching, Mr. T.H. was going to be found any day now. Found, filmed, and immortalized for people everywhere. On a global basis. Forever. Undismayed by the loss of the Taru team, we went to bed that night determined to work harder than ever and to find the elephant, come what may. We went to sleep filled with positive thoughts, good food, and the warmth of good campfire companionship. The date was November 30th.

The next day Hikmat arrived in camp. We heard his Jeep droning down through the forest while he was still a mile away. Shortly afterwards, wearing an impressive khaki safari shirt and looking quite smart in a British Kangol cap that Dede and I had brought for him from the U.S., he walked into camp. How, I do not know, but he heard about the problem with the Taru search team and had come to try and remedy the situation. He offered to let us have a couple of his own Taru men from a village that lay in his ancestral lands, the people of which had been known to his family for generations. The two men would be hand-chosen and he would guarantee that they would be thoroughly reliable and dependable. He did not guarantee that they would be honest and that they would give us an honest return for wages paid to them. He did not have to do that. That the men would be honest was taken for granted. That they would give us adequate return for wages paid was entirely dependent on what we asked them to do and on their interpretation of whatever it was that we asked them. This they would carry out to the best of their ability.

All of this being quite clearly understood, Hikmat called for two men who had been standing by his Jeep to come and join us. They came over quickly and squatted by the fire. One was big, heavily built, with bulging arm and thigh muscles. An unruly shock of black hair set off a hard face with thick lips and a low forehead. The other was slim and quick moving, with a face that was finely etched. Both were dressed in typical Taru fashion, short-sleeved cotton khaki colored shirts, gray-white loincloths wrapped around their middles, and black vests, or waistcoats. They squatted silently at the campfire, watching Hikmat as he spoke to us, and when he left they left with him, having said hardly a word to us. Later, they were both to prove their worth in many ways; we never saw them alone, only with Hikmat. But I knew that they spent quite a bit of time in the jungle; the amount of information with which Hikmat supplied us, much of it emanating from them, proved the truth of this.

The pattern of our days settled down. They were long days and good days. A good day on safari is when you set out to accomplish something starting in the pale blue hours before sunrise, spend all day out in the open jungle or grassland, complete what you set out to do or do your damnedest to get it done, and come back to camp with the sun going down and the air chilling, jungle debris — grass seeds, leaves, twigs — and the brown dust of the jungle roads in your hair and clothes and teeth. A hot shower is followed by clean clothes, the "ah" of sinking into a canvas-backed campfire chair, the heat of the orange-yellow flames on face and shins, the smell of woodsmoke, a drink in the hand, the taste of good hot food from a dining table in a big mess tent, the comfort of another quick warm-up at the fire, front and back, and then a big soft sleeping bag. To sleep, with the sound of a tiger moaning in the distance and the piping calls of Axis Deer responding in alarm. To sleep, with the stars marching down the Himalayan sky, a glistening band of light woven through the leafy mosaic of the trees, brighter in the Himalayan Terai than anywhere else on earth. To sleep, perchance to dream of a giant elephant walking ghostlike through the dark corridors of the jungle night.

The morning of December 2nd dawned bright and I set off with the video team to search the upper forest of the reserve for whatever we could find. Pasang rode in the front with me; Dick and Teresa were in the back with their gear. We left camp and drove west over the Bauni Bridge and into the reserve. The Suzuki was now the only vehicle I would trust to the old wooden bridge. Constructed to my design in 1969 and build of massive timbers on a sound cantilever principle, the structure was now rotten throughout its length. Bridges must be maintained, particularly when they are made of wood and subject to the onslaught of monsoon rain and tropic suns. But there is an odd psychology among the Nepalese about maintaining things, especially if they are the property of H.M. government and therefore the responsibility of the bureaucratic machine. The attitude is that whatever it is, if it is still standing, it must be all right. When it falls down, well, then perhaps something should be done about it. But until then the fates and the gods of the jungle would take care of all structures including the Bauni Bridge, and all those who cross it. Not for all the rice of the Terai, though, would I have attempted to run the Scout across it. As it was, every time I saw or heard Hikmat rattle its rotting timbers in his Jeep, I held my breath.

We crossed the reserve driving slowly and when we reached the guard tower that stands beside the huge *Peepul* that marks the north center of the grasslands, we stopped, got out, and climbed into the tower. We stayed there while I glassed the grasslands and Dick shot footage of my doing so for the film. Then we drove on, west and then north, following the main inspection road, the original alignment of which I had laid out in the building of the reserve. We drove to where it left the grasslands and turned into the forest and the northwestern enclaves of the reserve. We passed through a little grove of mango trees where the tiny and long since abandoned villages of Balma and Barcola used to be. Soon afterward, we forded a shallow stream that is one of the tributaries of the Bauni River. We came out of the forest again, drove through a big reach of elephant grass that is the permanent home of several tigers, and came to the Barcola guard post. Here we stopped and talked to the *sepoys*. They told us that two elephants had walked right between the houses of the post a few days previously. I did not believe them at first because what they were describing was unusual behavior for wild elephants. But they showed me several prints — prints of small wild elephant — right in the middle of a vegetable patch among the guard huts.

From the guard post, where we had obtained no new information on Tula Hatti, we drove on through to Majgaon. Here, at the

Majgaon guard post, two of the *sepoys* told us an odd story about some of their companions seeing a black tiger on the road near the post. They said that it had been seen twice. I wondered what they might have seen. A tiger that had lost its hair to some disease, such as mange? Or one that had been caught in a fire, and survived but lost its pelt? Only once had I seen the pelt of a true black tiger and that was in the store of a Kashmiri trader, on the Mall in Darjeeling, many years ago. Old Habeeb Mullick, who was a friend of mine, offered to let me have it for a few rupees but I did not buy it. He said that no one believed it was a real tiger skin and so he had been unable to sell it. It was certainly big enough to be a tiger and by holding it up to the light I could see, very faintly, dark stripes under the coal black hair of the pelt. A black tiger in the White Grass Plains? It was worth keeping an eye out.

We left the Majgaon post and drove slowly into the middle forest of the reserve, keeping our speed down to fifteen miles per hour. At this speed less dust came into the car. Keeping the windshield down also helped and, with the slow speed, gave us a better chance of seeing something like the gray, ghostly shape of an elephant in the shadows of the trees. Pasang watched the jungle on the right. The crew kept their eyes open right and left. I kept one eye on the road ahead, another on the road far ahead, another on the jungle on the left, and another on the rearview mirror.

It was the eye that I had on the road far ahead that picked up two dark shapes walking along the left-hand verge. They were tigers, and when we first spotted them it looked for all the world as though they were out for an afternoon stroll. But they were not. They were strolling along the road, all right, but they were doing it for a purpose. To cool off was my bet; two tigers together in the month of November, ambling down a forest road, meant love. And, as nature has designed that they mate every twenty minutes of the two to three days they spend together, they had probably just mated or were about to mate. Hence, in this case, a very uncharacteristic lack of caution on their part, which allowed us to get within a hundred yards of them before, hearing and then seeing the approaching vehicle, they exploded with alarm and hurled themselves into the forest.

The male, a big cat perhaps nine feet in length, went right. The female went left.

I whispered to Dick to get ready and, accelerating up to where they had left the road, slammed on the brakes and skidded to a halt. The female was not to be seen. The male had also disappeared and I accepted the fact that, as only tigers can, they had simply vanished. Nevertheless I swung my binoculars across the jungle on both sides in case there was an eye or an ear showing and a big cat lurking behind or beneath it. My binoculars were medium-powered, wide-angle Ranging 5x32s, very well suited for this kind of short range searching where a wide angle allowed one to cover a broad area. I glassed the left side of the road and then swung across to the right. Pasang was silent and still beside me. The silence from the rear of the vehicle indicated to me that Dick and Teresa knew the same was expected of them. Which was good because within a second of glassing in on the dense three- to four-foot-high undergrowth no more than twenty feet from the car, I found myself looking straight into the face of a large, very wide-eyed, very surprised looking tiger.

I did not know if Dick's video camera was rolling so I whispered to him, "Are you shooting?" When he did not reply I guessed that he was. The tiger was, with the exception of the face and head, mostly obscured and I wanted to edge the vehicle forward a little to get a clearer view of him. When the question to Dick, repeated, again received no answer, I kept the Suzuki where it was. I was amused and intrigued by the look on the tiger's face, a look that asked, "What on earth are you doing there and why are you staring at me?"

The big cat stood and watched us for probably a whole minute. Then it turned quickly and slid into the forest. I started the Suzuki and drove into the thick undergrowth to try and get ahead of him for some more footage. But driving in thick brush where the ground is not visible presents severe hazards for a small vehicle. In the Terai forest the main hazard is stumps. Equally dangerous are rock hard termite mounds. Either can tear the tie bars off a small vehicle, break a spring, or crack the oil sump. Before leaving Oregon my local Chevron garage mechanic had welded a quarter-inch-thick steel plate under the engine and steering mechanism for protection against such hazards. But even with this protection I had to drive very slowly and carefully over the unseen surface and Mr. Stripes, with no such hazards holding him back, quickly outpaced us. He disappeared and we did not see him again.

Back in camp that evening we ran the footage of the tiger on our generator-powered TV monitor. The look of wide-eyed surprise on the black and yellow mask of his face gave us a few chuckles and I wondered what he and his lady love said about us when again they joined up, as no doubt they soon did.

Getting tiger footage was exciting. Tigers are hard to find and hard to photograph and getting them out of the thick stuff, or the tall grass, means baiting them out or beating them out with men, either of which is often a major operation. Luck had smiled on us for a moment or two and the gods of the jungle had given us a little bonus for our film. Now, if they would just expand that generosity a degree or two to include a large elephant, all would be well. Viewing the footage of the tiger later I pictured in my mind a similar scene with the elephant, the massive beast standing and looking at us, posing. I knew that we would come to that eventually, that we would catch up with him. But the clock was running down and so far we had not even had a whiff of him.

In camp I was usually the first to awaken and get up. Sometimes Pasang would be up before me, or Jangbu, and the sounds that would drift in on my subconscious mind to awaken me would be the crackle of the kindling as they lit the cooking fires in the kitchen. But normally I was the first up. I like a big comfortable sleeping bag and I like to lie in it for a few moments when I awaken, even though I consider sleep and the hours we give to it to be a waste. Mornings are my best time. To me there is nothing as exhilarating as a winter morning on safari in the Terai jungles, with the sun coming up slowly to burn the gray mist out of the trees, the Black-Headed Orioles sweetening the air with their mellifluous songs, the smell of woodsmoke and good black coffee. Lord Baden Powell, founder of the Boy Scouts, said much the same thing when he camped at Singpur and hunted in the White Grass Plains in 1890. His *shikar* exploits are described in his book, *Indian Memories*, published in 1914.

Thirty years before him another Englishman, Sir Edward Braddon, one of the very few foreigners to get into the forbidden land of Nepaul, as it was called then, also waxed lyrical about the sylvan glades of the Terai. In his book, *Thirty Years of Shikar*, he described the White Grass Plains as "the very home of Oberon's court."

The light had barely begun to come through the trees this morning and I was only halfway into my first cup of coffee when I heard the rattle of a bicycle coming down the road. It was the game scout and he had interesting news. Elephants, in the night, passing the guard post at Singpur. He had not seen any tracks but had come immediately after he heard the news to tell me.

The camp was still quiet with almost everyone still sleeping and so I decided to run up to Singpur with him and see if we could find tracks. I asked Jangbu to tell Dede, when she awakened, that I had gone to Singpur and would be back in an hour. Then I grabbed binoculars and a measuring tape, and a jacket against the cold morning air. With Pasang and the game scout I drove up to Singpur.

At the guard post the scout quickly found the man who had seen the elephants during the night and had him point to where they had been. The place was at the edge of the big, elephant grass-covered *phanta* that lies behind the guard post, the original rice fields of the abandoned village of Singpur. I parked the Suzuki, walked down along the edge of the tall, dense grass, and soon found tracks. It was not necessary to measure them. I could see that they were the prints of medium-sized adult elephants, three of them, with a couple of calves. We thanked the guard post *sepoy* who gave us the information, and told him, as part of our campaign to encourage people to help us, to visit our camp any time he wanted for a cup of tea and a chat.

Back at camp I had a quick conversation with the scout. I asked him where he thought those elephants might have gone, the tracks having indicated that they were heading west along the edge of the Singpur Phanta. They might have gone into the lower Bauni forest, he said, and asked me if I wanted him to follow them. I told him no, that I would personally look into them in the hope that the little group might be joining a larger herd that might, just might, contain Tula Hatti. He could continue on his own and report when he found something.

By now the camp was alive. Joining the others for breakfast, I told them about the elephants that had passed the guard post in the night and about my theory that they might join another group. The other group might just have Tula Hatti with them, I hoped. A loner most of the time and certainly on all of the occasions that I had seen him over the years, Tula Hatti did join the Sukila Phanta herd on occasion, I knew. This possibility was, I thought, worth following up. I shaped the general plan for the day accordingly. I would take the camera team and, following the line of direction that the little group of elephants had taken, try and circle around by road and find them. I would have to circle because the lower Bauni jungles are too dense to allow the passage of even a small vehicle.

Dede, checking her lists and supplies, decided that she needed to replenish some of our fresh food and planned to go to Mahendranagar; Madhab, Jangbu, Pasang, and Rara would go with her. While there she would check with Hikmat to see if his men had brought in anything new on the elephant.

By eight A.M., with the winter mists gone from the jungle and the tents steaming off the heavy dewfall of the night in the morning sun, we were geared up and off on our separate projects. We drove up the road to Singpur together and then separated. Dede went with her group to Mahendranagar for supplies; Dick, Teresa, and I rattled in the Suzuki over the old wooden bridge into the deserted village of Singpur — the very house posts of which had disappeared in the dense growths that had overtaken the little hamlet within the space of the few years since its abandonment — and then headed south and east to Jillmillia and from there south and west, over the lower Bauni Bridge, where the Bauni, after disappearing into the Sukila Phanta swamp, emerges again to take its waters to the Sarda.

My feeling about the little group of elephants that had passed through Singpur during the night was that they would go down along the Bauni and then head for the lush grasses that grow on the edge of the Sarda wetlands bordering the southern part of the reserve. If this was the case then we might find them somewhere along the edge of the wetlands rather than in them. The prints that I had seen showed a couple of small calves, probably five-year-olds; the mothers would not take young ones of this size into the deep

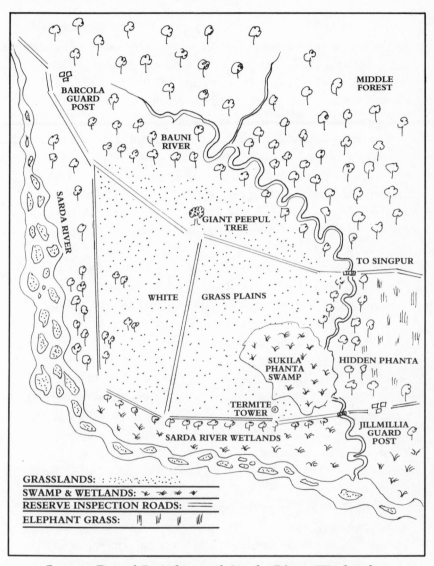

Lower Bauni Jungles and Sarda River Wetlands

cold water and thick soft mud of the wetlands. The prints were also heavy with dew, indicating that they had been made early in the night. Thus the group had enough time to have covered the distance from Singpur to the edge of the wetlands. At the same time we had the use, in our search for them, of the southern inspection road of the reserve that ran close to the area.

One way of finding elephants is to listen for them. As we had no tracks to follow and no specific place to search, this is the method that we now applied. We drove, stopped, listened. Drove, stopped, listened. Each time we stopped, if there was a convenient tree, I climbed up and glassed the area. In flat country — and all of the country of the lower White Grass Plains is as flat as a *chapatti* — a little elevation goes a long way.

We had stopped to listen for the umpteenth time and were admiring — while Dick was shooting — the graceful flight of a Painted Stork, when I heard a single sharp crack, the sound of a breaking limb. We had been driving west on the southern ring road of the reserve and the sound came from our left, about two hundred yards away, where a stand of big *Simul* trees marked the edge of the Sarda wetlands. We sat and listened. The sound could have been elephants. But it also could have been Langur monkeys ripping dead bark off a tree or tearing into a dead limb for grubs, sounds very similar to those made by elephants when they are feeding. Then we heard the sound again. As we did, very faintly, from the *Simuls* came the unmistakable high-pitched squeak of a young elephant.

I told Dick and Teresa to get ready. The sound indicated that there were elephants under the *Simuls*. Since I was fairly sure they would not enter the wetlands with their young, I thought we might be able to get near them for some footage. How many there were I did not know. But, and this was important, there was a group and where there was a group we might find Tula Hatti.

There were a good two hundred yards of tall grass between us and the line of *Simuls*. But it had been partially burned and was thin so I put the Suzuki into four-wheel-drive and low-ratio gearing and drove very cautiously into it, watching for stumps, termite mounds, dead logs, and holes and at the same time keeping an eye open for the elephants.

As we closed on the line of trees the grass thickened. Here the fire that had burned much of it had not penetrated. Thick clumps of tall, yellow grass and stands of small thorn trees meant maneuvering and in places even backing up to find a way through. I was navigating my way around a deep depression in the grass and at the same time trying to keep a branch of a thorn tree from forcing its way into the front of the car when I suddenly saw a large gray shape directly in front of me, no more than thirty feet away. Keeping the engine running I whispered to the crew and pointed. They were silent and when I looked around they were looking in the wrong direction. I whispered, "There, there," and pointed. As they told me later, it was as though the shape of the elephant grew slowly into their vision: one second not there, the next second materializing and taking shape right in front of them. I switched off the engine and Dick began shooting at once. As he did, the shapes of other elephants appeared and within half a minute we had a semicircle of ten of them around us, all within fifty feet. Some were still. Some were moving slowly, eating grass clumps they had torn out of the ground, beating them against their legs to rid them of dirt. Others were tearing small branches off the thorn trees and stuffing them into their mouths while their bellies rumbled their content.

I let Dick shoot while Teresa recorded the sounds. Keeping out of the way of the video lens I stood up and leaned over the front of the car, trying to get a little elevation to see further. Was Tula Hatti among them? Seeing and getting a nod from Dick indicating that he had some footage, I started the engine and moved the little car forward toward the herd, driving very slowly and keeping the engine noise to a minimum.

As we drove forward, most of the elephants continued eating and moving slowly. Then from the right loomed the shape of a very big male. For a moment I thought that it was Tula Hatti. The animal's trunk was raised, his ears were cocked up, and he was obviously taking an interest in us. I estimated that he was close to ten feet at the shoulder. But as he came closer I saw with a quick glance that he was not Tula Hatti but a *mukna*, a tuskless male. He slowly circled us from right to left and Dick managed to get a little footage of him. Then his interest in us was taken up by a female with a calf who raised her trunk and with a single short scream challenged us. Dick swung his camera toward her and she began to growl the deep, powerful muttering sound that elephants make when they are alarmed. At the same time, she started a slow, challenging advance, her calf tucked tight to her side.

Now the sound of her alarm was taken up by the other elephants and all began to growl. The sound, if one is not familiar with it, can be quite frightening in its power and volume. It has a tremor to it and sounds like the very deep growl of a very deep-throated and very large dog. A five-thousand-pound dog. To the sound of the growling was now added the high pitched squeaking of the younger elephants, especially the one that accompanied our advancing challenger, who, muttering powerfully, slowly came closer and closer.*

As we learned that evening on our camp monitor, Dick kept his camera rolling. Teresa, who admitted later that she was not at all happy about the big elephant slowly homing in on the open Suzuki, edged herself crabwise, inch by inch, away from the side of its approach but kept her sounding instruments running. For my part, my main focus of attention was the *mukna* whom I had lost sight of for the moment. I had no doubt that he was the herd leader and I am not happy around large, powerful herd leaders when I cannot see them. Was he circling behind us? Or standing in the grass some-

---

* Fairly recently a number of new discoveries have been made about elephants and their behavior. Among these is their ability to communicate with each other through the use of infrasound, the same sound that is used by Finback whales and certain other animals. I have discussed the "growling" of elephants when they are alarmed, and have to admit that until some recent reading on new elephant studies I have always believed this to be only a form of alarm call. New findings suggest that it may be something entirely different, a form of communication which, at its lowest frequencies (fourteen to thirty-five hertz, or cycles, per second) apparently has the ability, like the whistling of birds, to penetrate the foliage of dense forest. The studies of Cynthia Moss, Joyce Poole, and Iain and Oria Douglas-Hamilton in Kenya and Tanzania now clearly indicate that elephants, using infrasound, can communicate over great distances; perhaps, in certain atmospheric conditions, for as far as a mile or more.

where trying to make up his mind what he was going to do about us?

The big female came closer and closer, growling powerfully, slamming her trunk against the ground with resounding thumps, and flapping her ears, a technique elephants will also use to try and drive off a tiger or a leopard. Her calf squeaked mightily and this no doubt spurred the female on with her challenge. When she got to within thirty feet of us she stopped for a moment, giving me a chance to look around for the *mukna*. He was nowhere to be seen. But when the female started forward again, closing the last few yards that lay between her and us, I forgot about the *mukna* and gave her all of my attention.

Afterwards, my analysis of what happened was that in the little vehicle, still and silent, we presented to the elephant something that she did not understand. It is possible, in the little known and little visited country of the White Grass Plains, that she had never before encountered a vehicle. Perhaps her challenging advance was more curiosity than anything else. Whatever it was, when she began closing in on us and running her trunk along the ground to where, within the last few seconds of her advance, its tip was no more than six inches from the side of the vehicle, I decided it was time to act.

In sensational movies, this is where the elephant gets shot and collapses in a cloud of dust at the feet of the man with the cigar, the Stetson, and the triple-barrelled Magnum 929. Or perhaps the man misses and the Jeep, Land Rover, or whatever gets tossed high in the air with all of its occupants. (Actually, Teresa, somewhat unfamiliar with the habits of elephants, told me later that she was quite convinced at the time that the latter scenario was the big female's intention.) In this case what went in the air was my sweater, which was lying on the front seat beside me. I grabbed it and in the same movement threw it in the elephant's face.

I was taking a chance. I really had no idea whether this would stop the elephant, or infuriate her. I simply acted instinctively on the basis of something that was in the back of my mind, something that I had read about an Englishman charged by a tiger way back in the hunting days of the Raj. Somehow or other the man had become separated from his rifle and his companions and so he did the first thing that came to mind: he took off his Terai hat and tossed it in the tiger's face. The gesture, if it could be called that, worked. The tiger did not stop. But it changed course, went bounding past the hatless object of its onslaught, and disappeared into the forest. My sweater, which I retrieved later, had, fortunately, the same effect on the elephant.

She panicked instantly. She screamed and spun around and, her calf beside her, went crashing off through the grass. She was joined, just as instantly, by the rest of the herd including the giant *mukna*, which suddenly appeared from the right. All of them — as best as we could we counted twelve — screamed and trumpeted while the young ones piped and squeaked with them.

Then, in a cloud of dust and dry grass stalks spinning in the sunlight, they were gone. We did not go after them. They were startled now, even frightened, and in this state could have been dangerous, especially in protecting their young. We knew that we had great footage. This, combined with a little prudence, suggested that we leave our ponderous friends alone for a while.

That night in camp, with the game scout watching in awe and the Sherpas listening in silent wonder, our TV monitor showed us the whole story and, thanks to the courageous Teresa, growled and muttered and screamed and squeaked with all the power and majesty of the stars of the footage. Although Dede had no news to bring us from Mahendranagar and Hikmat's family, all agreed that it had been a full day, a real Terai safari day, one to be remembered. One that I think even Rara will remember, not only for what she saw on the monitor screen but for the arrival of a new friend by the name of Rosie. Rosie, a nice, brown, fat chicken, was purchased in Mahendranagar market for two dollars and was headed for Jangbu's cooking pot. Rara, seeing her bouncing around in a little basket in the back of the Scout on the way back from the market, suddenly realized what was intended for her. That was the end of any prospect of Rosie finishing up as the prime part of a good curried dinner, with *kalanonia* rice and steamed green vegetables. Rosie was removed from the basket and taken to the kitchen — to be fed, not to be fed to — and quickly became the camp mascot. Pasang built a little house for her and he and Rara made sure that she was locked into it every night, safe from jackals and other prowling chicken eaters. During the day she was given the run of the camp. While the winter jungles have very few flies, there was always one or two until Rosie arrived. After that the camp was totally fly free and one had only to see the speed of that yellow, snapping beak to understand why.

The clock was running down. The weather was great, we had a great crew, we had a professional team of video people, we had local backup, we had the know-how to track and stalk the big elephant and shoot the greatest footage in the world. But we had no elephant. If I had been a fingernail biting man, as the days slipped away toward the departure date of the video team — a fixed date timed to their work responsibilities — I would have been down to the quick on all ten fingers and nibbling toward my knuckles. I was still confident that we could find him and that I could get the video team in on him. Five minutes of footage was all that we really needed. More than this would have been great. But five minutes of tape is a lot of tape and cut and edited into the film it would have been quite sufficient for our needs.

But our problem was — and it slowly began to dawn on me, as the days slipped away — that not only could we not find the elephant, we really did not know where to start. Finding him in my mind was a matter of tracking him and then stalking him. But to track something you need tracks to start with and no tracks meant no tracking and no stalking. And, in this case, no elephant and no footage. No footage of the prime subject of the film? What kind of a film could we make? Could we even make a film? Who would even want to air it? Films about Bigfoot, the Loch Ness Monster, and the Yeti that show nothing at all of their subjects are somehow acceptable to viewing audiences. But a movie about an elephant with no elephant? Waking at night during the last few days of the video team's time with us I would envision a film that started with Jimmy Stewart (who was to narrate) saying, "Well folks, we want you to bear with us. We know this is a film about an elephant. But the darned filmmakers, headed by the ace tracker, stalker, and ex-big game hunter Mr. Peter Byrne, were, incredible as it may seem, unable to find the elephant! However, in a sequel, to be made when

Mr. Byrne emerges from the Sukila Phanta swamp, where he has been in hiding for the last two years, we promise you that . . . ”

On the evening of December 9th, three days before the video team was due to leave, we held a conference. Hikmat came down from Mahendranagar and had dinner with us. Afterwards all of us sat at the campfire and pondered the question uppermost in our minds. The game scout had a meal with the Sherpas, then he too joined us. Pasang came and sat with us and I opened the proceedings by stating the question that confronted us: where was the elephant and how were we going to find him within the two full days left to us before our photographic team departed?

Madhab wondered if he might have gone to Bardia. If he had then we were out of luck in terms of finding him in time to get footage. It would take all of one long day to get to the ferry on the Karnali River. If the ferry was working and if there was not a long line of truck traffic waiting to get on it and if the weather stayed fine we might get into the reserve late in the evening of the day we left camp, which, if we decided to try this, would mean tomorrow, the 10th. That would give us one day to search the area if we wanted to take a chance on getting the video team back to the airport at Dhanghari on the 12th. The logistics of getting to the reserve and getting back virtually ruled out a search there. And Hikmat, like me, did not think that Tula Hatti would have gone there. The ancient route, the cross country Elephant Walk that he would have used, was now almost certainly abandoned. Hikmat’s men, his two village Tarus, on whose information he placed a great deal of credibility, confirmed this; their village lay close to the old line of the Walk and they felt strongly that if the big elephant had gone that way they would have seen his tracks. Even if they had missed them, someone in their village, all now alerted to the need to report anything that looked like a twenty-two-inch track and all conscious of the huge sum of reward money to be paid to the person who made a find that would lead us to the elephant, would have told them. We ruled out Bardia and looked at other possible areas. There were two.

The first was the Sukila Phanta swamp. Could he be in there, moving quietly, eating, drinking, and not coming out? My opinion now, after all of the searching that we had done around the swamp, was that he was not. Somehow—and the feeling that I had was no more than intuitive—I just did not think that he was in there. Pasang confirmed this, saying that he felt the same way. When I asked him why, he said he did not know why and if he had asked me, I would have given the same answer. We both felt the same about the Sarda wetlands, south of the reserve. Earlier in the season the grass in there was tall and thick, good shade for an elephant against the midday sun, warm in the water against the chill of the winter's night, and with plenty of food. But much of the grass had now been burned and it was possible because of this to see—from a convenient tree—all the way from the northern edge of the wetlands, where we had encountered the elephant herd, to the river itself.

The same applied to the Haria Phanta and the dense grass around Rani Tal. At the edge of the lake the grass, its roots saturated with lake water, was still high and very thick. But it was only thick where it formed a band around the lake. Away from the water it thinned and the band itself contained too small an area to provide cover for the big chap. Pasang and I had searched this area, going in from the east side of Rani Tal, where there are some ferocious thickets of *Bhate*, and then walking and searching all the way around the back of the lake, coming out through the old Haria fields where the Singpur to Majgaon road sends a fork north to the Mangalserai guard post, the most northerly guard post of the reserve. In our hike Pasang and I had seen elephant signs close to the lake, but all of small elephants. We had found a domestic buffalo, foolish enough to wander away from his village and his companions, killed by a tiger. We had said hello to a big python that lived in a little canal dug by the people of Haria years ago to water their fields, now, like their village, abandoned. We had been snorted at by wild boar, screamed at by Macaques, peed down upon by an irate Langur, frozen into silence and immobility by the sight of a big dog leopard crossing the trail just in front of us, startled by a burst of peafowl from the brush right beside us, piped at by Axis Deer, and barked at by a little russet-coated *Kakar*, the Barking Deer of the Terai. But of our mighty friend we had seen no sign, not even an old sign which, even old and dried and dated in days or weeks or even a month, I would have welcomed.

We had been talking for a while when the game scout, who had said nothing until now, spoke. He hesitated, as though he felt that what he had to say would not be welcome and when he began to speak it was almost as though I knew, before he uttered a sound, why he had hesitated and what he was going to say. From his squatting position on the ground by the fire he leaned forward, picked up a little twig, tossed it into the flames, and said, "Maybe he has gone to India . . . "

This possibility had been in all of our minds. And it was not a pleasant possibility. If it were true, and if we were to follow up a confirmation of its truth with a search, it presented a whole multitude of logistical difficulties, not to mention bureaucratic ones. An international border lay between us and India. While the crossing of it on foot on a jungle trail or at night in a four-wheel-drive vehicle on a remote back road (something with which, over the years, to avoid the bureaucratic nonsense and interminable delays of border posts, we had become well experienced) was comparatively easy, trying to get a full film crew in with all of its equipment presented mind-boggling obstacles. Apart from this, even if we considered the prospect — which on the briefest of examinations we more or less dismissed — there were the time factors involved. These, comprising at least a month to get border crossing permissions and filming permits, ruled out all possibility of taking the search into the subcontinent. If Tula Hatti were down in the Indian forests, that was it. We would not see him. Nor would we be able to film him until he decided to come back to the White Grass Plains.

We thanked the game scout for his suggestion and told him that while what he said was a possibility, we as foreigners could not just four-wheel it across the Sarda and go looking for Tula Hatti in the Indian forests. However, what we could do, or at least what I could do with perhaps one other man, was follow up on Hikmat's search of the Sarda sands of some weeks before and look for tracks there. One thing about tracks in sand, any kind of tracks, is that for the most part they are clearly visible. Unlike tracks in dry grass or leaf mold that are often difficult to find and time consuming to follow, indentations in sand are much more quickly seen and identified and following them can be done at a faster pace.

I believed that Pasang and I could search out the five or six miles of each side of the Sarda, Indian and Nepalese, in a day. If we found tracks that indicated that the big elephant had taken up residence, however temporary, in the Indian forests, there was not a lot we could do about it; we could not take the video team in there. But if there were tracks on the Indian side moving toward Nepal, then we could act on them with the team. Thus, a search of the Indian side was worth a try. It was agreed that I would leave very early next morning with Pasang and carry out a full search of the Sarda sands, starting from Jillmillia and carrying out the first part of the search on the Indian side while it was still early and before Indian border patrols or forest guards started moving. With a bit of luck we would have some fog to cover our movements. While I was away, Hikmat would make another sweep of the northern part of the reserve with his men. Madhab would go to Jillmillia, Chicksua, and the Singpur guard post to check for information. Dick and Teresa would shoot stock footage in camp. Dede would hold the fort at base and be ready to act on any information that came in. Rara would direct fly-catching operations with Rosie and test the swinging possibilities of the huge hanging vines that draped the trees around the camp under the watchful eye of her great friend, Phurua. The game scout would start again from Singpur and sweep the roads north and east of camp. He also planned to walk down the bed of the Chaundari River which, although it had changed course some years ago and was mostly dry, still had a number of pools around which lush green vegetation grew, even in the winter months: attractive food for an ever hungry elephant.

Early next morning, dark early, I scratched on the canvas of Pasang's tent to wake him. He scrambled out and, quickly blowing up the embers of last night's cooking fire, boiled a pot of water. He made tea for himself, coffee for me. We drank the tea and the coffee, topped it off with a quick swallow of cold water, and then climbed into the Suzuki and headed out of camp, the headlights etching barred, black vertical shadows of tree on tree as we swung out onto the Singpur road.

We drove straight through to Jillmillia and had the Suzuki parked behind a big clump of cactus on the riverbank while dawn still lingered behind the eastern horizon. We were a mile across the soft white sand of the Sarda, had waded its swift, cold but shallow water, and were working our way down its southern bank hard against the Indian forests before the light had grown and the winter sun, climbing wearily out of the mists that grayed the eastern horizon, stretched weak fingers of light out across the white sand.

We set a fast pace and kept it up all morning. We stopped at midday, took a drink from the clean mountain water of the Sarda, and rested for fifteen minutes. Then we moved on quickly; over the years I had found that Pasang and I had the same physical capabilities and that anything longer than a fifteen-minute rest tended to stiffen his muscles as it did mine. Just as anything other than a very brief drink during the day tended to make us both feel thirsty all day. We moved quickly, not just because the instant visibility of tracks in the soft white sand allowed us to do so, but also because the possibility of meeting Indian border guards while on the Indian side of the border was a dangerous one. If we did, and if we were challenged, we did not intend to stop for possible questioning or even arrest. We intended to make a run for it. But as our escape route lay due north across the open sands of the river bed and as border patrols on the Indian border are very often accompanied by armed policemen who will not hesitate to shoot at a fleeing suspect, any attempt to run for the Nepal border would have been fraught with the possibility of a bullet. Our plan therefore, if challenged, was to duck back into the Indian forest itself. Once in the forest we were confident of our ability to elude anyone who might try and come after us and we would have immediate cover in the case of a shot or two. The problem, however, was that doing this would involve a long detour, upriver or down, on the Indian side, before we could venture out into the open riverbed again and head back for Nepal. It might even mean waiting for nightfall and a late return to a camp full of anxious people. So speed was essential, as well as frequent glassing of the edge of the forest ahead and behind.

We finished the five miles of the Indian side of the riverbed by midday. After a quick check for guards, we again waded the river—this year with all of its flow in a single course close to the Indian side—and then hurried across the open sands to the Nepal side. Breathing a sigh of relief, we rested for a few minutes and then started up the Nepal side. We finished the full five miles of this as the sun dipped down toward the western horizon and we were back at the Suzuki and on the way back to camp as twilight threw its gray cloak across the forests. The news that we brought back to camp was good in that it did not put the elephant on the Indian side. It was bad in that it did not put him anywhere. For we had not found the least sign of him in the ten miles that we had covered: two five-mile stretches that should have cut right across any route that he might have chosen when going south out of the reserve toward the Indian forest.

Pasang had an extra tot of rum that night. He liked it with hot water and lemon juice and a little sugar, as Dede and I did when we drank it, a good cold-weather campfire drink. And I had an extra scotch. I needed it when we gathered at the campfire and exchanged our negative findings for the day and when Hikmat, with what would have been a malicious smile if he were a malicious man, said, "Well Peter, it's the swamp for you. Better start packing some essential supplies."

For the clock had run out.

We spent the better part of the 11th helping Dick and Teresa to get packed and making plans to get them to Dhanghari Airport the following day. Hikmat went off to Mahendranagar to make sure that the plane was coming in and that the reservations he had kindly helped us to get for them were not lost, or forgotten, or cancelled, or, as quite often happens, annexed by some travelling V.I.P. bureaucrat. As a favor to us he took Lakpha and Jangbu Two with him. With the departure of the video team their services would no longer be needed and so we paid them off, gave them some extra bonus money for their good work plus bus fares and travelling costs from Mahendranagar, and said goodbye to them. Hikmat promised to make sure they got seats on a direct service to Kathmandu.

The headman of Radhapur came and drank tea and shook his head sadly when asked about the elephant, a gesture that with the Taru means yes and which in his case meant yes, I have no news for you. Madhab wrote up his reports and packed the single small bag of things that he had brought with him. He would leave with Dick and Teresa on the same flight. Accompanied by Rara, Dede and I did a last sweep of the roads around to Rani Tal, up to the Mangalserai fork, and back again through Singpur. We stopped at Rani Tal, climbed the watchtower and scanned the lake for a while until Rara, whose ability to remain still and silent is very good but has its limits, grew fidgety and we came down. We startled a big *Mugger* crocodile as we climbed down the rickety wooden ladder and he rushed out of the thick grass below the tower and plunged into the shallow water of the little lake. And we paused to remember a place close to the tower, where, long before it was built, we had spent a night sleeping in the back of the Scout in the dew-soaked jungle and having a big hyena walk around and around us curious and wondering, no doubt, if a Scout were edible — almost everything is to the ever hungry hyena. We drove back to camp with Rara sleeping in Dede's lap and with the sunset, a blood red band slashed through the patient trees, marking the end of another day, December the eleventh, 1989.

Next day I drove Dick, Teresa, and Madhab to Dhangarhi and got them on the plane. Dick was a trifle upset when he found that he could not get all of his equipment on the flight. But the plane, a little Twin Otter, was already bursting with baggage and he calmed down when I promised to get the remainder on the next flight to Kathmandu, where he intended to stay for a few days to shoot some commercial footage for his New York news service before leaving for the United States. He was, of course, disappointed at not seeing the elephant, at not being the first person ever to get film footage of him, at not being able to get what we vitally needed for the film. It was not until then that he pointed out to us the potential that existed with our own video gear, the Super VHS video cameras that Dede and I had brought with us as backup units. Now, as he was leaving, in some last minute discussions about the movie, he told us that while the video cameras that we had were not up to the high broadcast quality of the much larger and heavier equipment that he and Teresa used they would, in a pinch and with studio enhancement if that was needed, give us useable footage for the movie. Our cameras, both new models, had been brought for just this reason, to shoot backup footage for the movie where and when it seemed appropriate and to stand in for the bigger professional cameras when needed. Somehow, during the hectic time spent searching for the elephant, their purpose and use had never been discussed. Now, with the pro team departing, with no possibility of their being able to return—or our being able to afford their services again—and faced with the bleak prospect of a film without an elephant, I suddenly found myself with what I regarded as a heaven-sent reprieve. We had cameras. We knew how to use them. We could shoot Super VHS video footage that was very close to broadcast quality and that, with a new enhancement process, could be brought even closer. And we were still here, where the elephant was. *Where he had to be.* We could continue searching for him with our newfound ability to get video footage of him the minute we located him. Which I knew we would. Soon.

It was December 12th, the day that, had I been following Hikmat's tongue-in-cheek advice, I would be packing my bags and heading for the swamp. I drove back to camp whistling "The Road To Mandalay," Pasang smiling contentedly beside me. He knew that when that particular piece of music emanated from me it meant that I was happy. He also knew from experience that it might well mean that something interesting or amusing, or both, was about to happen.

171

6

BAN DEVI SMILES

H *atti, Sahib, hatti! Deri tula! Ek dum deri. Abi dekkahi, Sahib.* Singpur jungle!"

The game scout stood panting beside his bicycle. He had pedalled as fast as he could through the deep brown dust of the jungle road from Singpur and now, switching back and forth from Taru to Nepali, he pointed back in the direction from which he had come and told us with great excitement that he had just seen a *hatti* and that it was not just *tula*, big, but *deri tula*, very big. And, he continued, hopping from one foot to the other, he had seen it *abi*, just now, meaning within the last five minutes, in the jungle next to Singpur.

It was January the fifth and late morning on Hikmat's Hill. Dede and I were sitting at the campfire, having just come back from a round of the grasslands with Pasang and Rara. Growing increasingly conscious of the need to apply every minute of every day to the search for the elephant, we had left early, after coffee and a couple of hot *chapattis*, Rara complaining that it was the middle of the night and that she was still in the middle of her dream. Now we were back and relaxing at the campfire in the still cool day, looking forward to good brunch things coming from the kitchen and listening to Rara tell Jangbu about the big wild boar we had seen out in the *phantas*. Sitting with him in the kitchen area among the steaming pots, she told him how disappointed she was that we had not invited it back to camp. To her it had been such a friendly looking animal and she was quite sure, she said, that it would have made a great pet. And, she had promised us, she would feed it well and look after it, just like Rosie.

To Rara the big black boar was one thing. To us, another. When we first encountered it, out in the yellow grass of the *phantas*, it stood and watched us with cautious eyes, black and solid as a *Sal* stump. We sat quietly in the Suzuki and I rolled off a few feet of video, hoping to catch something of the cool, calculating fearlessness of *Sus Cristatus*, the most courageous of all the animals of the Terai forests. When he decided that we were not going to bother him he turned abruptly and trotted off into the high grass, back bristles standing rigid, tail up. He might have made a nice pet for Rara, but only in the first few months of his life when, as a small fat ten-pounder with a brown coat and horizontal stripes, he would have been playful and affectionate. Fully grown boars — and the record for the Indo-Nepal region is 450 pounds — are swift and powerful and fear neither man nor beast; they are not quite pet material, as we explained to our temporarily disappointed child.

We leapt to our feet when we heard what the game scout had to say. While I shouted quick orders to Pasang and Phurua and raced to get the video gear from the tent, Dede told Jangbu to cancel brunch, grabbed Rara, and ran for the Suzuki. I told the scout to leave his bicycle and jump in the Suzuki with us. Within three minutes of his arrival, we were off and racing down the road to Singpur in a cloud of dust — Pasang, Phurua, and the scout perched on top of a pile of equipment in the back of the bouncing Suzuki and poor Jangbu left standing among the steaming, bubbling pots and pans of his no doubt excellent brunch, now with no one to eat it.

The air pouring over the hood of the Suzuki was cool and the halls of the jungle on either side of the road were bright with the sunshine of the clear winter's day. Good visibility, I thought, both for seeing the elephant and for getting some footage of him at long last. As we pulled into the guard post at Singpur, Dede and I quickly formulated a plan of action. She would wait in the guard post compound while I determined if the elephant was still around. If he was then I would move in on him and try and get footage. I would then try and stay with him for as long as I could. While I was doing this Pasang would get up a tall tree and from there monitor my movements — which might not be visible to Dede if I went into the high grass — and relay these down to her. If the elephant had moved and was not immediately visible, I would also climb a tree as high as I could and try and see if he was out in the grass of the *phanta*. If he was, then I would try and stalk him. If not, Pasang and I and the game scout would try and find his prints, determine from these if what the game scout had seen was indeed Tula Hatti, and then try and track him. If the prints indicated that he had moved east then Dede would drive east on the Jillmillia road and circle ahead of us. If west, then she would do the same, moving slowly and watching for the elephant. If she saw him she would sound the Suzuki's horn three times and then, if he came out onto the road and stayed on the road, try and follow him, always staying in the car and always staying far enough away from him to allow for a quick turn and retreat should he take exception to being followed. She would try to stay with him until we caught up with her on foot.

The road from our camp on Hikmat's Hill to Singpur twisted and turned but on the whole took a generally direct route to Singpur. On either side was light forest, canopy trees with vine drapery, a few thick clumps of bush—dense and growing to heights of thirty feet—and small patches of elephant grass. From the road northwards, the forest stretched away for miles. But immediately to the south it formed a long single strip running roughly east-west, the southern edge of which was the grass covered *phanta* that had once been the rice fields of Singpur village. This strip was about a quarter of a mile in width. The big elephant grass-covered phanta, now known as the Singpur Phanta, reached all the way west to the Bauni and south to the edge of the reserve near the village of Jillmillia. The elephant grass, naturally seeding itself on the once pristine rice fields of Singpur, had within the space of a couple of years totally buried them in dense, almost impenetrable growth. The *sepoys* at the guard post, always nervous about the dark forest of grass that abutted their compound, had tried to burn it back. But their fires had burned only parts of it and big patches of it were still thick. One of these unburned patches ran along the south side of the guard post compound and it was here that the game scout had seen the elephant.

The sight that met us when we swept into the Singpur compound can only be described as comical. The compound has a number of tall trees growing within it and every one was festooned with *sepoys*, clinging to the branches, chattering excitedly with one another, and pointing in the direction of the phanta. As soon as they saw us they all began to shout, *"Hatti! Hatti!"* in loud voices.

I parked the Suzuki, told Dede to stand by, cautioned her to keep Rara in the car with her, told Phurua to stay with them in the vehicle, and followed by Pasang and the game scout, walked quickly through the compound to where it was enclosed by the edge of the *phanta*. When I stopped there, where the compound dropped off with a short steep embankment into the *phanta*, the scout came up beside me and pointed down into the thick grass. "There, *Sahib*. In there."

We stood for a moment and watched. When some of the *sepoys* dropped from the trees and tried to join us, I waved them back and told them to keep quiet. Pasang left at once and went up a tree about twenty feet. The game scout and I separated and from different viewpoints about thirty feet apart watched the edge of the *phanta*, I with one eye on Pasang, whose elevation gave him a visual advantage over us. We stood for a while and watched and listened. When the *havildar* in charge of the post came up, we asked him if he had seen the elephant and if he knew where it was now. He told us that he had not seen it but that many of his men had for a few moments. It had appeared at the edge of the *phanta* and then disappeared into the grass. When I asked him if he thought it was Tula Hatti he at once said yes, it was the big elephant. "That is why, sir," with a wave of his hand in the direction of the compound behind him and a smile, "all of my men took to the trees. They thought it was going to come into the compound and eat them."

I asked the game scout to point to exactly where he had seen the elephant and he did so. Then, gesturing to Pasang to go higher and to Phurua to join him, I went with the scout down to the edge of the grass to look for tracks. We searched for twenty minutes but were unable to find any. From time to time I checked visually with Pasang, now joined by Phurua, each a good fifty feet up separate trees. Each time I did Pasang raised his arm and, holding it vertically, turned his open hand back and forth in a gesture that meant no, nothing.

With the game scout, watched by a couple of dozen *sepoys* from

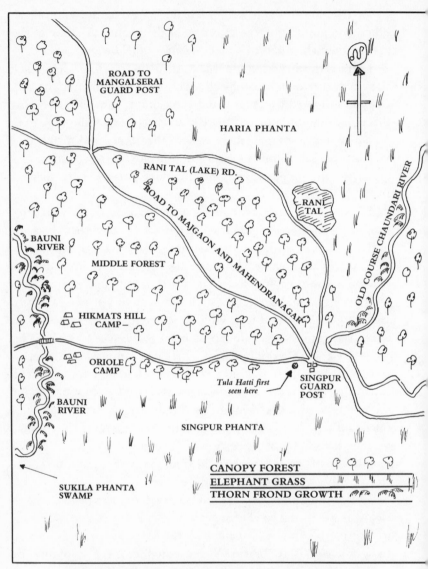

**Oriole Camp, Hikmat's Hill, and the place
where Tula Hatti was first found**

the compound above and behind us, I did a search of the edge of the high grass. I saw where something had gone in, breaking the dry stalks, crushing them. The size of the impressions indicated an elephant. But the hard ground and the dry grass showed no distinct prints and it was not possible to say if we were looking at the prints of Tula Hatti. I searched for a hundred feet in either direction and then went into the grass itself and ranged back and forth across where the animal had been seen. There was nothing, not even the marks of a passage through the grass. I went back to the edge of the compound and, climbing up, joined Pasang and Phurua in their airy perch. From there, slowly, looking for any irregularity in the pattern of the surface of the grass, the smallest movement, I carefully glassed the whole of the *phanta*. I spent twenty minutes doing this and saw nothing. In the time that it had taken the game scout to race to Hikmat's Hill on his bicycle and for us to get back to the Singpur guard post compound, probably twenty minutes at the most, the elephant had completely disappeared.

After a while I came down from the tree and joined Dede. Pasang and Phurua came with me while the scout, perhaps a little worried that his report of the big elephant had led to nothing, climbed another tree and stayed up. I told Dede that there were no tracks but that it was possible that the animal the *sepoys* and the game scout had seen was Tula Hatti. I also surmised with her that as we were moving into midday now, with the heat of the winter sun fairly strong and bearing down at a hard angle out of the upper southern sky, if the elephant had left the *phanta* it was not unreasonable to suppose it had done so to seek water. As the nearest water was the Bauni River, along the western rim of the *phanta*, it would be worth going down there to have a look. There was also water, in small shallow pools, in the old bed of the Chaundari to the east of us. But the Bauni jungle was thicker and the water deeper and I had a feeling that after being disturbed by the noise and shouting of the *sepoys* the animal would head for the more concealing cover offered by the Bauni, rather than the Chaundari. What I proposed now was that Dede take Phurua with her and, with Rara, slowly drive the Singpur road west toward camp. I would walk out the edge of the Singpur Phanta with Pasang and the game scout, and as we would be moving west, paralleling her course on the road, we could hear a beep on the horn from her if she saw the elephant up there or if she found his prints.

Phurua jumped in the Suzuki with Dede and together they left the compound, Rara waving and telling me, with a wise nod, that she would find Tula Hatti and not to worry. The game scout came down from his tree, frowning and shaking his head — how could the elephant have disappeared so quickly? — and joined Pasang and me as we set off on a little game trail that ran through the forest along the edge of the *phanta*.

From the high tree I had been able to see the northern boundary of the *phanta* where it bordered the forest along which we were now searching. I had seen nothing in the grass there to indicate that the elephant might be in it. Nevertheless, now, as we moved slowly west along the little game trail, we acted on the hypothesis that he was still in there and planned our movements and our search accordingly. We wanted to find him, of course. But at the same time we did not want to bump into him. So we stopped every ten yards, stood still, and listened. We did not expect to hear the elephant or even his movement. It was extremely doubtful that he would call out in the daytime and if he were more than thirty yards away, the sounds of his passage through either grass or forest would hardly be discernible to us. Not for nothing are elephants called the gray ghosts of the forest. Each time we stopped one of us shinnied up a tree and looked out into the *phanta* to our left. We took turns doing this. Tree climbing gets tiring after a while, especially when you are working on an empty stomach. And the scout, as we found out later, had a stomach as empty as Pasang and I — and Dede and Phurua and Rara — did, having leaped away from his morning cooking pot at the sight of the elephant to ride like the wind for Hikmat's Hill. Had any of us known the long, long day that lay ahead of us, I think that we would all have stopped to get some fuel inside before starting out.

We had gone halfway down the edge of the *phanta* toward the Bauni. Walk, stop, up a tree, down, move on. Look for tracks, listen to the sounds of the forest — the hum of insects, the chattering of Seven Sisters thrushes, the wail of a peacock, the scampering of

Rhesus Macaques above us, the rustle of small unseen things—and watch for movement ahead: the fleeting movement of deer, wild boar. Watch for it, see it, analyze it quickly, and then move on. And all the time register the hum of the Suzuki engine off to the right, a half mile away, travelling slowly west with us, stopping when someone saw something and got out to look, starting up again, changing gear, the hum increasing, decreasing as Dede worked our flank. Then, with half of the game trail to the Bauni behind us and half still ahead, thirty minutes into our search, suddenly came the beep, beep, beep of the Suzuki horn, followed by silence.

We turned as one man and ran into the forest toward the source of the sound. It took us a few minutes, dodging from clearing to clearing and avoiding the little patches of elephant grass, to reach the Suzuki. When we did it was to find Phurua standing on the road with a big smile on his face, Rara, eyes wide, with an even bigger smile, and Dede sitting in the front of the little vehicle silently pointing to a perfectly beautiful sight: a clear, fresh twenty-two-inch elephant footprint firmly set in the deep brown dust. After weeks of searching. After sending our disappointed camera crew back to New York. After enlisting half the people of western Nepal to search on our behalf. With the grim specter of P.B. heading for his hiding place in the swamp—a laughing Hikmat standing in the wings waving goodbye—hovering over us. After sleepless hours in the jungle night wondering if the great elephant was even alive anymore. With yet another deadline creeping up on us: our own departure date from Nepal, fixed to Dede's work schedule at her job as director of an Arts in Education program in Oregon. At last, bright and beautiful for all to see in the golden midday sun, the great elephant's personal signature quietly informing me, among other things, that I was quite wrong in my speculation that the heat of the day would send him toward water and the Bauni. A signature that added, "And not only did I not go toward water, Mr. ex-P.W.H., as you thought I might, I also chose to walk into the middle forests of the reserve, which, my clever friend, with its dry grass and hard ground is going to make tracking me something that may well defeat you and your merry band."

After four frustrating hours of tracking, backtracking, and trying to separate the prints of the big elephant from those of half a dozen other elephants, deer, and wild boar in the dry and broken grass, stick, and leaf debris of the forest floor, I was almost ready to concede that Mr. T.H. might be right. Then we hit the middle forest Elephant Walk and the elephant's prints turned onto it, making things a lot easier for us for a while. There was a nice set of faint but visible prints right down the center of the Walk, heading east. We turned after him, making sure that he stayed on the Walk with careful checks on both sides, quickening our pace in pursuit. As we did, as the clear broad trail of the Elephant Walk stretched ahead of us, I felt a calm come over me, a feeling that at long last we were closing in on our elusive friend and, with a bit of luck, a little bit of luck and a smile or two from the goddess of the forest, we would soon come upon him. When we did, when that great gray ghost came into view, the nagging thoughts that had been in the back of my mind since our failure to find him during the photo reconnaissance and even more since the departure of the camera crew, would, I knew, be instantly dissipated. And all of the doubts that had kept me company for so many weeks, especially since I had put Madhab and the crew on the plane at Dhanghari, would be forgotten.

After the camera crew and our liaison man, Madhab, had left on December 12th, two things happened. One: we got a message saying that a group of our sponsors would be in Kathmandu on the 16th of December. Two: I got a personal message from the game scout to say that while he was willing to work with us on the search for the elephant, and happy to be paid and more than happy to think that the reward might be his if he could lead us to it, we were not, in his opinion, going to find the big elephant, or even make any headway toward finding him, until offerings had been made to Ban Devi, the Taru's lady of the forest who controlled all these things, whose word in the forest was law, and whose whim it would be that we meet with Tula Hatti now, or not meet with him at all.

I thought that it was important that we have a chat with our sponsors, to bring them up to date on what was happening and to show them that we were working hard on the filming. So on December 15th, plane tickets having been miraculously obtained by

Hikmat and, even more miraculously, a plane having come in on time to Mahendranagar, we flew to Kathmandu and spent a couple of days basking in the ambiance of the Shangri La Hotel. I had all of our sponsors to lunch in the Shangri La's beautiful, brick-walled gardens and when I told them about our failure to find the big tusker they only asked me if I was going to go back and keep looking for him. When I told them "yes," their response, one that could not have been more encouraging to me, was, "Don't worry, you'll find him, we know you will. And you'll get great footage. Just keep in touch and let us know how you do."

Dede and Rara and I flew back to the western Terai on December 19th. The flight was an interesting one. We flew in a fully loaded Twin Otter. After taking off from Kathmandu we started the gradual climb toward the wall of the Kathmandu valley which, at plus or minus nine thousand feet, must be crossed by all flights headed south or west. Dede and I sat in the two extreme rear seats between the main door and the little emergency exit door and Rara sat immediately in front of us. The R.N.A.C. flight attendant sat next to us. She had come aboard with us, sat down in her seat, buckled herself in, and promptly fallen asleep. The remainder of the plane contained a two-person crew and fifteen passengers, mostly hill people and villagers, all clutching packages of food, clothing, live chickens, and personal belongings, probably an extra thousand pounds of weight which, had it gone into the baggage compartment where it should have gone, would have cost them half as much again in fares.

Soon after leaving the main airstrip the plane, instead of starting its climb for the wall of the valley, levelled out at about one thousand feet. It stayed at this level for three or four minutes and then began to descend. Below us the numerous little villages that dot the valley of Kathmandu slid by, red tiled roofs gleaming prettily in the morning sun. They began to look less pretty as we continued to lose height and they suddenly started to get closer and closer. A thousand feet soon became eight hundred. Then five hundred. Then something I estimated at close to two hundred. I looked at Dede. She looked at me and leaned forward to make sure that Rara's seat belt was fastened. I had a quick look at the flight attendant curled up beside us. She was still fast asleep and so, moving cautiously in case she awakened, I carefully opened and then closed the emergency door beside me, to make sure that it was working. (It, that little door, was the reason that we sat where we did and that we always sat in those rear seats: on more than one occasion over the years of flying with R.N.A.C., I have had a hand on the latch of that emergency exit door as my flight came hurtling in for another wild and wooly landing.)

The little blast of air from the opening of the door did not disturb the flight attendant, who slept happily on. In front of us the other passengers chatted, looked out at the distant mountains, laughed, smoked, ate, drank, and fingered their packages, totally oblivious to what was happening and to what we could see was now very close to a serious emergency. I raised myself in my seat and looked up toward the cockpit where the pilot and co-pilot were huddled over their instruments. Quick movements of their heads indicated that they were in intimate conversation with each other about their problem. Then they must have reached a decision, for as small trees and red tiled rooftops reached up at us, the plane made a sudden violent turn to the right, straightened out, and headed back to Kathmandu airport. No more altitude was gained or lost and within ten minutes we had made a slightly bumpy landing and were rolling down toward the airport tower. As we did, the flight attendant woke up and in sleep-dulled and robotic tones said, "We have now arrived at Nepalgunj. Not to leave the plane please. From here we go to Mahendranagar."

Later, after half a dozen little men had climbed all over the plane's engines and banged them with hammers and shouted back and forth at the pilot and co-pilot, we were once again in the air, climbing out over the wall of the valley, ascending, not descending. I waited until we were out of the valley and over the ramparts of the middle hills that enclose it. Then I turned to the flight attendant and asked her why we had returned to Kathmandu. Struggling to stay awake and looking straight ahead, she gave me her programmed reply. "Head winds, sir." Then she promptly fell asleep again.

Before we left for Kathmandu I had talked with the game scout about his concerns with things mysterious in the forest. I did not question them nor did I in the least way ridicule them. Like Hikmat, whose lifetime of experience with the supernatural beliefs of the jungle people was much broader than mine, I had and still have a serious respect for the power of myth, not just over the lives of primitive people, who hold them sacred, but also in other dimensions that are still beyond the understanding of the human mind. And so I had told him that when I came back I would help him to settle this little matter with Ban Devi and pay him for the offerings which he would have to buy. I did this on our return to camp. He asked for and I gave him two hundred rupees: about eight dollars. He used this to buy raisins, other dried fruit, and candy in the market at Mahendranagar. I also agreed to go with him to the place where he felt the goddess would be most likely to accept his offerings and hear his request, the ancient shrine of the Singpal Raja, in the forest just off the road to Rani Tal. (Not a lot seems to be known about the Raja of Singpal other than the fact that he had a fort here at one time surrounded by a huge compound in which he lived with his family and retainers. Long earth mounds, once walls of the fort, can still be seen in the jungle north and west of the Singpur guard post. Discarded pottery and cooking fire stones can be found in the forest. Even when Lord Baden Powell camped here a hundred years ago, the Raja and his people were long since gone. Baden Powell makes no mention of them in his book, *Indian Memories*, in which he describes a hunting and camping trip in the area about 1890. As a visiting dignitary he would almost certainly have been a guest of the Raja's had the jungle princeling been there. Another Ozymandias, gone into the sands of time.)

I stayed with the game scout and watched while, in the company of a young soldier who wanted to be part of what was going on, he laid the sweetmeats and raisins and other offerings at different places around the little piles of stones and the hanging brass bell that mark the age-old shrine. Then he and the young *sepoy* murmured some prayers together, and both bowed toward the shrine, hands held in front of them, fingers up, palms touching. The scout said *"Namuste,"* which has various interpretations but basically means greetings, and the two of them walked over to join me. They got in the car and I drove them back to the guard post. There the scout thanked me for doing what I did and said, "Now we will meet with

Tula Hatti. Soon." The date was December 26th, seven days after our return from Kathmandu and one day after Christmas in camp with the Bisht family, which included dinner in the big Eureka mess tent in a torrential downpour of monsoonal proportions and a huge Yule log that we had all dragged in from the jungle together struggling to stay alight on the campfire. Three days later, with the fading afternoon sun burning down behind the western trees, the game scout, Pasang, and I were on the middle forest Elephant Walk and moving briskly toward a long-awaited meeting with Tula Hatti, king of the elephants.

About a mile from where we came onto the Elephant Walk it crossed the Singpur to the Majgaon forest road. We emerged onto the road to see that our quarry had left the Walk here and, making an abrupt turn to the left, had gone up the road northwards. Like all wild animals that use roads, he had walked on the side of it rather than in the middle. In the deep brown dust his prints were easy to follow. We immediately started after them and had gone just a few yards when we heard a hum behind us. We looked back to see Dede driving up the forest road with Rara and Jangbu. Rara's smiling, "Did you meet Tula Hatti? Did you get a picture?" was delightful in itself. More interesting for the moment, however, were the flasks of hot tea, hot coffee, cold water, and little *chapattis* rolled up with jam and butter inside that Jangbu had brought with him. For by now the three of us had covered six miles of jungle on foot and, as well as being very dry, had stomachs that were beginning to growl from lack of food. Jangbu, our provider of good things from the cooking pot, leaped out as the Suzuki rolled to a halt and quickly spread his welcome offerings on the hood.

We took a quick break to eat and drink. Then Pasang and the scout climbed into the Suzuki with the others. Dede drove and I took a seat on the hood, right side forward with my feet on the front bumper. From here I had a clear view of the big elephant's tracks and we would be able to follow them a lot quicker in the vehicle than on foot, as long as he stayed on the road.

We tracked the elephant down the road for another two miles. Then, just as suddenly as he had left the Elephant Walk, he left the road and turned right, to the east. I raised my hand and Dede stopped the vehicle. Pasang and the scout jumped out. Without a word the three of us knew almost immediately where the elephant was going.

The forest road at this point ran for about a mile parallel to and west of the Haria Phanta, the big, grass-covered flatland that was once the rice fields of Haria village. As with the Singpur Phanta, the jungle had come in rapidly once the village was abandoned and now the whole area was eighteen to twenty feet deep in dense elephant grass.

We held a quick consultation. Our main problem was that the light was going. The sun was already far down on the western horizon and the short winter twilight was coming in fast. The stretch of forest that lay between the road and the Haria Phanta was barely a quarter of a mile thick at this point and I felt that the elephant would probably already be through it and into the grass of the *phanta*. If this was the case he was in an area inaccessible to us. Not only was the grass very thick along the western rim of the *phanta*, with visibility of three or four feet, the ground was also very marshy, with deep mud and cold water. It was difficult enough in the daytime; now prudence suggested that with the light fading and night coming in, it was not the most appropriate of places in which to try and get close to a large wild animal.

We formed a quick plan. Pasang and I and the game scout would keep going in the hope of seeing the elephant. Dede would wait until we came back, as we would do when the light closed down on us. She would turn the Suzuki south down the forest road toward camp and, with Jangbu, keep a careful watch all around in case our big friend, for reasons as obscure as why he did not go to the Bauni to drink but preferred to walk seven miles through the dry forest in the heat of the day, decided to turn around and come back toward the car parked on the jungle road.

I waved to Rara and we left. The tracks, like the ones that we had followed with considerable difficulty all day, almost disappeared when they left the road and went out onto the loam of the forest floor. A tuft of flattened grass, a crushed green leaf, a scuff mark in the dirt, this was all that we had to follow. But, now we had the

advantage of knowing almost certainly where the elephant was going and whenever the tracks disappeared, we simply followed their
general line of direction toward the *phanta*. By doing this, each time
we lost them we quickly came upon them again.

Within five minutes of leaving the car we came to the edge of the
phanta. The forest ended abruptly and in front of us stood a great
wall of tangled growth backed by twenty-foot-high elephant grass.
The elephant's tracks went straight into it. Down at its base, where
the water of the little stream from Rani Tal softened the ground, his
huge twenty-two-inch plates had sunk twelve inches into the mud.
He was gone, into the *phanta*, into an impenetrable sea of grass that,
like some vast creature from the deep, had opened its mouth and
swallowed him.

We stood and listened for a moment. Then I noticed a big tree,
one with a wide, round bole that grew out of the ground at an angle
of forty-five degrees and hung out over the edge of the *phanta*.
Handing the video camera to Pasang I told him to wait, and with
the game scout behind me, I went up the tree. About forty feet up,
there was a convenient perch, and, climbing into it and making myself comfortable, I was pleased to find that I could see well into the
phanta. I got my binoculars ready, waited until the scout had settled
down behind me and the tree had stopped quivering with his movements, and then started to glass the *phanta*.

The light was fading fast and in the jungle below us an army of
black shadows marched to the beat of the dying sun. But out in the
phanta the light was still holding and the excellent light-gathering
optics of my Coleman binoculars still enabled me to pick out even
small objects at distances of up to two hundred yards. A little
Screech Owl sitting on the limb of a thorn tree. The movement —
grass stems twitching — of a sounder of wild boar doing some last
minute foraging before the advancing night settled them down to
sleep. A Kite Hawk floating silently above the grass and terrifying
a fluttering group of little Red Munias. Closer at hand, two Crow
Pheasants, jumping from grass stem to grass stem in bursts of black
and russet as they used the last of the light to look for a meal. And
then, closer still, no more than fifty feet from the base of the tree

in which we perched, a large, gray, curved shape, still and silent among the tall stems.

I think I must have stared for probably ten seconds before I realized that what I was seeing was the back of an elephant. A very large elephant. Large enough to be only one elephant: our elusive friend of the long day's tracking and the weeks and months of searching and hoping. Tula Hatti at last.

I whipped the binoculars down and hissed at the game scout and pointed. He knew what I was pointing at at once. He told me later that he had in fact been looking at it and not realizing what it was. At the same time I looked down to get Pasang's attention while I fumbled through my pockets for some nylon cord to haul up the camera. For a moment I could not see Pasang. A good woodsman, he had concealed himself under a leaning hook of our tree while watching the jungle around him. I hissed. He did not hear me. I hissed louder. He still did not hear and suddenly I was in a dilemma. In a direct line from us the elephant was no more than fifty feet away and in the silence of the evening jungle, with the dampening air carrying sounds considerable distances, I was afraid that he might hear me. I hissed again but Pasang continued to stare impassively into the jungle around him. With quick thinking the game scout solved the problem. He broke off some tiny twigs and started dropping them down beside Pasang, one by one. Eventually their pitter patter attracted Pasang's attention and he looked up. I indicated the nylon cord and lowered it down. Pasang tied the end of it to the handle of the video camera and I hauled it up.

Quickly I untied the string, swung around in my perch, switched the camera on and steadied the viewfinder on the huge animal below us. As I did so, almost as though he knew what was happening, the elephant suddenly surged into motion and went lunging into the grass, moving rapidly away from us. Fifty feet, sixty, seventy. Then a hundred yards and then, turning to give me a brief side view of his face and head, he entered a dense clump of grass and disappeared.

I switched the video off and waited. In his sudden exit the elephant had made almost no sound. Now, with his disappearance, the *phanta* was completely silent. I looked at the game scout. He was

187

smiling. I looked down at Pasang. He was looking up at us and I gave him a thumbs up sign that told him that we had done it, that we had got the first footage. Not great footage. But footage nevertheless. And I felt that we had broken a barrier. That we were over a big hurdle. The gods of the jungle, led by Ban Devi, were beginning to smile at last. I felt, I knew, that we would see the great elephant again. Soon.

One thing bothered me a little about the elephant and that was his sudden movement and quick disappearance into the grass. We had been very careful about sound and I did not think that he could have heard us. In addition, there was no wind, no air movement that could have taken our scent into the thick grass and down to him. But he had detected us, I knew. What he had detected could have been no more than a whisper, a hiss, the falling of a twig. So why had he reacted so suddenly and so capriciously? What was it that made him extra sensitive to what could only have been the tiniest of sounds, sounds that could just as easily have been interpreted as having natural animal sources, such as squirrels or monkeys. Indeed, we had made far less noise than a feeding Rhesus Macaque, the common monkey of these jungles.

Was there a more sinister reason for his unusual caution? I tried to put it out of my mind, but it kept coming back. Did Tula Hatti have a bullet in him? Had he been shot some time in his life? Had he been able, then or afterwards, to associate the shooting with man or, at the very least, with something very dangerous to him — something to be watched for, listened for, scented for, and avoided at all costs? Was this why he was so spooky? Later, much later, I was able to look more closely at his hide and to examine it with binoculars. I found then that he did have marks on him that might have been those of a bullet, or bullets. Three of these were on his forehead in a pattern about fourteen inches in diameter. Another was in the left rear side of his back. All were small round scars, dried and healed. They could have been bullet marks but that is all that I can say about them at this time, except to add that I hope they are not.

If they are, two questions arise. The first is how he got them and the second, when. The first is probably the easier to answer. My guess is that they were wounds inflicted either by poachers shoot-

188

ing at him with inadequate firearms such as ex-army .303 rifles, the common weapons of the Indian poachers, or by irate Taru farmers trying to drive him out of their crops at night with muzzleloaders. The second question is more difficult to answer. All that I can contribute is that when I had met him from time to time in earlier years, he had always appeared to me to be calm and undisturbed by my presence, the presence of a human. On the basis of this I would say that the gunshot wounds—if that is what they are—were recently inflicted, which would account for what I do not hesitate to describe as a recent and definite change of personality in the animal.

Dede drove us back to camp and the bright spark of the campfire, seen through the trees in the darkening night, was a welcome sight. Jangbu who, like Phurua, does not drink alcohol, headed for the kitchen and a cup of tea. Dede and I headed for the mess tent where, with movements deft from practice, we quickly created four giant Safari Specials—big mugs of Nepalese Kukri rum mixed with hot water, lemon juice, raw sugar, and cinnamon—for ourselves, Pasang, and the game scout, both of whom joined us at the campfire. Rara raised a glass of orange juice in a toast to the great elephant and if her smile was a big one, the smile on the face of the scout was even bigger. For he would receive the reward for finding the great elephant together with the status among the Tarus that would accompany it. He left camp half an hour later, promising to return at the crack of dawn. Tomorrow we would go back to the Haria Phanta, tree-search it, listen to it, and if necessary walk all around its ten miles of trails to find the elephant. He was in there now and by heavens if he stayed in there we were going to get more footage of him. If he came out we were going to be on his trail within a minute of his leaving. When we had done with him we were going to have the most magnificent footage of the most magnificent animal in the Terai jungles. In Nepal. In the world.

7

FACE TO FACE

It was the first week of the new year and it was the week of Tula Hatti. He was not in the Haria Phanta next day. During the night he apparently lay up and let a few thoughts run through his head about the odd little noises that he had heard in the still of the previous evening. Either he analyzed them correctly and knew them for what they were — man — or he did not know other than that they bothered him. In any case, early next morning, with a blue-gray fog swirling above the surface of Rani Tal, with the big *Muggers* watching silently from their waterside lairs and Fish Eagles screaming their eerie calls, he left the *phanta* and headed south. He bypassed Rani Tal, staying just east of the little lake, and walked over toward the old bed of the Chaundari, now dry with the exception of a few shallow pools. He forced his way through the thorn belt that separates it from Rani Tal and then, heading south, walked into the forest close to Chicksua village. About two hundred yards west of Chicksua he turned and headed due west, crossing the Singpur to Jillmillia road about half a mile north of the Jillmillia guard post. Two *sepoys*, doing an early morning run from Jillmillia to Singpur on their bicycles, saw him crossing the road and raced to the Singpur guard post to tell the game scout. But the game scout was by this time — just after first light — several miles away and perched high in a tree with Pasang and me, glassing the Haria Phanta and listening to its messages. Listening to a Barking Deer tell us repeatedly that it was disturbed by something large moving down toward the Chaundari River. Listening to Jungle Ravens cawing to each other about something big moving toward the

Chicksua forest. Listening and analyzing and then climbing down and getting into the Suzuki and racing toward Chicksua.

The two *sepoys* who had seen the elephant were waiting for us at the Singpur guard post. We did not meet them because we took a short cut—the old road that used to run to the Chaundari Bridge—and bypassed the guard post. But when we got into the Chicksua forest, we did see a small green branch with fresh leaves on it lying on the road. When we stopped to look at it, we found that it was lying in the middle of a nice, twenty-two-inch footprint. The little branch had obviously been dropped by a moving, eating elephant and the size of the print told us instantly which elephant had made it. In addition, its placement told us where the elephant had gone: into the little pocket of forest that lies between the road and the Singpur Phanta.

We parked the Suzuki and left it. Left it open with tools and shovels and axes and all sorts of things quite fascinating to a native passing on the road all loose in the back and in plain view. Left it in a land where, in all of the years I have spent there, I have never known theft. Left it knowing that when we got back, no matter how many Taru walked by and stopped to look at the strange machine and its wondrous contents, everything would be untouched. Left it and walked quickly into the forest, where we found a happy sight: short, two- to three-inch-high burnt grass stems growing out of a thin layer of charcoal in which the elephant's footprints showed clear and sharp, stretching away from us toward the Bauni jungles. They were visible ahead in a line for more than fifty feet at a time, which meant fast tracking, fast follow-up for us.

We caught up with Tula Hatti an hour later. Knowing the direction in which he was going and being fairly certain that he would stay on the east side of the river, we did not follow his footprints, which at times went through thick brush, but instead used a little game trail, one that runs between the eastern edge of the Bauni jungle and the Haria Phanta grassland. On the trail we were able to move faster than if we had tried to follow him through the thicker jungle. In addition, the hard dirt center of the trail was ideal for quieter movement. Doing this, however, somehow or other we managed to get ahead of him.

We heard him first, coming up behind us and to the left. Then we saw him, a gray shape that suddenly materialized out of the shadows of a big *Jamun* tree. One second nothing; the next a huge floating grayness moving to the faint sounds of leaves and branches running down its flanks. His course was a straight line and we could see that it would take him past us at a distance of about thirty yards. I switched on the camera and started filming. As I did so the elephant stopped. Stopped, raised his trunk in the air, carefully scented the air, and then listened, his huge ears turned forward to pick up the tiniest of sounds. We froze where we were, hardly daring to breathe. Then the elephant moved on. However, he went no more than twenty yards when he stopped again and repeated his performance. Trunk up, check the air. Ears forward, check for sound. Wait, watch, listen, and then move on. While he was within sight of us he did this four times and as he moved away the game scout whispered to me, "*Bahut chelak, Sahib, bahut chelak.*"

He used the Taru word "*chelak,*" meaning cunning. He might have searched for another word and not found it or, having found it, thought — quite possibly correctly — that I might not understand it. The word that he wanted, I think, was cautious. In Nepali it is "*hosh.*" But his meaning was clear; he had seen what I had seen. Here we had further evidence of the elephant's unusually sensitive attitude. I do not think that he could have heard the video camera. It ran very quietly and it was inaudible to the human ear at more than twenty-five feet. Yet in the time he took to pass in front of us, probably two minutes, he stopped four times to scent the air, listen, and watch. On each occasion, while he did this, he stood absolutely still, as if rooted to the earth.

We stayed with the elephant all day, but we got no more footage. Once he passed us on this first sortie, he was ahead of us. The dense jungle of the Bauni forest prevented us, all through the afternoon, from getting past him or ahead of him. There were a couple of times when the jungle thinned and we considered trying to get in front of him. But the risk was that the sound of our quicker movement, even in the thinner areas, might alert him. Alerted, he would have quickened his pace and we might not have been able to catch up with him again. We saw him half a dozen times. But each time the camera view of him was rear end on and while I did collect some footage of him walking away from us, it was not good. Around five o'clock, as the light began to dim in the forest and the flashing green of Alexandrine Parakeets racing to their roosts heralded the onset of night, we left him and started back. I felt confident now, as I had done when we first came upon him in the Haria Phanta, that we would find him again on the morrow and with this thought in our minds we walked up the Bauni and back to camp. The night came in on us as we single filed our way through the Bauni forest. There was no moon and twilight quickly gave way to darkness, creating a phantom forest of spectral trees, their roots set in pools of ink. But there is a good game trail through the eastern Bauni jungles and our knowledge of it, aided by a band of starlight that wound its way through the canopy above us, enabled us to reach camp within an hour.

That night we ran the footage that we had shot on the camp monitor. It was, like the Haria Phanta footage, fair. But we needed something better. Something closer and more dramatic and with plenty of extra footage that we could edit out for the film. We were not, I realized now, going to be able to get extended footage of the animal itself, eating, drinking, being with the other elephants, in the time that we had left. A great deal of time would be needed for that and we simply did not have it. The ordinary difficulties that might be encountered in getting that kind of footage of another elephant would be multiplied by Tula Hatti's spookiness. Evidence of this was the day that we had just put in. We had been after him for hours and four-fifths of our entire time had been spent maneuvering around him to take advantage of cover, working with the wind, watching and waiting for him to change position, and then changing ours to avoid having him detect us. Now what we needed was good, clear footage of the big elephant, close up, and in good light. We planned to go after him and try for it again next day.

Once again I sent the game scout off to his headquarters at Singpur with instructions to return at the crack of dawn. It was January the first and we had only six days left. But somehow, I could not tell why, I knew that we would get the footage that we needed and

I went to bed that night confident that the next few days would crown our efforts with success.

That evening we had a visitor. Her name was Jessica and she was a Peace Corps volunteer. We had met her at the Bisht house a couple of times and after getting to know her had invited her down to camp. She had been in Nepal for a couple of years at this time. She lived in a Taru village rather quaintly named Mousa Pani, which means "mouse water," and her work with the Tarus seemed to be mainly related to fish farming. She was about twenty-five years of age, fair-haired, blue-eyed, almost elfin in build, and she rattled around the Taru buffalo cart roads on a bicycle. She had ridden the twenty miles from Mahendranagar to our camp that day and she planned to stay with us for a couple of days. She was, as a visitor to camp, something of a rarity, for although, as was our yearly practice, we had invited a number of friends to be our guests on safari, very few ever seemed to manage to work out the logistics of getting there. Apart from the Bisht family, Jessica was our only visitor that winter. We set her up in a nice big Eureka safari tent and made sure she had a campfire chair. In return she offered to look after Rara from time to time. The very next day, in case more than a few hours with our small jungle girl changed her mind, Dede and I left Rara in her care. Instructing Pasang to hold the fort at camp and the game scout to continue his independent searching, we went out together after the elephant.

We left camp early on foot and, crossing the forest road, walked through the clearing of Oriole Camp and made our way down through the vine-draped trees to Python Corner. Our fifteen-foot friend was not waiting to greet us this morning. He was probably enjoying the warm waters of the Bauni until the sun came up. We stood beside the little clearing where he sunbathed during the day and listened to the sounds of the early morning jungle. A *Murghi*, the Common Jungle Fowl that is the ancestor of all of the domestic fowl of the western world, challenged everyone and everything in the forest with raucous crowing. Peacocks, still in their nocturnal perches, meowed to the morning sun. Deer, far down the Bauni, called to the forest folk to tell them there was a big cat on the move. And, almost in answer to Dede's question as to whether I thought

A young tuskless male elephant in the Bauni River.

Dede Killeen and Jangbu Sherpa explore the big swamp in the White Grass Plains Reserve.

The guard tower and the giant *Peepul* tree that marks the north center of the White Grass Plains.

A Langur monkey in the White Grass Plains middle forest.

Dede glasses for Tula Hatti atop the giant termite mound in the southeastern corner of the reserve—the largest mound ever seen by Peter
Byrne in thirty-five years in the area.

Wild elephants in the Terai grassland, as seen through the window of a Land Rover.

An Asian One-Horned rhinoceros in the central Terai.

Mugger crocodiles sun themselves on the bank of the Bauni River. The crocodile's metabolism demands a daily intake of sunlight.

The elusive Tula Hatti, as photographed through Peter Byrne's video camera. Note the broken tusk.

Measuring the footprint of Tula Hatti—twenty-two inches across.

Another video shot of Tula Hatti. To date, no one has managed to get a still photograph of the great elephant.

Dede, Peter, Rara, the game scout (Mr. Pant), Phurua Sherpa, and Jangbu Sherpa stand next to a tree snapped off by Tula Hatti the night before.

The *Tula Hatti* film crew. Top row (left to right): Pasang Sherpa, Jangbu "Two" Sherpa, Lahkpa Sherpa, Dick Fisher, Madhab Battarai, Peter Byrne. Bottom row (left to right): Dede Killeen with Rosie, Phurua Sherpa, Rara Gael Byrne, Teresa Powlovsky, and Jangbu Sherpa.

we could actually find the elephant again, we heard a single sharp, heavy crack, the sound of a thick limb being snapped off its parent trunk. I turned to her with a knowing smile and whispered, "There you are. See? I told you we could find him. Q.E.D."

We set off immediately toward the sound and, when we got to where we thought it came from, stood and listened. Directly ahead of us the forest ended in a clearing covered with thick brown grass about four feet high. When we did not hear anything more we moved up to the edge of this clearing. Again we listened and now we heard more sounds, the sounds of an elephant eating. Giving Dede my best professional nod, one that said, "There you are; I told you so," I led her forward to a little mound just inside the clearing. We walked up onto this and looked. Sure enough, there was an elephant standing eating not more than than thirty yards away. A big elephant. But not Tula Hatti, as we saw instantly. Quickly erasing the knowing look from my face I whispered, "There you are. An elephant. A big elephant. Which is better than no elephant, OK?"

We stalked the big elephant for about half an hour. He was a *mukna*, probably the one that we had encountered with the herd some weeks ago, when the video team had shot the footage of the female and calf that had done their little dance with the Suzuki. When I had shot some video of the *mukna* and Dede had taken some stills of him, we moved south down through the jungle in the hope of finding Tula Hatti. But we had only gone a short distance when we ran into a segment of the Sukila Phanta herd. They came toward us from our right and forced us to drop back into the tree jungle at the edge of the clearing where the *mukna* was still feeding. We climbed into a small tree and watched them for a while. There were three tusked bulls, five adult females, and four calves, all about four to five years old. They were part of the White Grass Plains herd but not the group that we had encountered and filmed down on the edge of the Sarda wetlands. One of the calves was a young male with surprisingly large tusks. He stood about four feet at the shoulder and probably weighed about six or seven hundred pounds. He was very active and moved back and forth around the herd all the time they were passing in front of us. When they reached a point directly in front of where we were perched in our little tree, one of the females suddenly got wind of us. She rolled her trunk up tight and then, unrolling it with a quick downward movement, slammed its tip against the ground, making a hollow booming sound. Instantly all of the group closed in and stood while it was determined what the danger was and where it lay.

The females herded their calves together and tucked them into their flanks; the bulls ringed the little group, trunks high, while they tried to pinpoint the source of the scent. They all stood like this for about a minute and then, to our delight and surprise, the little four-year-old with the outsized tusks suddenly came dashing around the side of the herd, making what he obviously considered loud screams of challenge but which only came out as mighty squeaks, and charged directly at us. I do not think that he saw us; he was probably only guessing at our location. But his charge was determined, fast, and furious and he held it for about fifty yards. Then he skidded to a halt about thirty yards away, lashed the grass with his trunk a couple of times and shook his head from side to side, ears flapping, all of this making it quite clear that if we came any closer we would have to deal with him! As the herd moved away after a few minutes he remained out on the flanks, charging up and down, squeaking mightily and making it known to all that he was ready to take on the world. We instantly named him Son of Tula Hatti.

After the herd left we went on down the Bauni looking for Tula Hatti. We did not find him and in the early afternoon we turned and walked back, getting into camp at sundown. We told Rara about the little elephant and she was quite disappointed that we had not brought it back to meet her. We told the game scout about him also and he agreed, with a smile, that we might well have encountered an offspring of Tula Hatti. What I did not tell him was how I had led my wife in to stalk Tula Hatti only to spend an hour stalking the wrong elephant. But then, hearing about the *mukna*, he probably worked that out for himself.

As to Tula Hatti and his whereabouts, he agreed that the animal was still in the Bauni forests. He had done a round of the eastern side of the area on his bicycle and had gone all the way to Jillmillia and back. He had checked for signs in case T. H. had decided to go back to the Haria area and talked with villagers and the guards at both the Singpur and Jillmillia posts. He had seen no sign and had heard nothing from guards or Tarus, which suggested fairly strongly that T. H. was still in the jungles on the east side of the Bauni, south of the road. Our familiarity with this area would enable us to search it from end to end in a single day. Which we planned to do again, starting early next morning. And which was confirmed as being quite the right thing to do by a near visit from Tula Hatti himself during the night.

One question that often came up in conversations during our research on Tula Hatti and our filming was, "What if he should walk into camp at night? Is this not a possibility and is it not a danger?" The fact is that it was a possibility and, should it have happened, one with hazardous potential. Elephants had walked close to our camps on several occasions over the years, once along the edge of the river at the base of the little hill that was our campsite, no more than thirty yards from our tents. All that we could say in answer to the question and all that we could believe in was the basic rule, which is that all things being equal, elephants stay out of campsites and, for the most part, stay away from them during the night. If, of course, one is foolish enough to build a campsite on an Elephant Walk, or even close to it, then one is asking for nocturnal visitors perturbed at the sights and sounds and smells of humans in a place they have no right to be. Big visitors weighing tons. Powerful visitors who, with a flip of a trunk, could pick up a Suzuki and toss it in the air. But, according to the law of the jungle, one does not do this. One goes to sleep at night knowing that all sensible creatures, among which the most sensible and indeed the most intelligent is the elephant, also know the jungle law and the penalties for disobeying it. I have had leopards in my camps twice, a buffalo once, and rhinos twice. Both of the leopards—not Hollywood leopards which either charge into camp intent on seizing the cook (always the cook who, unlike the gunbearers and trackers and other staff, is large and fat and slow moving) or leap from trees onto the back of the client's blonde mistress—were simply big curious cats that wandered through camp on little tours of inspection. One actually sat down ten feet from where I was sleeping—on this occasion in the open and without a tent—until I shooed it gently away.

The rhino that came in did much the same thing. While there is no arguing that rhinos can be very dangerous, especially at night, on both occasions a quiet and controlled approach helped us to avoid what might otherwise have been a calamitous situation.

In the case of the rhino, the occasion took place far down the Sapt Gandaki River, in central Nepal. I was guiding the trip and my client, C. W. Ennis from San Antonio, Texas, was having what he called a last safari. He had hunted with me twenty years before and we had been friends ever since then. On this night we had both gone to bed and I was near sleep when I heard a familiar fluffing sound, the sound that a rhino makes when it is moving and is a little alarmed. It is a sound that is hard to describe but it is similar, though a lot more regularly paced, to the noise made by a bed sheet hanging on a line and blowing in a stiff breeze. I slid out of bed and looked out through the tent flaps. There was a bright moon and I was quite horrified to see two huge One-Horns—the Asian One-Horned Rhino is bigger than either the African Black or the African Wate—standing side by side with their noses almost touching the back of my client's tent. All they needed, I thought, was the least provocation, the slightest sound, and they would lunge forward and go right through it. There was only one thing to do and that was try and draw them off it in some way. So, barefoot and clad only in a pair of blue striped cotton pyjamas, I slipped out through the flaps, dropped to all fours, and went slowly on my hands and knees around to the back of my tent. Then I stood up and crept silently into the jungle until I was behind both of the huge beasts and about thirty feet from them. From there I called them both, very gently, very softly, "*Ao, ao.*" There are times when words in another language—in this case Nepalese—are softer than in one's own. This was one of them. "Come, come," somehow or other did not seem suited to the occasion. "*Ao, ao,*" I called again and I kept calling until both of the giant prehistoric-looking beasts turned slowly away from my client's tent, turned to stare in my direction, and then began to move toward me. As they did I moved carefully back and when I had drawn them a good hundred feet from the tent I gave them both a good British bellow that sent them thundering into the jungle, tails up, huge feet pounding the ground, snorting and fluffing in alarm.

The second occasion was some years later, again on that great jungle river, the Sapt Gandaki. Dede was with me and on this occasion our client was a single person, Cynthia Fagen, a reporter from New York having her second safari with us. She had booked a ten-day photo safari of the river and its wildlife. Once again two armor-plated giants decided to visit us in camp at night. But this time, remembering the previous incident and applying the jungle lore of the years, I had hung white cotton bedsheets around the campsite. These effectively held our nocturnal visitors at bay until the three of us, gently clapping our hands and saying, "Shoo, shoo," eased them off into the night.

The buffalo was different, as buffalos can be. It was in Assam and my client on a hunting safari was a very large German lady whose husband had recently passed away, leaving her with several billion marks and a yen to spend on safaris. She had had a little too much to drink at the campfire and, getting up to go to the loo in the small hours of the jungle night, came face to face with a buffalo. The buff was an Asiatic, wide of horn and narrow of mind. The piercing scream that she gave on seeing him, one that woke up every sleeping monkey within half a mile, probably scared him as much as it did me. I remember erupting out of sleep, straight up (in the P.W.H. trade, to lose a client was the End), grabbing for flashlight and rifle and thinking, "Oh my god, she's walked on a scorpion, or a centipede," they being about the limit of what might attack a large respectable German lady in the middle of the night. The buff did not wait around. It whirled and bolted for the jungle. Unfortunately the course it chose took it right through the kitchen tent; when it left the tent, pots, pans, kettles, and cooking utensils went with it. We found the tent later and got most of the stuff back. The Sherpas, Pasang in particular, had a good laugh about the incident, as did I. But we refrained from laughing in front of our client who complained with a look of Teutonic horror on her ample features that, "*Mein Gott*, that feelthy beast nearly killed me."

Normally, putting aside the indisputable fact that there are always exceptions to the rule, large wild animals stay out of camp-sites. Human scent plus the sight of unfamiliar objects such as tents or parked vehicles will tend to keep them away. There is also, usually, the smoke of the dampened campfire as a deterrent; the big dead logs that we always used for our campfire, ones that we found lying on the jungle floor and chained up and dragged in with one of the vehicles, often smouldered well into the wee small hours. So when Tula Hatti nearly visited us in the dark of the jungle night, it was just that, a near visit.

The path that he used was the middle forest Elephant Walk. How he got into the northern end of it from the southern Bauni I do not know. But he did. When he woke us up, he had been up in the northern end and was coming south, passing our sleeping camp on his way back to the Bauni forests. He woke us with a powerful scream just as he was passing our camp. It was a sound that sur-passed and surmounted all other sounds. It started with a low-pitched roar, almost a growl, so deep it was, and then rapidly ascended into a powerful, trumpeting cry. Immediately on reaching its crescendo it tapered off and descended into a long moan. He repeated the call once as he crossed the Singpur road and after that he was silent.

Next morning, checking Tula Hatti's prints on the road — prints that confirmed that it was he who had passed us in the night — we also looked for tiger pug marks. A tiger on the road would have been a good reason for that mighty nocturnal scream, the great animal's way of saying to a big cat, "Move aside," or, at the least, "Keep back and do not try anything foolish with me." Though they do not fear them, elephants do not like tigers; the dislike also in-cludes leopards which, though not a threat, have a similar scent. And while a tiger is no threat to a fully grown tusker, a hungry tiger is a ferocious animal that will attack almost anything in its need for food, including elephants. But we found no tiger pugs. Why then did the normally silent and unusually sensitive elephant call out as he was passing us? I do not know. Before we went back to sleep and again next morning at breakfast, Dede and I discussed but did not resolve the question.

With the game scout I went to where the elephant had crossed the road in the night. We quickly found his tracks again and set off to follow them. They were fresh and clean in the deep dust of the road. Where they passed into the forest, they still glistened with the night dew. Leaving the road the elephant had turned south toward the lower Bauni jungles. For an hour we followed without difficulty his zigzag route southwards through the forest that lies between the river and the Singpur grasslands. Then, after about two miles, the tracks suddenly turned and led us toward the river. We followed them right up to the edge of the Bauni and I gave a mental groan when I saw that they appeared to go straight into the water. If the elephant had crossed the river this would mean a backtrack for us all the way to the Bauni Bridge, a round trip of four miles, to get to the other side. The Bauni was not too deep at this place, probably about five feet, and in a pinch we could wade it. But I hated to do this unless I really had to; some of the *Muggers* of the lower Bauni are really big. Although we would be in the river only a few minutes — it was about thirty feet wide at this point — wading it was a risk that I preferred not to take; in fact the very thought of it sent shivers up my spine.

We stood looking at the prints in the dirt for a few seconds. On the edge of the bank where the seeping river water had softened the earth, the animal's forefeet had gouged two deep grooves as he lowered his immense weight down to the water to drink. I checked carefully for *Mugger* and then got down on my hands and knees close to the water to look at the last print that he had made as he slid in. Close to my face the water, its dark, inscrutable surface hiding the secrets that lay below it, inched its way downstream. A Snake Bird screamed and a large brown frog, startled out of a midday reverie, broke the brown mirror of the river with a dull plop.

I studied the print. As I did, a tiny movement caught my eye. It was infinitesimal and so slow that, had my face not been within inches of it, I would not have seen it. Embedded in the soft dirt of the print was a tiny fragment of green grass. It was fresh and clean and it was set into the dirt in the form of a half-spiral. As I watched, it slowly raised its tip an eighth of an inch, a quarter of an inch, three-eighths, as it straightened out to regain its former shape.

When it stopped moving I let my eyes follow the direction in which it pointed. As they did I saw, a little less than three feet away, barely visible in a pile of dead leaves, the faint impression of another footprint. I moved over to it. Beside it was another and just beyond that, another. Tula Hatti had not gone into the river. He had only gone up to it, lowered himself to drink, and then, stepping back and turning on a single foreleg, stepped away from it. A tiny piece of grass told us the whole story.

We set off at once to follow the tracks. They went about twenty feet and then turned sharp right, doubled back across the tracks that we had been following on the way to the river's edge—we had missed them—and then turned south. We turned with them and as we did the rain, which had been threatening all morning, suddenly began to come down.

One of the problems of being out in the forest when it is raining is, of course, that you get wet. Another more serious problem is the noise and movement caused by the raindrops falling on leaves and small branches. When one is stalking large game of any kind, movement in the vegetation plays a large part in the detection of animals and in ensuring one's own safety. The turning of a leaf. The bending of a single blade of grass. The swaying of a tree branch: all contribute to seeing whatever it is that caused the movement. The smallest sound, from the snapping of a tiny twig to the faintest rustling of leaves being overturned, can play a vital part in the game of detection and identification.

For about ten minutes it rained quite lightly. Then it began to get heavier. Within another fifteen minutes, the steady drumming of the raindrops on the leaves obscured many other small sounds, sounds that might warn us of the proximity of the elephant when our eyes could not see him. As it was, we almost bumped into him. Had it not been for the fact that he had a young bull with him, we might have done so. We saw the young bull first, a nine-footer, tough looking, quick moving, standing in the tunnel of the game trail we were following about thirty feet away. We froze into stillness and watched. We were standing together, motionless, when a very slow moving single white object caught my eye about twenty feet away to the right, just off the trail and in a dense clump of brush.

It was a tusk. It was the very faint movement of its tip that caught my attention. We stood and looked as the vast bulk of Tula Hatti took shape, seeming to grow out of the very earth. At the same time, the young bull moved slowly away from us and disappeared down the trail.

The big elephant was looking directly toward us. The density of the brush prevented him from seeing us. The muted roar of the falling rain prevented him from hearing us and there was no wind for him to scent us. Slowly, very slowly, to avoid a movement that might catch his eye, I sank to my knees and with an arm stretched behind me and a finger hooked into his shirt front, pulled the game scout down with me. Crouched on our knees, we waited. I had the camera ready but the brush in which he had buried himself was much too dense to record anything other than his vague outline and the blurred white of his tusks. "I will wait," I thought. I'll wait until he comes out of there and then flip the ON switch and get some nice footage of him. I'll wait as long as I have to. With which thought I took off my Terai hat, placed it over the camera to protect it against the rain, and settled into a more comfortable position on the ground.

I waited for three hours.

The light was fading when the elephant at last moved. For three hours he had stood in the dense thicket, three frustrating hours during which his only movement was a minimai, slow, up-and-down or side-to-side movement of his head, signalled to us through the only thing that we could see at all clearly: the single tip of his right tusk. The tip of the other tusk did not show at all. It was only after an hour of studying it through my binoculars and, whenever it moved, with the naked eye, that I saw it was snapped off; where the tip should have been was a shattered stump. It was here that I learned, for the first time, that one of Tula Hatti's tusks was broken. Where that happened and how, we shall probably never know. The other, his right, was perfect. Once, while we were watching him, he hooked his right tusk into a little fork in a tree in front of him and rested it there. At least I thought that was what he was doing: resting it. I based my impression on having read that big elephants with extra heavy tusks will often lay them against something solid to ease the weight. I found later that I was wrong about this. When the tusks are not extra heavy, as is the case with Tula Hatti, there is another reason.

When the light was almost gone, the elephant at long last moved. He turned suddenly to his right and in a smooth almost gliding motion, without any sound, slipped out of the thicket and onto the game trail and walked away. I managed only a few seconds of footage of him, rear end on, and then he disappeared. It was frustrating and another whole day had suddenly slipped away. But it was not without its amusing side. For as the elephant disappeared I turned, for the first time in three hours, to speak to the game scout squatting behind me. At least that is where I thought he had been all of this time. But he was not there. I looked back and had to raise my eyes to find him. He was a hundred feet away and thirty feet up a tree. When I walked in his direction he slid down the tree and joined me. To my unspoken question he said, "Too close, *Sahib*, much too close. If Tula Hatti saw you that close he would not like it."

Having put me in my place and, as far as he was concerned, exonerated himself for slipping away and leaving me alone, he led off up the game trail, away from the direction taken by the elephant, and back to camp.

The footage on the monitor that night, our sturdy Honda generator droning away in its little hole in the ground a hundred feet from camp, showed us rain-sodden leaves dancing against a solid wall of greenery through which, from time to time, faintly, as in a dream, a minuscule cream-colored object was seen to perform a snail-like ballet. There was nearly two hours of it. American audiences would love this, I thought. Rara and Phurua, the latter worn out after a long day of playing jungle games with Jungle Girl, both fell asleep watching.

During the night the rain clouds that had soaked the forest slipped away to the northeast, leaving the skies blue and the air in the jungle around the camp breathtakingly clean and clear. While Dede, Rara, and Jessica slept I sat at the fire in the cool air of dawn and waited for the game scout. When, after an hour, he did not appear, I took Pasang and we left camp and walked out down the Bauni. It was January 4th.

213

We took water and rolled *chapattis* with butter and jam with us. We envisioned a long day ahead. I was determined to follow the elephant all the way to the Sarda if necessary, a hike that might take us late into the night. Pasang carried a shoulder bag containing, in addition to the food, batteries for the video, and an assortment of small equipment, two five-cell flashlights. We might have left them behind; any additional weight counts when one is carrying it. But the weather was changeable and whereas we could have made our way back through the Bauni forests in starlight, should cloud come in we would lose that. When this happens in the Terai, the stygian darkness that envelops the jungle, deep down under the tree cover, has to be seen to be believed. And it can be seen — as a curtain of impenetrable blackness that seems to hang an inch in front of one's eyes.

We picked up Tula Hatti's prints an hour after leaving camp. They were clear and fresh on the floor of the jungle and we followed them south for another hour. Then, about two miles downriver, they suddenly turned and headed into the Hidden Phanta. We continued after them through the jungle to the rim of the *phanta*.

We stopped at the edge of the ten-acre grass-covered clearing to watch and listen. A Giant Hornbill boomed from deep within the *phanta* and two Serpent Eagles flicked their shadows across us as they cruised the tree canopy above. Some of the grass of the *phanta* had been burned and the air was heavy with the smell of damp charcoal. But, like the Singpur grasslands, there were still big patches of high, green grass. We were watching one of these directly in front of us when we heard branches cracking and bark being ripped, the sounds of an elephant feeding. We headed for the sounds at once but instead of going directly toward them through the thick grass, we cut left around the east side of the *phanta* to where a little stream fringed with big Strangler Fig trees ran into the grass. We climbed into one of these and got as high as we could. We had been there only a moment when we saw something long and thick and gray come up out of the grass about three hundred feet away. It seized a limb from a tree and snapped it off. It was the trunk of an elephant.

We climbed down and very cautiously began to move toward where the trunk had appeared. As we got closer we moved slower and slower, listening carefully, watching for the least movement

and generously feeding the wind with handfuls of grass seed in return for which it told us where it was coming from and where it
was going. When we got to where we had seen the trunk, we stood
and listened. The elephant was not there. He had moved. Then we
heard him again. The sound came from off to the left where there
was dense grass in which grew a scattering of small thorn trees. We
moved in that direction and found a short, thick Strangler Fig, its
root system laced around the hollow core where its long dead host
tree had once been. In it, about twenty feet up, was a triple fork that
offered a perch for us. We got up into the tree, glassed the grass and
the thickets in front of us for about five minutes, and found the elephant. It was Tula Hatti.

He was in a thicket about a hundred feet away, standing quite
still. Most of him was obscured by the leaves and branches of the
thicket and only his tusks showed at all clearly, pale white through
the foliage. We considered trying to get closer. But between us and
the thicket that held the elephant was dense, tall grass. Visibility
would be two to three feet at the most; as it ran right up to the edge
of the thicket, we would not be able to see him until we came right
up against him, at a distance of probably three or four feet. Pasang
remained silent as I examined the ground between us and the elephant. But he knew what I was thinking. When I whispered that I
thought that we had better stay where we were, he said nothing.
Pasang is one of the few men I know who is afraid of absolutely
nothing. Had I said to him "Let's go, Pasang. Let's get in that grass
there and see how close we can get," he would have followed me
unhesitatingly. And if I had asked him to lead the way he would
have done so, *kukri* in hand, fearing neither man nor beast.

We had a lovely afternoon. So did Mr. T.H., who spent it doing
nothing, nothing at all other than airing his tusks and staying camera shy. When the light began to fade, and when the not-too-
comfortable limb crotch in which we had been wedged for four
hours had begun to bite into our bones, our friend suddenly moved.
He walked out of the thicket, contemplated the grass for a
moment — the moment it took me to get the video rolling — and then
walked into it and sank gracefully and silently out of sight. I think
that he lay on his side. I was not sure. We could not see a hair of

him once he went down. Even when he had come out of the thicket, his eleven-foot-high shoulders only briefly showed in the tangled greenery. Now, down in the grass, he completely disappeared. He lay there for about half an hour — he must have been tired after his hectic afternoon — and then rose and moved rapidly off to our left. We saw only parts of his back as he moved quickly away in the fading light. Just before he stepped out of the *phanta* to disappear into the forest, he raised his trunk once, high in the air. Just once. Up. Then down again. I really do not know if he knew that we had been there most of the afternoon watching him. It is possible that he did not for with the heightened sensitivity to human presence that I suspected he had, he would surely have moved away on detecting us. But if he did know we were there, I had no doubt at all about what he was saying to us now. "Goodbye. Hope you had a nice afternoon. I did. See you tomorrow. Maybe."

Pasang and I had a pleasant hike back to camp. I should have been frustrated, but I was not. I was amused. Somehow or other I felt that our giant friend was playing games with us. That it was January 4th, and that we had only one day left bothered me not a whit. Two can play your game, I thought. One of us will win. It's playing the game that counts more than winning. And what a game it was, in what a setting. I could think then, and now, of no more exciting game on the face of the earth, in no more exotic a setting.

When I got back to camp, there was a note for me from the *havildar* in charge at the guard post. It was to say that the game scout had been called away for special training. He had to leave almost immediately. He would be away for three months and asked that I please pay his money and whatever else he had coming to him to Colonel *Sahib* Bisht. The note explained his non-appearance of the morning. I guessed that he had been busy making preparations for his departure. From now on I would be working without him.

January 5th dawned bright and clear. The Black-Headed Orioles heralded the morning sun in tones soft and melodious. An orange and black Tree Pie perched in the tree canopy above our tents and, in low staccato tones, just as he heard them floating up to him from thirty feet below, mimicked our voices. We were all up early, even Rara, excited at the prospect of breaking camp and heading again for Captain Doo and her beloved Shangri La Hotel, source of such delights as ice cream and apple pie. While Jangbu prepared breakfast, Pasang and Phurua had already started taking down the extra tents. Soon boxes and bales were being carried through camp to the vehicles and the trailer. Dede had been at work since dawn getting our personal things packed and Jessica, when she came to the mess tent for breakfast, already had her tiny bag of clothes and toiletries tied onto her bicycle and was ready for the twenty-mile ride through Mahendranagar to Mousa Pani.

I was all ready to go out again and have a last crack at our giant friend of the forest and this time I was going to do it alone. Pasang had developed a cough within the previous few days and I noticed that when we were out together he was having great trouble suppressing it. He would stay in camp and help the others pack. I would leave immediately after breakfast and would if need be spend the whole day out. The only contingency plan that I made with Dede was that if I was not back by nine that night, she would drive the roads a bit to look for me. She would drive down to Jillmillia in case I went all the way down the Bauni and came out there, or into the big *phanta* of the reserve—the real white grass plain for which it is named—and down its eastern inspection road, should I come out the other way. This, coming out of the Bauni jungles on the west side, was an unlikely prospect and one that I would only use in an emergency. Coming this way would mean wading or swimming the Bauni at some point. Although as a hunter in years gone by I had waded it many times, it was always with rifle in hand, loaded and cocked and ready for instant use. I now travelled the jungles of the Terai without a gun and without fear of any animal. I had learned, over the years, that if one has even a glimmering of jungle lore, one knows that it is possible to walk the Terai forests from end to end in complete safety. Walk. Not swim. Not wade. Because swimming or wading in the Terai jungle rivers or lakes puts one into the territory of the one animal that holds not to the jungle law, the one creature to which all living things are, simply, food. The animal that Kipling called "the belly that runs on four legs." The *Mugger* crocodile.

217

Tula Hatti

The Nepal Terai has two species of saurian. One is the big, long-nosed, fish-eating crocodile that the Tarus call the *Naka*. The name is self explanatory; "*naka*" means "nose." The books call the animal the Gharial and they describe a huge amphibian that will grow to a length of twenty-five feet. But one could swim in a pool surrounded by Gharial and be as safe as if they were goldfish. The Gharial is strictly a fish eater and no other food interests it.

Not so the other member of the genus, the *Mugger*. The name, in its western connotation, conjures up images of faceless beings lurking in dark alleys waiting to prey on the unwary. The image that I have of the *Mugger* crocodile is not far from this. The only creature in the Terai of which one must always be aware, the *Mugger* of the little jungle rivers and the shallow forest lakes sees all moving things as food. To its small, undeveloped brain, man is but another moving thing, whether he be in the water or out of it. In camp on the Bauni, at first when Rara was two and later when she was five, we were confident that with the exception of the *Muggers* lurking in the dark brown waters of the river we had nothing to fear for her from any animal. But that exception was always there, a hundred feet from camp, as a result of which anything closer than fifty feet from the river was strictly out of bounds for her. The rule applied even during the day when we knew that the big saurians usually kept well away from the activity of camp, spending most of their time basking in secluded, sunlit clearings up- or downstream.

Being taken by a crocodile is a nasty business. I have always been very aware of what actually happens if one gets grabbed by one of the big, powerful, very fast animals. The *Mugger*'s method of catching and killing its prey is to seize it in its powerful jaws, submerge with it, and hold it — deer, wild boar, monkey, man — underwater until it has stopped struggling. When the victim's struggles have ceased the big saurian will take the body to one of its food lairs. This may be under a bank or in the roots of a submerged tree. The lair is jealously guarded against other members of the species. After three or four days the victim's body will begin to decompose and emit the gases that tell the *Mugger* it is ready to eat. The croc will then take the body out of the lair and break it up into pieces. Having no cutting teeth, the *Mugger* is unable to chew its meat. The breaking up is done by seizing the body in its jaws and rolling over and over with it until it begins to come apart. Then the *Mugger* gulps down the various parts, whole and unmasticated.

Very few victims escape the *Mugger* once those steel trap jaws close down. I have seen *Mugger* take deer and monkeys. There is something chilling about the speed with which it happens and the silence of the aftermath, a silence broken only by the faint popping of bubbles as they rise to the surface, grim indicators of the hopeless struggle below. During my hunting years I had seen not a few dead *Muggers* opened up for skinning after they had been shot. In their bellies, often, were the pitiful mementos of their human victims, mostly women and children: silver and copper bangles, metal nose rings and earrings, children's glass ankle bracelets, brightly colored. No, I told Dede, it was most unlikely that I would come out into the big *phanta* west of the river—to get to which I would have to cross the river—if I were late. More likely I would walk straight back to camp, up the east side of the Bauni and be back before dark. If I got stuck somewhere—and one can always fall over a root and break a leg, I suppose—and if it were in the deep jungle where a vehicle could not go, I would simply light a fire and bed down for the night, something that I had done many a time while running hunting safaris.

When we had eaten breakfast, we assembled outside the mess tent. There was one thing that we had to do before I left for the day. This was to have a quick look at a tree not far from camp that we thought Tula Hatti had snapped and broken off just before dawn. I had been sleeping at the time and the sound had awakened me instantly. Indeed the crack it made as it snapped was like the report of a small cannon through the forest; only an elephant could make a sound like that. Earlier, to save time searching for it, I had sent Pasang out to find it. He returned just before breakfast to say that he had found a big tree broken by an elephant—almost certainly by Tula Hatti—close to the Singpur road and only about three hundred yards from camp.

Leaving Lakpha and Jangbu Two to hold the fort at Hikmat's Hill and to continue with the packing, Dede and Jessica and I got

into the Suzuki joined by Jangbu One and Phurua, who were keen
to see Tula Hatti's handiwork. Pasang handed Rara into the back to
Phurua and we set off toward Singpur. When Pasang said "Stop,"
we parked the vehicle and got out. We were about to head into the
jungle with him when we saw the game scout coming down the
road toward us. He had heard about a big tree being broken by Tula
Hatti—how, I do not know—and having a few minutes before an
army jeep would take him to Mahendranagar for the beginning of
his new training, he wanted to join us and have a look. Led by
Pasang we all walked into the forest together.

Within a hundred feet we came to a big tree cleanly snapped off
about six feet above the ground. We all looked at it in awe. The tree
was a strong young *Sal* with a bole about fourteen inches in diameter. Although I could not estimate with any accuracy the power
needed to break it off, my guess was that a force of not less than six
or seven thousand pounds must have been applied to snap it at that
height. The elephant—and we had no doubt that it was Tula
Hatti—had done this without even using a tusk to push. The tree
was clean of any tusk marks, indicating that it had simply been
seized in the great beast's trunk and then slowly bent down, down,
until it snapped. Described as a wasteful practice by some, the
elephant's habit of pulling down whole trees just to eat part of the
foliage at the top has a simple explanation. The tenderest part of
most trees, the most succulent shoots and leaves, are at the top. The
time-honored phrase, "two leaves and a bud," applies to the tea
bush and to that part of it that makes the highest grade tea: the top-
most tips of the bush. I have no doubt that elephants learn early in
life where the sweetest munchies are to be found: the "two leaves
and a bud" at the top.

We stayed at the tree for a little time and took a few quick pictures. Jessica took a picture of us and then we said goodbye to the
game scout, telling him that his reward money as well as a gift of
a big Coleman Bowie knife would be waiting for him with Colonel
Bisht when he got back. Then we separated. I went alone to the
lower Bauni jungles for, I hoped, a final rendezvous with Tula
Hatti; the others went back to camp to pack, load, and generally

fold tents. The next day, January 6th, we would say goodbye to the White Grass Plains for 1989.

When I got down to Python Corner I stopped to check my equipment and to allow my senses to adjust to the light and sounds of the deeper jungle of the Bauni. Mr. Hiss, as Rara called him, was there, curled up in his corner and waiting for the morning sun to reach in a finger or two of warmth. He eyed me somewhat coldly and his tail flicked a couple of times. But he did not move away; I think he was getting used to me. When I made no motion toward him his tail stopped moving and he remained still. Pythons are constrictors and kill their prey by crushing it in their coils. To do this the tail must be hooked around a solid object, so at the sight of prey, or a potential enemy, the first thing they do is seek an anchor for the tail. They are very ancient creatures and have probably changed but little in millions of years. The theory that they were once a different kind of creature, something closer to a lizard, is supported by the vestigial claws to be found lying close to the anal orifice at the nether end of the body. Like the tiger's "wing" bones, or "floating" bones, that lie unattached in the muscles of the shoulders, they are remnants of life as it was in the primeval world. When hunting with clients I never allowed them to kill python, even though some of them wanted skins. We limited our intrusion into their lives to temporary capture, examination, photographs, and then release. It takes a minimum of five strong men to pin down and hold a fifteen-foot python. If there is a struggle the main thing to watch out for is the teeth. A big python has a powerful bite. Although there are no toxic glands, decayed particles of food lodged in the teeth can cause septicemia if one is bitten.

I had taken some care to dress carefully for this last meeting with the elephant; if Mr. Hiss had had any interest in what I was wearing, he would have noted that I had on my dark brown Terai hat and a light nylon camouflage jacket over a khaki shirt, a handful of grass seed in the left-hand pocket of the jacket. Worn khaki pants were held up with a leather belt. Over light woolen socks, I wore a pair of Coleman Lightweight Hikers, the laces of which I had cut down to lengths that would just allow for a double reef knot. No bows in the jungle. They have a nasty habit of getting snagged on things.

Tula Hatti

For my basic equipment I carried a small compass and matches in a waterproof container, with a striker. The compass was to guard against the possibility of getting caught out in the dark in a fog that would prevent me from seeing the stars and finding my way home. The matches were for a fire in case I had to bed down for the night, particularly in the open country. In January, nights in the jungles of the White Grass Plains Reserve have temperatures that move around the mid-forties, Fahrenheit. But in the open country, the grassland, they can be fifteen degrees lower, with even a couple of degrees of frost. A Coleman Bowie knife, a small sharpening stone, a length of nylon cord, binoculars hung on a leather thong around the shoulders and under the right arm—to keep them tight to the chest—and the video gear completed my equipment. The video gear consisted of the camera, an SVHS Magnavox, one of the two that we had in camp, and, in a small canvas bag slung on my back, extra batteries, one extra SVHS tape, some lens cleaning tissues, and a small air brush.

I did a last check of everything, said goodbye to Mr. Hiss, and stepped into the jungle as the first yellow beams of the winter sun cut down through the trees like swords. I walked slowly, watching the ground underfoot and mentally photographing it every second step to reduce to a minimum the time needed to keep my eyes on it. Doing this I hoped to avoid snapping a twig while at the same time using my eyes more advantageously on what was more important: what lay ahead. I stopped every fifteen to twenty feet to listen to the sounds of the jungle. Each time I did so I tested for air movement with a little pinch of grass seed. There was some movement. It was minimal and coming from the south. Even without the seed I could at times feel it gently touching my face. I knew that if and when I got close to the elephant wind direction would be vital; if I made the mistake of getting upwind of him for even a few seconds he would spook and be gone.

I knew of course that elephants are almost uncanny in their ability to detect scents and determine their direction and source. It is a capability that is only paralleled by the tiger's ability to pinpoint sound stereophonically. One thing that an elephant can and will do is use his trunk to pick up ground scents from tiny feeders of air that sometimes run just a few inches above the ground *against* the direction of the wind. A deer, picking up a scent that is foreign and needing analysis, will turn and face the wind, the only direction it can conceive of as the source of the scent. But an elephant will check both directions, from the strong breeze twenty feet in the air all the way to the little currents and flows that run through the grass and leaves at its feet. Being downwind of an elephant is not enough. One also needs a bit of luck. And maybe even something else. Something else that I found I had and was very lucky to have, later in the day.

There will come a day when my eyesight, my hearing, and my ability to detect and analyze scent on rivers, in mountains, in jungles and grasslands, will not be as good as they are now. (I do not look forward to that day.) Right now I measure all three as fair, the result of many years of use under demanding conditions. (I do not measure them as expert. Indeed, an expert, in my opinion, is someone who has nothing more to learn.) If they are fair, then I think it is because my fields of application, particularly the Terai forests, have made imperative their use to the very limits of their ability. With eyesight—to look and look and look again, even when common sense is saying that there is nothing there, nothing at all: a shadow, a natural shape that demands no further attention, a trick of the light. With smell—to stop and analyze and analyze again until, after running it through the olfactory nerves six or eight or ten times, it identifies and registers itself on the brain. With hearing—to apply total alertness of the mind not so much to what one hears, or what one thinks one is going to hear, but to what is barely heard, to what barely impinges itself on the mind, to what barely registers. A leaf rustles. A tiny twig snaps. A tall blade of grass sighs as something moves against it. The brain instantly asks a question. Was that a sound? Was there really a vibration there? Did I imagine it? This instant of the slightest sound, so faint as to be almost nonexistent, is when a vital message can be received, analyzed, understood, and acted on. Or ignored, discarded, and lost, together with all of its meaning.

The sounds that I now heard were like this. Faint, shallow, and barely registering themselves on my mind. But experience—not expertise—had taught me not to ignore them. Though at first I was quite unable to interpret them, I opened my mind to them and continued to listen to the very limit of my ability. The sounds were of the faintest rustling of leaves and grass stalks and they seemed to be coming from a thicket about a hundred feet ahead of me and to the right. They could have been made by a *Murghi*, the wild jungle chicken, scratching in the dry leaves for insects. Or a Langur turning over twigs to look for beetles. Or a deer browsing. Or a wild boar quietly nuzzling for roots. Or an elephant . . .

The ground was clear between me and the thicket, and its surface—bare of leaves and debris—allowed me to move forward quickly to the cover of a jumble of fallen trees and broken branches. I slipped into these, jammed my shoulder against a thick branch to steady my camera stance, got the video on my shoulder, pulled my hat down over my eyes and settled down to wait.

I did not have to wait long. The little collection of sounds I was hearing was suddenly totally obliterated by the most thunderous crack. In front of me, deep in the thicket, a sixty-foot *Sal* tree leaned over and went crashing to the ground. Since *Murghis* and Langurs do not pull down trees and since ordinary elephants do not snap off sixty-foot *Sal* trees with fifteen-inch trunks, I knew that the thicket could contain only one animal: Tula Hatti. I also knew by now from frustrating experience his fondness for getting into thickets and staying in them for hours and hours and hours. But I was determined to wait all day if necessary. For this was it. This was the last sortie, the last chance. As of the evening of this day, the clock had run down to zero. Tomorrow, in answer to the unalterable schedules demanded by our private and business lives, my family had to leave and head home. There was no way out of this; a whole series of events, tightly scheduled, would be set in motion by our departure on the morrow. A four-day drive to Kathmandu. A Thai International flight that would take Dede and Rara out of the magic kingdom on January 12th. An American President Lines ship that would hoist the valiant little Suzuki and the old International Scout on board at Bombay on January 24th and steam across the oceans with them to Portland, Oregon. And, at home, an organic blueberry orchard coming out of winter dormancy and needing attention, not to mention Dede's work and my lecture schedules . . . This, my giant friend, I silently whispered, is it. Will you please, please, please not stand in that damned thicket all day until the light is gone and my chances of getting you on tape are gone and your chances of becoming a household word to several million people are gone, quite possibly forever. Please. There's a good chap.

The elephant stayed in the thicket for about five minutes. Then I heard him move. I could not see him when he was in the thicket eating at the tree that he had pulled down and I could not see him when he started to move. But a *Murghi* suddenly dashed out on the left side of the thicket directly in front of me and, with a loud cackle of alarm, went racing off on foot into the undergrowth. Immediately afterwards, slowly, majestically, massive head nodding to the rhythm of his stride, Tula Hatti appeared from behind a big *Jamun* tree and began to walk directly toward me. As he approached, I saw something that sent the hair on the back of my neck prickling and my heart pounding. On either side of his face, halfway between the eye and the ear, a stream of black mucous fluid streamed down in a delta-shaped flow. The stuff was rutting fluid. The bull was in heat.

Are Asian wild elephants dangerous to man under normal circumstances? The subject is much debated but I think that the answer is that they are not. Normal circumstances means unprovoked. Provocation, however, takes many forms and various facets of what are called the Instances of Provocation can be applied to tiger, or bear, or rhino, or even to a mouse, for that matter, for a provoked mouse will bite in self-defense with all the ferocity of any wild animal. So too can they be applied to wild elephant. The I.O.P.s that can be applied to elephants are: *A*. Surprise. Elephants do not like to be surprised and may react aggressively if they are. *B*. Cul-de-sac driving. This means driving or forcing an elephant into a dead-end corridor such as a ravine or *nullah* from which there is no exit; again the elephant will react defensively and possibly quite aggressively. *C*. Closing in on females with young. Female elephants are fiercely protective of their young. While their first instincts are always to get their young away from the source of the threat, if they feel that they cannot do so—if, for instance, deep water is between them and their line of flight, water in which a young one might get into difficulties—then they will stand to the challenge of the danger, protecting their young to the very limit of their abilities, even unto death. *D.* Injuries. An injured wild elephant, regardless of how he or she got the injuries, is an animal to stay away from at all times. Hurt, confused, wanting only to lie up and be left alone, a wounded wild elephant, at the approach of someone foolish enough to try and get close, can quickly become the most dangerous of animals. *E. Musth.* This is the name given to the physical and mental condition of female elephants in estrus and male elephants in rut. I include it among the Instances of Provocation because a bull elephant in this condition is, without any outside or additional impetus, already actually in a state of provocation.

The condition of *musth* in elephants is still not fully understood. Male elephants in *musth*, which may occur several times in a year and which will last from four to six weeks each time, become extremely agitated, short-tempered, and irritable to the point where the least thing will send them into paroxysms of rage. When this happens they become extremely dangerous. Their natural wariness of and respect for man will completely disappear. Wild elephants will charge through villages trumpeting and screaming, attack domestic animals, and challenge anything that moves. Bulls in *musth* have been known to chase cars on highways, challenge buses, and even take on trains. One bull in Burma is recorded as having derailed a train and lived to trumpet about it. Even domestic elephants, born in captivity or captured as young animals, have to be chained and tied up during this period. No one, not even their keepers of years, can approach them; water has to be piped to them through a hose—usually a hollow bamboo stalk—and food tossed in front of them from a safe distance.*

Now, remembering what I had read about elephants in heat, it suddenly came to me what Tula Hatti had been doing when, during

---

* For years it has been believed that the condition of *musth* was a periodic phase of sexual excitement, the same as the rutting phase in the male deer. My own observations have always suggested this, and the males that I have seen mating have always

the long hours that we had watched him in the rain-soaked thicket, he had placed his tusk from time to time in a tree fork in front of him. Pressure on the tusk, it is believed, eases the irritation caused by the emissions from the glands in the temples and helps it to flow more freely. When I thought that he was just resting his tusks in the tree, something big elephants with heavy ivory may do, he was actually performing a biological function related to his sexual state of the moment. Not suspecting that he was in rut—through the rain-soaked leaves I never did see either side of his head where the temporal glands lie—I had not realized the significance of what he was doing.

As to why he was not with the herd and its females at this time, my feeling was that he probably visited them as he wished and as he desired. Only a large and dominant elephant can do this. A smaller male, leaving the herd for more than a day or so, may well find the young bulls he left behind have closed ranks against him, preventing him from returning. With his huge size, Tula Hatti would not encounter this problem; to an animal of his dominance, the door to the herd—young bulls notwithstanding—was always open. Since the only time that we encountered him was during the daylight hours, his visits to the herd could all have been nocturnal, when we would not have known about them.

I had the camera rolling when Tula Hatti appeared from behind the *Jamun* tree. I kept it rolling when he turned and, without breaking his stride, began to walk in my direction. When he first appeared from behind the tree, he was about seventy-five feet away and he quickly closed the distance between us. As he did, and I laugh now thinking back on this, I heard a peculiar thumping noise coming from somewhere close. It was not his footsteps, which were almost silent; it took me seconds to realize that it was my heart thumping in alarm inside my chest. The elephant closed to about thirty feet and then he suddenly stopped and stood still. He sensed something; whether it was my scent or whether he had seen me, I did not

---

had the telltale streams marking the sides of their faces. Now, however, scientists are beginning to think that *musth* is not related to sexual desire. If this is so, as of this writing they really do not know what its meaning is.

know.* He stood for a few seconds and then slowly began to use his trunk to check the air for scent. He raised it several times for high scents and then swung it to the ground for the low flows. This done he stood silently, as though considering what to do next. Then he again stepped forward and continuing walking toward me. The camera kept rolling.

When the animal was about twenty-five feet away, I began to think that perhaps he was close enough. He was beginning to tower over me and I had to raise the camera a fraction now to frame his face and head. There was nothing aggressive in his approach. It was slow and steady, almost plodding. But it was, to me, alone in the deep jungle and with my heart banging away against my rib cage, something close to an irresistible force. It was as though a mountain was moving against me, something that no power on earth and cer- tainly no means at my disposal could halt. So I coughed. A little cough. A small cough. One that I had used before with tigers and other animals. It is a sound that is a human sound without quite be- ing a human sound. Wild animals do not like human sounds. They are very sensitive to them and to the dangers that they represent. Their usual reaction is one of instant wariness often followed by quick retreat. The cough has worked for me with tigers and buffalos and leopards. And it worked with Tula Hatti, to a point. He stopped. But he did not retreat. He could see me now, I was fairly sure of that. But what he was seeing—a figure, crouched in front of him, head and face almost totally obscured by hat and camera, still and noiseless—confused him. In addition, he had not yet been able to pick up an identifying scent.

---

* New studies regarding the use of infrasound communication by elephants suggest that my interpretation of some of the behavior of Tula Hatti, during the times that we got close to him, may be partly wrong and that what I believed to be extreme wariness on his part, when I saw how frequently he stopped to watch and listen, may well have been a listening phase, or pause. Elephants are very silent creatures but they do make some noise when they walk through dense forest; the "freezing" that we saw in Tula Hatti, if a listening pause, could have been to eliminate even those small sounds of his own movement. Infrasound, coming to him from other elephants over considerable distances and through dense foliage, must at times be close to inaudible. In Africa it has been noticed that whole herds will sometimes freeze simultaneously to listen to what must be the calls of other elephants.

When he stopped this time, he remained perfectly still for a few moments directly in front of me, looking right at me from a distance of twenty feet. He towered over me, the immense bulk of his body filling the camera lens, the bulging frontal lobes of his forehead twelve feet above me. With steady eyes he stood and looked at me, his incredible sixteen- to eighteen-thousand-pound body still and steady as a huge gray rock. He stayed like this for about ten seconds. The camera kept rolling.

Then he began to use his trunk again. Up, high in the air, twenty feet above me. Then down. He did this several times. It was at this moment that I realized in addition to the little bit of luck that I had which was keeping him where he was and getting me the long awaited footage that we so badly needed, I had the other ingredient, the "something else" that made it all possible. I had a body odor that was totally unique, totally foreign to the elephant and completely different from what he was used to in his brief encounters with the indigenous peoples of the jungle. His previous encounters with me were spread across the space of years, and too brief, I think, for him to have developed a memory of the scents I emitted, foreign and distinctive as they were. What the elephant was now encountering—something he was obviously having great difficulty analyzing—was the body smell of a meat and potatoes westerner. This was what was holding him where he was, this and the sight of a strange object—a jumble of hat, camouflaged clothing, half-concealed face, and video camera, all as still and silent as himself.

He may have heard the video camera. It did emit a faint hum as it ran. But unless he was able to separate that from the general level of sound created by birds and insects that vibrated all around us, I do not think that it registered with him to any appreciable extent. (Though how he could not hear the pounding of my heart at this time I do not know.)

Then he took another step forward. When he moved this time, his single step brought him to within seventeen feet of where I was standing. (Later that day, to help reconstruct the event, Hikmat and I went back to the scene and measured the distances involved with a steel tape.) He loomed over me. When his enormous trunk swung toward me I finally decided that he was close enough. I decided in an instant that I must either move and leave immediately or try and stop him again. The latter idea seemed best under the circumstances and so I gave him another cough. This time it was louder with a bit more volume behind it and it did the trick. It did more than that. It startled him, I think, and perhaps annoyed him. With a continuation of the forward momentum, he swung his huge body to the left (his right), gave a single trumpeting scream, and powered off into the jungle. The camera kept rolling.

I followed him with the camera until he went out of sight. As the distance between us lengthened, so the thumping in my chest decreased proportionately. When he disappeared into a thicket of greenery about a hundred and fifty feet away I stepped out of the tangle of dead limbs and moved forward a few feet. I switched the camera off and stood listening for a few moments, trying to decide whether to follow him or to be content with the footage that I had. Great footage, the best that could be expected. One half of me said, "You have enough. Be content with it and go home." Another half said, "He's there, he'll wait for you, go and get some more." Yet a third half said, "Wait. Wait, watch, and listen." This was my professional side, the one with a bit of experience behind it. What it was saying to me now was that when he swung away like that and trumpeted, he was telling me something. He was telling me that whoever or whatever I was under the hat and the camouflage and with the weird body odor, I had perturbed him. I had upset his balances and disturbed him. Whatever the extent of his disturbance, it was undoubtedly enhanced and expanded by his condition of *musth*, for within five seconds of disappearing from view he decided that not only had I upset him but it was appropriate that I should know about it. Having made this decision, he turned and charged me.

He came out of the thicket of greenery like an express train. The sound of smashing and bursting shrubbery was accompanied by a series of powerful screams and the ground trembled under tons of angry elephant. His huge trunk lashed from side to side and his enormous head bobbed up and down in time to the pistonlike pounding of his twenty-two inch feet. I immediately turned away from the sight of the charging animal and looked behind me. I did not run. Animals, from the tail-waggers that are man's best friend on up, like to chase things that run. What was important at this precise moment was to see *where* I was going to run if I had to do so. I was in fairly dense jungle, confronted by an enraged elephant, one that I have to admit I was to blame for enraging—I and the *musth* condition, that is—and it was vitally important that I have a line of retreat that would enable me to get away as fast as possible. Fast meant as fast as I could run in that line of retreat.

Elephants, massive in size, ponderous of movement, give the impression that they are incapable of anything other than a plodding approach when on the move. Something quite the opposite is nearer the truth. They can accelerate quickly with long, swinging strides that are really a fast walk rather than a run, and reach speeds of thirty miles an hour for short distances. A man, running away in the open from an elephant enraged for some reason and determined to wreak vengeance on the object of his rage, has no chance of escape. The animal will quickly catch him and that is that. However, in forest or in light jungle there are a number of ways of getting away from a pursuing elephant. My quick study of the ground behind me was an effort to see if one or more of these might be available.

One way to escape is by using the trees. If there are trees within one's line of flight, one can run between them and use them to break the speed of the elephant's charge. The animal will come through fairly fast, but its speed will be reduced by having to dodge around the trees. Then one may be able to get far enough ahead to get out of the animal's sight, in which case it may give up the chase. Another avenue of escape is via a *nullah*, or ravine. It must be at least six feet deep and have steep, almost vertical sides. One jumps into this and runs up or down it. An elephant cannot jump and to get into the *nullah* must lower its great weight slowly and carefully. It may even have to slide in on its knees. Once again its speed will be broken and the object of its dire intent may escape. A third way, one that has produced quite hilarious results on occasion, is to run as fast as possible and at the same time, as a delaying tactic, to drop as many articles of clothing as possible in the path of the oncoming beast. Perhaps seeing these as parts of the object of its pursuit, the elephant will invariably stop to savage them, ripping them to pieces with its trunk and tusks and pounding them into the dirt with its feet. First goes the hat. Then the shirt. Then the pants. Then the underpants, socks, whatever, until, naked as a newborn babe, one comes panting into camp to be greeted by the riotous laughter of one's companions.

Tula Hatti did not press home his charge. When he was about fifty feet from where I stood ready to run for my life, he suddenly skidded to a halt in front of a big, fire-blackened stump, four feet in height and width. He wrapped his trunk around this, gave a mighty scream, tore it out of the ground and hurled it in the air. He stood for a few seconds looking at me. Then he suddenly whirled and walked away. His demonstration was over and, in his mind at least, its message was clear. It was, "Leave me alone. Leave me alone and stay away from me. You confused me and bothered me and you startled me and I do not like being startled. Or confused. Please keep that in mind for future reference."

I was back at camp an hour later. I walked in holding the camera over my head like a trophy. Rara came hopping, skipping, and jumping to meet me. "Did you see Tula Hatti? Did you meet him and get his picture?"

"Yes," I said. While Pasang fired up the Honda generator to give us power for a viewing, I set up the monitor inside the big Eureka stores tent, one of the last left standing. When all was ready, we closed the tent flaps and turned on the monitor.

The footage was perfect.

The footage was perfect and had we had a bottle of Dom Perignon '68 in camp we would have broached it instantly and shared it with everyone. The Sherpas were delighted, Dede was relieved that I was back and all in one piece (I did not tell her about the elephant's charge until later), and Rara, with Rosie sitting in her lap, said, "Did you touch him? Did you pet him? He was close enough."

A little later Hikmat drove down from Mahendranagar and we ran the footage for him. Then we put it away, wrapped against damage, dust, and moisture, and we did not view it again until we got home. Soon after, Hikmat, Pasang, and I walked down the Bauni for the last time to view the scene of my encounter with the elephant and take some measurements. Tula Hatti was gone. But he had come back again after I left and, to amplify his little warning to me, had taken the stand of dead branches where I had stood and torn it to pieces. Not a stick was left standing. After smashing it all down, he had trampled it into the ground. Hikmat, viewing the destruction after measuring the distance between where I had stood and where my last cough had turned the elephant away, raised an eyebrow and said, "A little close, what?"

That evening Hikmat drove back to Mahendranagar. It had begun to rain again. When it stopped, Dede and I left Rara with Jessica and the Sherpas and drove out in the little Suzuki to do a last round of the white grass *phantas*. We left camp in the cool of the late afternoon, rattling over the old wooden bridge and driving slowly through the corridors of forest that lead to the open grassland. We drove slowly to the great *Peepul* tree that stands at the head of the grassland and stopped there to listen, glassing for animals and breathing the cold, clean air of the *phanta*, heavy with the scent of wet grass. We watched the sun go down into the Sarda reaches, watched a line of Black-Backed Vultures floating down the evening sky. A perfect day was rounded off with the single trumpeting call of an elephant from the dark line of trees that marked the southern boundary of the reserve. Rain clouds, violet tinted in the light of the dying sun, rose out of the southwest. They slowly built, layer upon layer, until they covered all of the sky above the sea of white-tipped grass that waved in a gentle wind. We left the *phanta* and drove back through the dark tunnel of forest to camp. As we did the light faded and suddenly it was night.

We closed camp next day and drove to Mahendranagar. We unloaded about eighty percent of our gear there, including the utility trailer, and left it all with Hikmat. He would store it for us pending another visit. Another safari. Another dream time. When? At this time we did not know.

One last task at Mahendranagar was to put aside the reward money for the game scout. We left it for him with the Bishts. To it I added what I had promised when I said goodbye to him—a premium steel, ten-inch Coleman Bowie knife in a leather sheath. I had carried one myself most of the time that I had been out with the scout and I had noticed him admiring it. My bet, knowing how a Taru treasures something like this, is that it will stay in his family for generations.

We said goodbye to Jessica at the Bisht home and she peddled off to her Taru home at Mousa Pani.

Next day, with rain falling steadily, we left the Bishts and drove east on the first leg of our run to Kathmandu. As we pulled out of the Bisht compound, Hikmat voiced my feelings when he said, "Good luck for your journey. It's not going to be an easy one with all of this rain. You'll get there, I know. But you'll be lucky if you can do it in four days." He and his wife then gave Rara a hug. She needed it. There had been a flood of tears when it was decided that Rosie should stay with the Bishts rather than go to Captain Doo. (She has since quite recovered from the incident however, having learned in letters from Hikmat that soon after we left Rosie got married, had twenty-four little ones, and is well and happy in Mahendranagar.)

The drive to Kathmandu was . . . murder. There may be other and better words to describe it, but murder seems appropriate. It is a rough enough cross-country trip at the best of times, but the unseasonable rain had turned the whole of the Terai into a giant quagmire and the three-hundred-mile run took us nine days. Nine days of slogging through oceans of mud and muddy water, of bogging down in mud holes that could swallow a truck, of fording swollen streams and rivers, of winching out of sinks and wallows a hundred times. Of mud that covered the vehicles, crept inside, crept into the gear, into our sleeping bags, into the food. Of rain-soaked camps on the side of the road and soggy fires and wet tents and cold food. Of a little girl who never complained but who ate something along the way that gave her a bad stomachache and gave us a lot of worries.

I drove the Scout and we towed the Suzuki on a triangular towbar behind us. Dede, Rara, and I rode in the Scout and the three Sherpas rode in the Suzuki. The Scout, with its powerful V8 engine and its high clearance, handled most of what the rain-soaked roads, tracks, and buffalo cart trails had to offer. But were it not for its eight-thousand-pound Warn winch, the trip might have taken nineteen days instead of nine. After the first day, as we slowly oozed through morass after morass, the most important thing in the world became a log, or a tree, or even a stump, something that we could hook onto to winch out. The Suzuki, with its little engine and low clearance, would not have made it alone.

We broke the towbar to the Suzuki. It snapped clean in two when we put close to eight thousand pounds of Warn winch power to it to get it out of a wallow full of gluelike mud. We repaired it with nylon rope. We broke a spring on the Scout in a giant chuck hole that we did not see in time. We repaired it with wire wrapping. We crossed the roaring waters of the Bhabai River courtesy of some kind Korean engineers. The Scout pulled the Suzuki and in turn was towed by a giant construction machine with nine-foot-high wheels. The Scout, even though it went underwater to the door-handles, stayed dry inside. But the Suzuki completely flooded when water rose to the windows and then rushed in under the sides of the canvas hood. Pasang made one of his very few jokes when we came out of the river. "We should have had the life jackets on, *Sahib*."

On the last day, we drove non-stop for nineteen hours, arriving at the haven of the Shangri La at two in the morning. Kathmandu meant access to medical facilities for Rara (who recovered in a day), hot baths and hot food and clean sheets, and the happy smiles of the Sherpas as we put them all in taxis and sent them home.

Dede, Rara, and I spent three days in Kathmandu together. The nine-day drive from the west had completely discombobulated all of our carefully laid schedules and so we simply had to make new ones. Sitting in a comfortable suite in the Shangri La, in clean, dry clothes — no mud! — and nursing glasses of Glenlivet, Dede and I smiled and said to each other, "This is Nepal. This is what happens in the magic kingdom when one defies the gods by trying to make exact plans and follow exact schedules in a land where nothing is exact, where little can be scheduled, and where time does not matter." We smiled, and then our smiles turned to laughter as we thought back to some of the deliciously amusing things that had happened to us there over the years. Like waiting for a "scheduled" flight with Royal Nepal Airlines from the northwestern Himalaya after an expedition to Rara Lake—the lovely mountain lake after which our daughter is named—waiting seven days camped on the grass airstrip at Jumla, eyes fixed on the skies for the plane that came not. Like having a packet of precious personal mail sent down to us in the west, only to find, when we flew down there, that it had been sent back to Kathmandu, only to find, when we got back to Kathmandu, that it had again been sent back down to the west. Like ordering Christmas pudding to be taken on a Himalayan Abominable Snowman expedition. Christmas pudding. The traditional British after-dinner dessert served once a year on Christmas day is made with raisins, sultanas, candied fruit peel, and spices. As well as being quite nutritious, it has been considered an essential item of the food supply of British Himalayan expeditions since the turn of the century. The order, placed with an enigmatic little institution called the Kichipokri Cake House in Kathmandu's inner city, was for ten one-pound cans of pudding. Somewhere along the line the one-pound became translated into fifteen-pound. So for weeks three bewildered porters hauled fifty-pound loads of Christmas pudding up and down and over the mountain trails. Like having a Nepali mountain trekking company equip us for a river run when our own equipment temporarily disappeared into the maze of Royal Nepal Airlines' baggage systems en route from Pokhra to Kathmandu. The run was on the Trisuli River, with ten clients. The first night out we opened up the gear they had smilingly supplied us with to find that they had smilingly omitted pots, pans, plates, knives, forks, spoons, and mugs. Like . . . like many other hilarious experiences that only the magic kingdom can bestow and in return for which it asks only that one maintain a strong and imperturbable sense of humor from Himalayan dawn to Terai dusk.

We spent much of our three days in Kathmandu in talks with the people at the King Mahendra Trust. The main purpose of the talks was to lay the groundwork for some kind of official recognition of the great elephant, for the magnificent animal that he was, for the symbol of nature and the ecoweb that he represented, and as part of the natural heritage of the people of Nepal. Our proposals were well received and our friend Dr. Mishra, Secretary of the Trust, promised to carry them to higher authorities. When we left Nepal that is where things stood.

Rescheduled, Dede and Rara flew out of Kathmandu on January 20th. I spent five more days there, closing down the project, storing equipment and having the Scout overhauled for the overland run down to Bombay. I left Kathmandu on January 26th. After another nerve-wracking run across India — although this time I did not have the highway madness of another Indian *puja* to contend with — I reached Bombay on February 5th. Pasang, his cough not better, had elected to stay in Kathmandu but Jangbu came with me for the run. We saw the vehicles containerized and hoisted aboard an American President Lines ship after a mere three days of paperwork, and flew back to Kathmandu on February 11th. There I paid off the Sherpas, gave them all well-earned bonuses, told all of them how much we valued their loyal and hardworking contribution to the project and the movie, promised to send them VHS tapes of the film when it was completed, climbed on a flight out of Kathmandu on February 16th, and was back in the U.S.A. via London within five days. I came back to the rolling hills of Oregon, the dark green forests, the snow-capped beauty of Mount Hood, and the brooding rimrock that etches the skyline above our little place in the mountains, the place that we call the Weed Patch. Home.

EPILOGUE

By the time this book goes to press we may have achieved for Tula Hatti what these writings and our film documentary with Jimmy Stewart's wonderful narration were designed to do: have him declared a National Treasure, or a National Monument. (This was done with great success for a giant tusker in northern Kenya some years ago; although his huge tusks made him a prime target for both poachers and unscrupulous foreign trophy hunters, Ahmed, as he was called, remained unmolested for many years and eventually died of natural causes.) As of late 1990, however, the Nepalese government has not moved to do this. In Nepal, as in most other countries, the wheels of government grind exceeding slow and recent events in that little kingdom, the results of the winds of change from communist Europe, have slowed things even further and, in some cases, dropped them down the ladder of priority. Nor has any change been made in the status of the White Grass Plains. It is still a reserve and as such open to licensed hunting and tenuous in its status.

However, the very fact that both matters have been accepted for consideration is heartening, and when one considers what Nepal has done in the field of conservation within a very few years, the prospect of having both proposals accepted and gazetted in the not too distant future is real and encouraging. In consideration of the probability of this achievement, one has only to view the concern of the kingdom for its wildlife in its shining record. With a population that has grown twenty-five percent within the last fifty years (in the U.S. this would be the equivalent of an increase of more than fifty million people), with ongoing and seemingly incurable politi-

238

cal problems with its southern neighbor, India, with erosion-induced land scarcity, and with all of the ills that modern civilization has brought to its people, the little country of Nepal has within the space of seventeen years gazetted five new national parks (Chitawan, Sagarmatha, Langtang, Rara, and Shey) and three reserves (Kosi Tappu, Bardia, and Sukila Phanta). In addition it has established the internationally respected and locally influential King Mahendra Trust for Nature Conservation, a conservation body with interests that reach to all corners of the Nepalese econet and the leading light of which, Secretary Dr. Hemanta Raj Mishra, was awarded the prestigious J. Paul Getty Award for valuable achievements in wildlife research in 1987. With committees in the U.S., Japan, and Britain, and under the august chairmanship of H. R. H. Prince Gyanendra Bir Bikram Shah, brother of the king, the King Mahendra Trust is the instrument by which our proposals are being carried to government decision makers and through which we hope to bring to Tula Hatti the protection and security to which as a National Monument he would be entitled. Once this is done, a natural continuation of the gesture will be the gazetting of the White Grass Plains as a national park, thus ensuring its safety and security for all time.

Both gestures would serve as examples to people everywhere of what can be done even in the face of trying and adverse conditions when good intentions are followed by positive action, the kind of action that in Nepal only started in 1973, but which as of 1990 grows daily stronger. The relatively recent but extraordinarily successful efforts of Nepal on behalf of its wildlife represent a sharp contrast in many ways to the U.S., where well before the turn of the century there were people who stood up and made clear the need to look to the future, not just of wildlife but, with wildlife as an integral part of the dependent whole, of the world in which we live. Prominent among these early advocates, indeed a clarion voice of his day, was a Native American of the Pacific Northwest, Chief Seattle. Unheard by some, dismissed by others as just another cry in the wilderness, Seattle said in a letter to Franklin Pierce in 1854:

This we know: the earth does not belong to man, man belongs to the earth. All things are connected like the blood that unites us all . . . Man did not weave the web of life, he is merely a strand in it. Whatever he does to the web he does to himself.

What Chief Seattle was saying, in a voice at one time faint but now loud and clear to millions of concerned people, is that the future of wildlife everywhere, from Tula Hatti in the jungles of Nepal to the owl that calls from the Big Leaf Maple in our own backyard, both as a single concern and as a vitally interdependent part of the ecoweb on which we now precariously balance our very future, is the responsibility of all of us.